Italian and Italian American Studies

Series Editor
Stanislao G. Pugliese
Hofstra University
Hempstead, NY, USA

This series brings the latest scholarship in Italian and Italian American history, literature, cinema, and cultural studies to a large audience of specialists, general readers, and students. Featuring works on modern Italy (Renaissance to the present) and Italian American culture and society by established scholars as well as new voices, it has been a longstanding force in shaping the evolving fields of Italian and Italian American Studies by re-emphasizing their connection to one another.

More information about this series at
http://www.palgrave.com/gp/series/14835

Penelope Morris • Perry Willson
Editors

La Mamma

Interrogating a National Stereotype

Editors
Penelope Morris
School of Modern Languages and Cultures
University of Glasgow
Glasgow, UK

Perry Willson
School of Humanities - History
University of Dundee
Dundee, UK

Italian and Italian American Studies
ISBN 978-1-137-55986-9   ISBN 978-1-137-54256-4   (eBook)
https://doi.org/10.1057/978-1-137-54256-4

Library of Congress Control Number: 2018937885

© The Editor(s) (if applicable) and The Author(s) 2018
This work is subject to copyright. All rights are solely and exclusively licensed by the Publisher, whether the whole or part of the material is concerned, specifically the rights of translation, reprinting, reuse of illustrations, recitation, broadcasting, reproduction on microfilms or in any other physical way, and transmission or information storage and retrieval, electronic adaptation, computer software, or by similar or dissimilar methodology now known or hereafter developed.
The use of general descriptive names, registered names, trademarks, service marks, etc. in this publication does not imply, even in the absence of a specific statement, that such names are exempt from the relevant protective laws and regulations and therefore free for general use.
The publisher, the authors and the editors are safe to assume that the advice and information in this book are believed to be true and accurate at the date of publication. Neither the publisher nor the authors or the editors give a warranty, express or implied, with respect to the material contained herein or for any errors or omissions that may have been made. The publisher remains neutral with regard to jurisdictional claims in published maps and institutional affiliations.

Cover illustration: ©Fototeca Gilardi/Associazione Maraja Designer: Fatima Jamadar

Printed on acid-free paper

This Palgrave Macmillan imprint is published by the registered company Nature America, Inc. part of Springer Nature.
The registered company address is: 1 New York Plaza, New York, NY 10004, U.S.A.

PREFACE

This book stems from an interdisciplinary project, entitled "La Mamma: Interrogating a National Stereotype," led by the editors of this volume and funded by the Arts and Humanities Research Council (AHRC), UK. This project included four interdisciplinary workshops and two public events which explored Italian motherhood and the maternal in both Italy and its diaspora from the Risorgimento to the present day, with a particular, albeit far from exclusive, focus on the stereotype of *mammismo*. The workshops, held in Scotland and Italy between May 2012 and May 2014, brought together scholars from a range of disciplines.[1]

All but one of the contributions published in this book originated as papers in these workshops. The project as a whole demonstrated the importance of understanding the stereotype of *mammismo* within the context of a wider investigation into the lived experience and representation of Italian motherhood. The selection of papers for this volume is guided by the same rationale, with some focusing on the stereotype itself, or areas of Italian life where the stereotype has made its presence felt, while others point instead to conspicuous absences or completely different understandings of motherhood.

The first of the interdisciplinary workshops—"The Maternal Role and Representations of Maternity in the Late Nineteenth and Early Twentieth Century"—was held at Dundee University in May 2012. Alongside the academic workshop there was a public event—"La Mamma: The Invention of a Stereotype"—in which sociologist Chiara Saraceno discussed the themes of historian Marina d'Amelia's book *La mamma* with the author herself. Papers in the workshop, presented by historians and

v

literary scholars (Ursula Fanning, Benedetta Gennaro, Katherine Mitchell, Enrica Moretti, Marjan Schwegman, Katrin Wehling-Giorgi, Perry Willson and Sharon Wood), examined the ways in which maternity and mothers had been represented (and, to a lesser extent, the lived experience of Italian mothers) during the period from the Risorgimento to the Fascist *ventennio*.

The next workshop, "*Mammismo*, the Emergence of a National Stereotype," focusing on the mid to late twentieth century, was held at the University of Glasgow. The papers, given by historians and literary scholars (Joyce Antler, Maud Bracke, Niamh Cullen, Adalgisa Giorgio, Ruth Glynn, Gabriella Gribaudi, Penelope Morris, Silvana Patriarca and Molly Tambor) and a sociologist/psychoanalyst (Lesley Caldwell), ranged over a number of areas, including politics in the postwar years; literary and cinematic representations of motherhood; personal diaries, magazines and advice columns; female terrorists; feminism in the 1970s; and comparisons with stereotypes of the Jewish mother.

The third event of the project, "La maternità in Italia: un percorso ad ostacoli" (Motherhood in Italy: An Obstacle Course), was a public one, held in the Parliamentary Library in Rome, which focused on motherhood in present-day Italy. Keynote papers were given by sociologist Chiara Saraceno and historian Sandro Bellassai, and they were then joined by Senator Livia Turco, trade unionist Lidia Obando and journalist Alessandra di Pietro for a lively round-table discussion.

In the final workshop, "The Stereotype Abroad: *Mammismo* in the Italian Diaspora," held in Edinburgh in May 2014, our focus shifted from Italy itself to Italian diaspora communities. There were papers on North America by Silvia Barocci, Maria Susanna Garroni and Maddalena Tirabassi, on Australia by Francesco Ricatti and on New Zealand by Adalgisa Giorgio. The workshop explored both how motherhood and maternity has been represented as well as how such representations in the host countries have contributed to the development of the stereotype itself.

The formal academic workshop was followed by a public event which turned its attention to the local context. This event—"Maw or Mamma: Mothers and Motherhood in the Italian-Scottish Community"—held in the Edinburgh Story-Telling Centre, focused, as its title suggests, on the Italian-Scottish community. Combining personal testimonies, a photographic display and a theatrical performance, it engendered a lively debate that pointed to a notable depth of feeling about mothers and motherhood among present-day Italian-Scots.

PREFACE   vii

We owe thanks to many people who have helped us in the course of this project. First and foremost, we would like to thank the AHRC (and their anonymous peer reviewers) who chose to award us funding for this project. Our grateful thanks are also due to Emily Ryder, the project's very efficient administrator; to Carlo Pirozzi, who generously gave up his time to help organise the project's public event in Edinburgh; and to Marina d'Amelia, who provided us with invaluable assistance in organizing the Rome workshop. We would also like to thank the many contributors to the four workshops, who are far too numerous for us to have included all their papers in this book (although some of their papers, we are delighted to note, have resulted in publications elsewhere). Over the course of a succession of interesting discussions and debates, their contributions helped us and the various chapter authors to think through and develop our ideas on the issues raised in these pages. We would also like to thank those involved in the public events and the audiences of those events, who also contributed interesting ideas and questions. Silvana Patriarca, Ursula Fanning, Gabriella Gribaudi and Mark Seymour all provided extremely helpful comments on an earlier draft of the first chapter. Finally, our thanks are due to our translator Stuart Oglethorpe for his excellent, careful work, to the series editor Stanislao Pugliese and to the production team at Palgrave Macmillan.

Glasgow, UK

Dundee, UK

Penelope Morris

Perry Willson

NOTES

1. Abstracts of the papers from the Dundee, Glasgow and Edinburgh workshops are available on the La Mamma: Interrogating a National Stereotype project website at https://lamammaitaliana.wordpress.com

CONTENTS

1 La Mamma: Italian Mothers Past and Present   1
   Penelope Morris and Perry Willson

2 *Mammismo*/Momism: On the History and Uses
   of a Stereotype, c.1940s to the Present   29
   Silvana Patriarca

3 Mothers, Workers, Citizens: Teresa Noce
   and the Parliamentary Politics of Motherhood   51
   Molly Tambor

4 Problems and Prescriptions: Motherhood and *Mammismo*
   in Postwar Italian Advice Columns and Fiction   77
   Penelope Morris

5 Conceptualizing the Maternal: Representations, Reflections
   and Refractions in Women's Literary Writings   105
   Ursula Fanning

6 Neapolitan Mothers: Three Generations of Women,
   from Representation to Reality   131
   Gabriella Gribaudi

ix

x CONTENTS

7 *Mammas* in Italian Migrant Families: The Anglophone
Countries   161
Maddalena Tirabassi

8 Queer Daughters and Their Mothers: Carole Maso, Mary
Cappello and Alison Bechdel Write Their Way Home   185
Mary Jo Bona

9 Beyond the Stereotype: The Obstacle Course
of Motherhood in Italy   215
Chiara Saraceno

Index   237

Notes on Contributors

Mary Jo Bona is Professor of Women's and Gender Studies, Italian American Studies and Chair of the Department of Cultural Analysis and Theory at Stony Brook University. She is past president of the Italian American Studies Association. Her publications include: *Women Writing Cloth: Migratory Fictions in the American Imaginary* (Lanham, MD: Lexington Books/Rowman and Littlefield, 2016); *By the Breath of Their Mouths: Narratives of Resistance in Italian America* (New York: State University of New York [SUNY] Press, 2010); and *Claiming a Tradition: Italian American Women Writers* (Carbondale: Southern Illinois University Press, 1999). With Irma Maini, Bona co-edited *Multiethnic Literature and Canon Debates* (SUNY Press, 2006) and is editor of the Multiethnic Literature Series at SUNY Press. http://www.stonybrook. edu/commcms/cat/people/cat_faculty/MaryJoBona.html

Ursula Fanning is Senior Lecturer in Italian at University College Dublin. Her research interests lie in the areas of nineteenth- and twentieth-century women's writing, as well as in Pirandello studies. Publications include *Gender Meets Genre: Woman as Subject in the Fictional Universe of Matilde Serao* (Dublin: Irish Academic Press, 2002); a chapter on "Maternal Descriptions and Prescriptions in Post-Unification Italy," in Katharine Mitchell and Helena Sanson (eds), *Women and Gender in Post-Unification Italy: Between Private and Public Spheres* (Bern: Peter Lang, 2013). Her most recent book is *Italian Women's Autobiographical Writings in the Twentieth Century: Constructing Subjects* (Madison, NJ: Fairleigh Dickinson University Press, 2017). http://www.ucd.ie/ research/people/languagesliterature/drursulafanning/

xii NOTES ON CONTRIBUTORS

Gabriella Gribaudi is Professore Ordinario in Contemporary History at the Università di Napoli Federico II. Her publications include "Donne di camorra e identità di genere," in *Donne di mafia* (special issue of *Meridiana* co-edited with Marcella Marmo), 67 (2010); (ed.) *Traffici criminali. Camorra, mafie e reti internazionali dell'illegalità* (Turin: Bollati Boringhieri, 2009); *Guerra totale. Tra bombe alleate e violenze naziste— Napoli e il fronte meridionale 1940–44* (Turin: Bollati Boringhieri, 2005); *Donne, uomini, famiglie. Napoli nel Novecento* (Naples: L'ancora, 1999); *A Eboli. Il mondo meridionale in cent'anni di trasformazione* (Venice: Marsilio, 1990). She is on the editorial board of *Quaderni Storici*. https://www.docenti.unina.it/mariagabriella.gribaudi

Penelope Morris is Senior Lecturer in Italian in the School of Modern Languages and Cultures at the University of Glasgow, Scotland, UK. Her research interests lie in the social and cultural history of women in modern Italy and in the role of emotions in history. Her publications include *Giovanna Zangrandi. Una vita in romanzo* (Verona: Cierre, 2000); (ed.) *Women in Italy 1945–1960* (Basingstoke: Palgrave, 2006); (co-editor with Francesco Ricatti and Mark Seymour), *Politica ed emozioni nella storia d'Italia dal 1848 ad oggi* (Rome: Viella, 2012). She is General Editor, with Mark Seymour, of the journal *Modern Italy*. http://www.gla.ac.uk/schools/mlc/staff/penelopemorris/

Silvana Patriarca is Professor of History at Fordham University, New York. Primarily a cultural historian, her publications include (co-edited with Lucy Riall) *The Risorgimento Revisited: Nationalism and Culture in Nineteenth-Century Italy* (Basingstoke: Palgrave Macmillan, 2012); *Italian Vices: Nation and Character from the Risorgimento to the Republic* (Cambridge: Cambridge University Press, 2010), Italian translation: *Italianità. La costruzione del carattere nazionale* (Rome-Bari: Laterza, 2010); *Numbers and Nationhood: Writing Statistics in Nineteenth-Century Italy* (Cambridge: Cambridge University Press, 1996), Italian translation: *Costruire la nazione. La statistica e il Risorgimento* (Rome: Istat, 2011). http://www.fordham.edu/academics/programs_at_fordham_/history_department/faculty/silvana_patriarca_70076.asp

Chiara Saraceno former Professor in Sociology at the University of Turin and Research Professor at the Berlin Social Science Centre, is currently Honorary Fellow at the Collegio Carlo Alberto in Turin. Her, often comparative, publications on families and gender include: *Coppie e famiglie. Non è questione di natura* (Milan: Feltrinelli, 2013); (with Manuela

Naldini), *Sociologia della famiglia* (Bologna: Il Mulino, 2013), 3rd edn; (with Manuela Naldini) *Conciliare famiglia e lavoro* (Bologna: Il Mulino, 2011); (ed.) *Families, Ageing and Social Policy* (Cheltenham: Edward Elgar, 2008); *Mutamenti della famiglia e politiche sociali in Italia* (Bologna: Il Mulino, 2003); (with Marzio Barbagli), *Separarsi in Italia* (Bologna: Il Mulino, 1998). She has also co-edited with Jane Lewis and Arnlaug Leira the two-volume reader *Families and Family Polices* (Cheltenham: Edward Elgar, 2011). http://www.carloalberto.org/people/faculty/honorary/chiara-saraceno/

Molly Tambor is Assistant Professor of European History at Long Island University Post campus in New York. Her publications include *The Lost Wave: Women and Democracy in Postwar Italy* (New York: Oxford University Press, 2014) and the English translation and preface of Gian Giacomo Migone, *The United States and Fascist Italy: The Rise of American Finance in Europe* (New York: Cambridge University Press, 2015).

Maddalena Tirabassi is Director of the Centro Altreitalie sulle Migrazioni Italiane in Turin. She is also Editor of the journal *Altreitalie. Rivista di studi sulle migrazioni italiane nel mondo* and Deputy Director of the Association of European Migration Institutions. Her publications include *I motori della memoria. Le piemontesi in Argentina* (Turin: Rosenberg and Sellier, 2010); *Ripensare la patria grande. Amy Bernardy e le migrazioni italiane* (Isernia: Cosmo Iannone Ed., 2005); *Il faro di Beacon Street. Social workers e immigrate negli Stati Uniti* (Milan: Franco Angeli, 1990). http://www.altreitalie.it/Chi_Siamo/CV_Maddalena_Tirabassi.kl

Perry Willson is Professor of Modern European History at the University of Dundee, Scotland. Her research interests focus mainly on twentieth-century Italian women's and gender history, particularly of the Fascist period. Her publications include: *Women in Twentieth-Century Italy* (Basingstoke: Palgrave Macmillan, 2009), Italian edition: *Italiane. Biografia del Novecento* (Rome-Bari: Laterza, 2011); (ed.) *Gender, Family and Sexuality: The Private Sphere in Italy 1860–1945* (Basingstoke: Palgrave Macmillan, 2004); *Peasant Women and Politics in Fascist Italy: The Massaie Rurali* (London: Routledge, 2002) and *The Clockwork Factory: Women and Work in Fascist Italy* (Oxford: Oxford University Press, 1993). She was Chair of the Association for the Study of Modern Italy 2006–9 and is currently Vice-Convenor of Women's History Scotland. https://www.dundee.ac.uk/history/staff/details/perry-willson.php

CHAPTER 1

La Mamma: Italian Mothers Past and Present

Penelope Morris and Perry Willson

Motherhood, as an idea, has been and remains fundamental to how Italian women, whether mothers or not, think about themselves. It has also strongly shaped how Italian men view, and have viewed, women and it is part of how Italians have been perceived and represented by others in the wider world. The Catholic Church, with its emphasis on women's essential maternal duty and destiny, and its veneration of the Madonna as an (impossible) ideal of chaste motherhood, has played an important part in this. As historians and others have argued, however, both the lived realities of Italian mothers, and the cultural constructions of their role, have varied greatly over time, in different regions of Italy and between social classes. Even the Catholic vision of maternal duty was not immutable. From the middle of the twentieth century, the Church gradually began to accept new roles for women, including in politics and employment, albeit without abandoning an emphasis on the importance and sanctity of maternity.[1]

Translations from Italian source material are the authors' own.

P. Morris (✉)
School of Modern Languages and Cultures, University of Glasgow, Glasgow, UK
e-mail: penelope.morris@glasgow.ac.uk

P. Willson
School of Humanities - History, University of Dundee, Dundee, UK
e-mail: P.R.Willson@dundee.ac.uk

© The Author(s) 2018
P. Morris, P. Willson (eds.), *La Mamma*,
Italian and Italian American Studies,
https://doi.org/10.1057/978-1-137-54256-4_1

2   P. MORRIS AND P. WILLSON

Beyond the Church there have been many lay figures, particularly "experts" of various kinds such as medical doctors, who have been interested in how mothering should be done. In many of these discussions of the maternal role there has been a tension between notions of mothering as innate, instinctive or "natural" and ideas of different ways of doing it, of motherhood as practice, with the two often coexisting uneasily. From the Risorgimento to more recent times, moreover, various political movements have, in their own and differing ways, based their arguments regarding women's role and destiny primarily on the maternal. The meaning of this, however, has been far from uniform. While many have invoked women's maternal role as a reason to curtail their access to the public sphere, others, including certain types of feminists, have presented it as legitimizing such access. Italy has not, of course, always been entirely distinctive in its historical emphasis on women's maternal role, nor in the diversity of opinions about the meanings and practice of motherhood. Attitudes to and debates about motherhood in other European countries have often been not dissimilar, and indeed changed in similar ways, to the Italian example.

MAMMISMO

There is, however, one particular representation of motherhood that is very much Italian—*mammismo*. Indeed, the idea of the "*mamma italiana*" and her dependent, spoilt, offspring (particularly sons) is one of the most widespread and recognizable stereotypes in perceptions of Italian national character both within Italy and beyond its borders. As historian Anna Bravo has described her, the *mamma* of the stereotype is:

> Incomparably loving, servant and owner of her children, often in tears but always on her feet holding the family together … Adored, feared and caricatured, in discussions about the Italian family, "*la Mamma*" has become a glorious archetype … the enduringly popular image of the Italian mother is of a strong woman who dotes on her son and dedicates herself to him intensively. In exchange she gets the right to veto his choices, his constant attentions and an unrivalled emotional and symbolic dependency. As eternal sons, Italian men struggle to grow up and find it hard to accept new roles for women: Italian women, whether mothers or not, treat men with the sort of indulgence that is normally reserved for children.[2]

This primitively possessive, domineering and, at the same time, indulgent figure makes frequent appearances in jokes and other forms of popular culture, but references to it have also abounded in serious media debates about Italy's social fabric. *Mammismo* has been cited, for example, as a contributing factor to many of what are perceived to be recent and current "problems" with the Italian family, such as Italy's dramatically low birth rate and the extremely unequal gender division of labour within Italian households. Of all such "problems," the one that gives rise to the most persistent references to the stereotype is the advanced age at which many Italian "children" (particularly, but not only, male "children") leave the parental home. The causes of this phenomenon lie, of course, in a number of factors, including very concrete economic and social ones like high levels of youth unemployment and housing shortages. Here, the focus has shifted to an extent from the role of the mother to the adult "children" themselves, seen as far too unadventurous and comfortable in the "golden cage" of the parental home.[3] The flames of this debate were fanned when, in October 2007, the Italian Finance Minister Tommaso Padoa-Schioppa famously referred to stay-at-home adult offspring as "*bamboccioni*" (big babies). He thereby launched an unfortunate expression (the use of which has proved remarkably persistent) that led to a furore in the Italian media.[4] This is a good example of a persistent, unhelpful tendency for politicians and the media to blame Italy's economic problems on supposedly embedded "cultural" traits, sets of beliefs or values which create behavioural patterns that hinder economic development.[5]

A quick internet search suffices to demonstrate that this term (or the similar "*mammone*"), and the idea of Italian men as immature, perpetual children who struggle to grow up and disentangle themselves from the suffocating, protective web of their mothers' apron-strings, is well known not just within Italy but also crops up in foreign observations about modern Italian society. A typical example, randomly selected from many, is an article in *The Guardian* newspaper in 2010 on "Why Italy's mamma's boys can't cut the ties."[6] References to *mammismo* and to overly mothered, dependent sons abound in the Italian media and on websites. One example was a quiz included in *PourFemme* magazine in 2015 to help Italian women investigate the extent to which the man in their life was a *mammone* at heart.[7] This was obviously meant as a light-hearted diversion but it epitomizes the fact that the idea of *mammismo* is an instantly recognizable one to Italians today. Even quite serious news articles often find it hard to resist references to the stereotype, the term *bamboccione* enjoying especial popularity.[8] Two stories that were particularly widely reported, both in Italy and abroad, were the assertion by Cardinal Angelo Bagnasco (Archbishop of Genoa) in 2014 that *mammismo* was one of the greatest threats to marriage in Italy and the claim by Gian Ettore Gassani (lawyer and president of Italy's matrimonial lawyers' association), that 30 per cent of marital breakdowns were caused by interfering mothers-in-law and their over-dependent sons.[9]

The stereotype, or versions of it, has also sometimes surfaced in films and novels, particularly, but not exclusively, those with comic intent. Hollywood and American sitcoms have been important vehicles for this but home-grown products have also played a part. Unlike the perhaps better-known stereotype of the overbearing Jewish mother, in *mammismo*-inspired comedy it is generally—as Silvana Patriarca points out in her chapter in this volume—the son, rather than the mother herself, who is the main comedic figure.[10] The comic actor Alberto Sordi's classic screen performances as a *mamma*'s boy in a series of 1950s films were important in helping embed the figure of the weak and dependent male in the Italian popular imagination. Such portrayals are not, however, simply a feature of the past. For example, Gianni Di Gregorio's film *Gianni e le donne* (2011) in which a man, despite being 60 years old, a husband and father, continues to be dominated by his demanding elderly mother, suggests the enduring appeal of the weak downtrodden male as a comedic trope.[11]

There are recent literary examples too, like the novel *Confessioni di un mammone italiano* (2014) by David Leone, which focuses, as the title suggests, on the protagonist Alfredo's obsessive and dependent relationship with his mother.[12] Similarly, Alberto—the main character of Giuseppe Culicchia's novel *Ameni inganni* (2011)—seems a classic *mammone*. At the age of 41 he still lives with his mother and is even financially supported by her pension. Instead of working he hides at home, devoting his time to reading soft porn and building model spaceships.[13] Both novels focus on what happens, albeit in different ways and with different outcomes, to these overgrown adolescents when they attempt to face up to the outside world and the complexity of adult relationships.

It would be ridiculous, of course, to suggest that Italian literary and cinematographic production has only, or even particularly often, represented mothers in this way. Much more common, particularly before the 1980s and in works by male authors, were one-dimensional portrayals of mothers, seen purely through the eyes of sons and reduced "to a single emotion: unconditional devotion to their offspring."[14] Alongside such depictions, however, there has also been a wide range of more nuanced representations of mothers, as indeed Fanning's chapter demonstrates, and the last four decades in particular have seen a flourishing of explorations of the maternal in literature by women.

Nor has the "mama's boy" been the only representation of Italian masculinity. For many, until fairly recently, the stereotype (and, often, the lived reality) of men as authoritarian husbands and fathers—the *padre-padrone*"—has been a more familiar image than the weak son spoiled by his mother. Representations and ideals of masculinity have not, of course, been unchanging, with, for example, the militaristic hyper-virile fascist model succeeded by the idea of the *"uomo di successo"* during the economic miracle.[15] Various scholars, moreover, have seen the second half of the twentieth century as a period of "crisis for masculinity," a crisis which has been particularly evident in film, with "the fragile male [...] central to Italian cinema."[16] Indeed, Italian films of this period often dwell either overtly or implicitly on this theme. Jacqueline Reich, for example, has argued forcefully that Marcello Mastroianni—perhaps the best-known male film star of this period—was, rather than a "Latin lover," more often seen in the role of the *"inetto"* (inept man), who, "underneath the façade of a presumed hyper-masculinity," is really "an anti-hero [...] at odds with and out of place in a rapidly changing political, social, and sexual environment."[17]

STEREOTYPES

Stereotypes are, of course, a far from easy, and often uncomfortable, subject for scholars to approach. Some, including the American writer and journalist Walter Lippmann who first used the term in its modern sense in the early twentieth century, have argued that stereotypes should not always be considered negative as they can be useful as organizing mechanisms, generalities that help us make sense of human society.[18] Lippmann did acknowledge that they were not unproblematic, warning that it is important "to know that they are only stereotypes, to hold them lightly, to modify them gladly,"[19] but nonetheless felt that "the abandonment of all stereotypes for a wholly innocent approach to experience would impoverish human life."[20] Likewise, some psychologists, particularly recently, have found positive aspects of stereotypes, seeing them as contributors, for example, to cognitive economy or as a means of helping people build identities as group members.[21] Beyond the world of scholarly psychology journals, however, stereotypes have tended to be viewed in a more negative light.

Many stereotypes point to problematic and embarrassing aspects of a group or society, exaggerating and distorting them. Their sheer negativity quite understandably makes many want to distance themselves from them, for the act of scholarly research itself (and some journalistic writing) is often essentially an attempt to dispel stereotypes, to get beyond their generalizations and simplifications to various kinds of deeper truth. This is particularly true of those studying disadvantaged social groups, for, as many have pointed out, stereotypes are often forged by those with power: they usually reflect and perpetuate the views of dominant social groups. One particularly problematic aspect of stereotypes is the fact that, although they are rarely, if ever, a faithful representation of reality, they almost invariably include some kind of relationship to it. The relationship may be tenuous but it is often a troubling one.

It is, however, important not just to go beyond stereotypes but also to examine the stereotypes themselves. Stereotypes may seem frivolous, crude or simply inaccurate, but they are, nonetheless a means, whether rightly or wrongly, that people use in their attempts to make sense of the world and their own lives. They are important because they are stories (whether embraced or rejected) that people live and interact with. Doubtless the majority of Italians do not really believe in the stereotype of *mammismo* fully (or, in many cases, at all) but it is, nonetheless, a widely recognizable cultural element that Italians use to think about themselves, their society and their "national character." It is, moreover, a stereotype that shapes how foreigners perceive, and have perceived, Italians and Italian society and, in particular, Italian gender roles. This is relevant both for Italians who live in Italy itself and for those belonging to its sizeable diaspora. In the diasporic communities, such as in the United States (explored in Maddalena Tirabassi's contribution to this volume), or indeed the Scottish context discussed below, *mammismo* is often seen as just one element of a wider portrayal of the Italian family as a close, protective unit, one that is both supportive and suffocating.

The stereotype of *mammismo* has been mentioned in the growing body of scholarly work on national identity in Italy, with, for example, an important study by cultural historian Silvana Patriarca suggesting that it is part of a wider culture of national soul-searching and self-denunciation.[22] Despite this interest, however, and despite the widely acknowledged importance of the family in any understanding of Italian society and culture, *mammismo* has largely tended to be regarded ahistorically and taken for granted rather than investigated. As yet there has been very little systematic academic analysis of the stereotype and its social and political consequences.

Many scholars have, of course, been interested in motherhood, and there is now a considerable bibliography about it in various disciplines across the social sciences and humanities.[23] Scholars of Italian literary works, for example, have shown a particular interest in motherhood in recent years, although the focus of much of this has tended to be the mother–daughter relationship: far less attention has been paid to mothers and their sons.[24] Historians of women and gender in Italy, conversely, have shown only a fairly limited interest in mothers.[25] Of course, historians have not totally ignored this theme, but motherhood has tended to be discussed as part of other topics like the emphasis placed on it in patriarchal gender ideologies of various kinds, or its role in first-wave feminist ideology. There has been less interest in the practice and experience of motherhood, apart from the related topic of pregnancy and childbirth.[26] In this, Italian historians have not differed greatly from historians of women in other European countries: such (relative) neglect is not unusual in Western historiography.[27] Overall, where they have written about motherhood, both Italian historians and literary scholars have largely ignored (or possibly studiously avoided) the stereotype of *mammismo* and neither have they displayed much interest in the mother–son relationship, perhaps unsurprisingly given that the study of masculinity in Italy remains at a fairly early stage.[28]

THE "BIRTH OF *MAMMISMO*"

In 2005, Marina d'Amelia opened up debate on the stereotype of *mammismo* with her book, *La mamma*,[29] which raised the interesting hypothesis that the idea of a particularly strong relationship between Italian mothers and their sons is far from the universal, timeless feature of Italian society that many assume it to be. Instead, she argued, *mammismo* is an excellent example of an "invented tradition,"[30] one that was forged just after the Second World War as a means of explaining Italy's ills, and the consequent anxieties about Italian masculinity, in the aftermath of twenty years of dictatorship and the recent military defeat and occupation. According to d'Amelia, it was the writer and journalist Corrado Alvaro who was the first to use the term *mammismo*: it appeared in the title of an essay he published in 1952.[31] In this essay, a kind of nostalgic lament over the recent changes to Rome, he mourned things like the influx of people into the city from the provinces and the replacement of the old-fashioned *osterie* (taverns) of days gone by with modern, and, in his view, less appealing, bars. A prime focus of the essay was what he saw as the deplorable behaviour of the young men of Rome. The typical modern Roman youth was, for him, an idle good-for-nothing who spent a great deal of time lounging around doing nothing in particular. As he wrote: "There the older boys are, on the low walls in the sun, watched with envy and dismay by foreigners who have the satisfaction of seeing Italians doing sweet nothing."[32] A striking element of this particular sentence is the fact that it includes what has been a core preoccupation for much of Italy's self-blaming literature—the theme of how Italians are viewed (negatively) by foreigners. Alvaro is, quite simply, embarrassed.

Rather than blaming the lazy youths themselves, however, Alvaro directs his disapproval at their mothers. Responsible for this state of affairs, in his view, was the great exaltation of motherhood in Italian culture and the consequent pernicious influence of the overbearing Italian mother. It was important, he felt, to go beyond sentimentality about this issue and he complained (invoking a frequent theme of Italy's copious literature of self-denunciation—that of comparison with other, "more civilized," societies) that:

> In contrast to what happens in modern societies, where young people are brought up with a sense of order, obedience and respect for the needs of society [*un senso collettivo*], each of these young men is the centre of his mother's life, the sole person who has a right to everything…[33]

Alvaro did not, of course, simply conjure up this idea from nowhere. He may have been the one to coin the actual term itself but he was essentially just giving a name to a pre-existing concept. Ideas that we would recognize as part of the stereotype can be found elsewhere prior to the publication of Alvaro's essay. Anna Bravo has noted, for example, that the idea that Italian men were spoilt, vain "mama's boys" was widespread among Allied soldiers in the Second World War.[34] Another example is the publication, in 1945, by the historian Fabio Cusin of a wide-ranging critique of the ills of the "Italian character," one of whose sources he saw as the pernicious influence of mothers over their children's development. Cusin blamed mothers for what he saw as an Italian tendency to exhibit "feminine" traits such as emotionalism and sentimentality.[35]

Long before this, moreover, gender had played a role in the laments of many who wrote about the "failings of Italy": many nineteenth- and early twentieth-century writers had expressed their desire for a regeneration of the national character in terms of the need for a re-virilization of an effeminate Italy, albeit without specifically mentioning the role of mothers. The Fascists, too, took this approach. They venerated motherhood for its potential contribution to Italy's national strength, but virility, in their view, sorely needed to be shored up. Good Fascist women were meant to produce many sons and then be prepared to let go of them as they marched off to war and imperial conquest for the glory of the nation.

Where then did Alvaro and others get the idea of Italian mothers as powerful figures? As the speakers at our workshop at the University of Dundee indicated, in the late nineteenth and early twentieth centuries, there had, indeed, been a great deal of attention paid to motherhood. Their papers covered such diverse topics as the depiction of mothers in realist, modernist and feminist literary texts to Risorgimental, first-wave feminist and Fascist ideas about maternal roles, to (grand)motherly figures in fairy tales. As they demonstrated, maternal figures in this period might be heroic; or long-suffering; or sacrificial. They might be theatrical and performative, or simply unruly. They might be strong or weak. They might be praised for carrying out a patriotic duty or castigated as in need of advice to make them better mothers. Motherhood was invoked to legitimize women's political participation but equally mothers were blamed for all sorts of things and were repeatedly exhorted to match up to the standards of various paradigms of good motherhood. Some of this was, of course, not particularly dissimilar to other European countries in this period, although the emphasis on the importance of motherhood was, arguably, somewhat stronger in Italy than in northern European and in mainly Protestant countries. Despite the great range of different, and sometimes contrasting, ways in which Italian mothers were represented in this period, however, none of the representations discussed in this workshop seemed to echo or foreshadow in any meaningful way the stereotype of *mammismo*. The specific ill of this blaming stereotype, and the theme of women ruining the nation by spoiling, indulging and smothering their sons, was noteworthy for its absence.

One idea discussed in the Dundee workshop, however, did seem to shed some light on where the idea of the strong Italian mother came from (albeit not specifically the indulgent mother of *mammismo*). This was the patrilocal family norm, still widespread in certain types of peasant families in the nineteenth and early twentieth centuries, particularly, but not only, in northern and central Italy.[36] As Rita Cavigioli has argued: "The widespread cultural norm of patrilocal postmarital residence has favoured the development of family relational patterns that have been traditionally associated with the 'Italian matriarchate' stereotype: a strong mother–son bond and alliance and complex female intergenerational ties..."[37] In patrilocal families, upon marriage brides went to live with their husband's family where they found themselves at the bottom of the household's pecking order, often tyrannized by their mothers-in-law. A daughter-in-law had influence only over her own children and it was only through her sons that she could exert authority in the family. Daughters did not bring the same status as they would eventually leave to marry. Thus, for a large group of Italian women, the only power they had was as mothers of sons (even though their massive workloads usually left little time for actual mothering). Patrilocal families, in practice, are generally associated with societies where women have very low status, in which sons are valued more than daughters. In such peasant families, there is no particular suggestion that excessive maternal love led to weak, ineffectual sons, since all peasants, of either sex, had to be tough and hardworking. In all families, moreover, whether rural or urban, patrilocal or not, it was the power of the male head of family, his authority bolstered by a combination of cultural norms and the force of law, that prevailed. Even a woman with a strong relationship to her own sons still had to submit to the authority of the male head of family.

The idea of strong mothers was, nonetheless, present in parts of the South too, a region where the patrilocal norm was less common. Gabriella Gribaudi's chapter for this volume (originally given at the Glasgow workshop) looks at one example of this, the works of the Neapolitan playwright Eduardo De Filippo—many of them written and performed prior to the publication of Alvaro's essay. Although De Filippo's work was, of course, a portrayal of strong southern mothers (and weak southern men), as Patriarca has pointed out, in many of the negative stereotypes about Italian national character there is a degree of slippage between ideas about the South and ideas about the nation as a whole: the South was often seen, not as separate from Italy, but as "an exaggerated version of Italy, that is, possessing all its defects in accentuated fashion."[38]

The cultural and social milieu of the postwar years must also be considered in discussing where the idea of *mammismo* comes from. As Silvana Patriarca argues in her contribution to this volume (which focuses on the history and diffusion of the stereotype from the 1940s to the present day), Alvaro's ideas about the nature of Italian motherhood, and its deleterious effect on Italian men and society more broadly, should be understood in the context of the broader intellectual environment at the time, both in

LA MAMMA: ITALIAN MOTHERS PAST AND PRESENT 11

Italy and beyond. This included the equally critical idea of "momism" which had gained currency in America and predated *mammismo* by around a decade. Within Italy, the growing tendency in the postwar period to use psychology as a means of analysing, and indeed criticizing, Italian identity and society, was an approach that drew in particular on the maternal, on ideas such as the "great (Italian/Mediterranean) mother" and "maternal civilization." As she goes on to show (and as we will explore further below), however, it was not through intellectual debate but rather through mass culture, and films in particular, that the stereotype took hold, and in a simplified form in which the much-ridiculed *mammone* and misogyny are the dominant tropes.

The postwar years were, moreover, a time when unprecedented numbers of Italian women became housewives, and this might help explain how the idea of *mammismo* came to take hold in the popular imagination. Although for many women the chance of becoming a housewife could seem like a liberation from the backbreaking toil of life on the land, and the opportunity, denied to many of their own mothers, to take proper care of their children, there were also downsides to this new situation. As Anna Bravo has written:

> Now stuck at home, she can turn it into a claustrophobic nest. She can begin to see her children as her own private, exclusive, property, scrutinising their lives, projecting her own unsatisfied ambitions onto them, suspicious of their every foray into the outside world, feeling guilty about their every failure, and devastated when they leave home.[39]

This idea that the overzealous mother figure stems from the unhappiness of the housewife of the postwar era was recently echoed by Italian psychologist Giuliana Proietti. In an interview with *Psychology Today*, she argued that the roots of the over-mothering Italian mother should be sought in what she calls the "traditional" role of the Italian (and Latin) woman, frustrated with her life in a period before divorce and career were options available to them: "She thus poured her love into her children. Over time the son became a sort of husband to his mother without the sexual component."[40] While the notion of "traditional" is always open to question, and indeed problematic in the sense that women's employment was widespread in Italy before the economic miracle, it is true that postwar Italy had a considerably higher proportion of housewives than some other European countries in those years.

As Penelope Morris notes in her chapter in this volume (based on a paper given at the Glasgow workshop), echoes of this surface in advice columns of the postwar period, a useful "window into the private sphere" of those years of change.[41] Morris compares the problems and advice regarding motherhood in the magazines *Grazia*, *Famiglia cristiana*, *Noi donne* and *Epoca*. As she demonstrates, the advice offered varies from normative prescriptions to genuine attempts to respond to readers' anxieties and predicaments. The notion of *mammismo* is undoubtedly present, if never named, and examined particularly closely by the novelist Alba de Céspedes in her column "Dalla parte di lei" in *Epoca*. In answers which are highly attuned to gender inequalities and the challenges of modern motherhood, it is striking that the stereotype is assumed to exist. For de Céspedes, such domineering—and essentially unhappy—mothers are the product of a society that denies women respect or influence other than as wives and mothers and traps them, in the absence of divorce, in loveless, and sometimes abusive, marriages. Admittedly, this is just one of many forms of mothering that appear in de Céspedes' column. It is also true that while the solutions proposed in "Dalla parte di lei" are never facile, the overall tenor is one of optimism, as in the magazine itself, designed in many ways to sell a modern, happy lifestyle. It is in her best-selling novel of the same period, *Quaderno proibito*, by contrast, that the intensely tragic implications of *mammismo* are played out. Here, de Céspedes paints a far bleaker picture of motherhood, "failed" masculinity and power relations within the family.

Of course, *mammismo* was far from the only, or even the dominant, vision of motherhood in these postwar years. Many celebrated motherhood, rather than condemned it. In the immediate aftermath of a catastrophic war, many returning soldiers yearned for the comfort and safety of their families, and particularly their mothers.[42] Catholics, moreover, who dominated Italy politically after the war through the Christian Democrat party, continued to praise women for their motherly virtues. Even many female ex-partisans, whether actual mothers or not, on the defensive given the attempts to brand them as women of loose morals, often claimed that it was maternal values that had led them to fight for their nation.[43]

In the Glasgow workshop, some of the rich variety of ways in which Italian mothers were represented in the postwar years and the following decades were explored. In this period mothers were both criticized and idealized; seen as both problematic and positive; strong, but overbearing and self-sacrificial. The Glasgow papers also showed how the meanings and experiences of motherhood changed over generations, and how those generational differences themselves could be problematic, as emerged in women's diaries, or in anxious letters to magazines from women trying to deal with cohabiting with mothers-in-law, or in the oral accounts of 1970s feminists who spoke both of a revolt against their mothers (of the postwar, housewifely, generation) but also of transgenerational connection and solidarity.[44] In this complex and varied picture of maternity, "traditional" and patriarchal assumptions about motherhood—which now also included the stereotype of *mammismo*—continued to play a fundamental part. Indeed, many of the workshop papers did not discuss the stereotype directly, as, in those years, it seems to have appeared mainly in popular culture—particularly films—or in the exchanges with readers writing in to advice columns.

Some of the papers in the workshop demonstrated how maternity could be used to reassure or "normalize," as in the case of the use of maternal discourses to rehabilitate female terrorists,[45] or to create consensus, as Molly Tambor's chapter in this volume shows. Tambor explores how, in the same period as Alvaro launched the idea of *mammismo*, others were deploying ideas about maternity to quite different, more positive and empowering, ends. She examines how postwar female parliamentarians (many of them ex-partisans) in the newly born Italian Republic skilfully drew on ideas about the social value of maternity to push through a raft of legislative reforms relevant to gender equality. Here, Tambor focuses on one particularly significant moment—the passing of Teresa Noce's law on maternity leave for working women. Through the story of the campaign for this legislation—passed in 1950—Tambor explores both a successful use of maternalist politics for women's rights, as well as the ambivalent consequences of politicizing maternity. Alvaro himself (as Silvana Patriarca notes in her chapter) was negative about women's new influence in the world of politics. Perhaps his slating of the mothers of postwar Rome was at least in part a reaction to this deluge of empowering maternal ideology.

Mammismo Abroad

No discussion of the stereotype of *mammismo* would be complete without regard to the role that it has played beyond Italy itself. The importance of the Italian diaspora was raised even in the first workshop in Dundee, when

Chiara Saraceno aired the idea that the stereotype of *mammismo* may be primarily one whose origins lie mainly outside Italy, constructed by migrant Italians as well as non-Italians. Although d'Amelia's work does seem to suggest that it would be wrong to describe *mammismo* as nothing more than yet another anti-Italian stereotype stemming from the scornful, orientalist gaze of foreigners and then taken on board by Italians themselves, the popularization and dissemination of this stereotype certainly did occur to a great extent beyond Italy's borders, particularly in the New World. Corrado Alvaro may have been one of the first to speak of it in Italy but cultural representations of gender roles in Italian diaspora communities, particularly American films and television programmes, have played a role in disseminating such ideas and reinforcing them in the popular imagination.

As the papers on North America given at the Edinburgh workshop demonstrated, the specific idea of *mammismo* in this diaspora community seems to have appeared at roughly the same time as it did in Italy.[46] In the USA, it was not evident in the late nineteenth century and early twentieth century, emerging only (shortly after a not dissimilar American equivalent—the "momism" mentioned above) in the second half of the twentieth century. When it did appear, it was popularized mainly in films and literary representations, although always alongside a range of representations of the Italian maternal figure, far from all being of the *mammismo* variety.

The North American example is the focus of Maddalena Tirabassi's chapter for this volume, based on her paper given at this workshop. Here she explores the emergence of the *mammismo* stereotype in America where an image of a "traditional Italian family" developed that was quite different from the realities of life in the Italian South that migrants had left behind. She argues that, over time, a series of stereotypical images of Italian Americans emerged. The early representations of Italians—primarily as organ grinders, downtrodden workers and romantic lovers—were increasingly replaced by images of strong mothers and "mama's boys" (as well as, of course, macho gangsters). Tirabassi's chapter examines a number of films, and literary and televisual representations, which, to varying degrees, have conveyed such ideas, as well as some recent independent films that offer more nuanced and less stereotypical representations than the dominant Hollywood narrative.

Overall, however, the contributors to the Edinburgh workshop demonstrated, in the examples they studied at least, how the lived experiences of many Italian diaspora mothers can be viewed through the lens of the stereotype only with difficulty, since the relationship between migration and motherhood is, and was, multi-layered and complex. The two papers on the Antipodes, for example, showed strong family ties in diaspora communities but a range of realities, often quite different from idealized or stereotypical images.

This complexity was also evident in the views aired at the Edinburgh public event focusing on the Scottish-Italian community, particularly in the discussions following the talk by keynote speaker Mary Contini,[47] and the round-table event where a diverse group of Italian-Scots (whose ages ranged over a number of generations—the youngest being a 14-year old boy) shared their ideas through personal testimonies. A notable feature of these discussions was the idea, expressed by some of the third- or fourth-generation migrants that a mother's tendency to spoil and depend on a particular male child, usually the oldest son—identified light-heartedly by some speakers as "the chosen one"—and her desire to provide food, together formed a defining feature of their identity as Italians. Some even presented these tendencies as some kind of innate (or even "genetic") feature of Italianness. The latter idea was contested, however, by a first-generation Italian migrant in the audience, who felt that the more established migrant community was essentially evoking a nostalgic idea of a bygone Italy which was out of touch with more recent changes in Italian society. One of the speakers in the round table mentioned this too and spoke of her own mother's approach to how her daughter should behave as based on "a time warp" in her failure to grasp that the Italy she had left had changed in her absence. The discussion, however, was far more nuanced than this simple contrast seems to imply, with many speakers pointing out differing or more ambivalent stories, based on their own particular life experiences. Others, moreover, were dismissive of whether or not this was how things were done in Italy since, as they pointed out, their identity was not Italian but Scottish-Italian, an identity that they saw as taking "the best from both cultures." Some pointed out too that aspects like expecting girls to do more housework than boys, and the favouring of the men of the household ("serve the men first"), was far from an exclusive feature of Italian households, but occurred in some Scottish families too. The figure of the (male) "chosen one" was, moreover, presented as different from the *bamboccione* of the *mammismo* stereotype, for this figure was seen as more a potential strong protector of the family in times of trouble, than a spoilt, coddled son. There was much agreement, however, on the importance of family values and of food (and the social nature of its consumption) as defining features of an Italian-Scottish identity in both the past and present.

BEYOND THE STEREOTYPE

As should be clear from much of what has already been said, many of the papers from the various workshops, and some of the contributions to this volume, demonstrate that *mammismo* is, and has been, but one of a diverse range of images of Italian motherhood. For example, as Ursula Fanning's chapter shows, although many Italian writers, particularly women writers, have found a rich seam of inspiration in the topic of mothers, motherhood and the maternal experience, in the main, they have (with good reason) simply ignored such negative representations. Fanning discusses what is perhaps the best-known example in Italian women's writing of the rejection of motherhood—Sibilla Aleramo's articulation of issues of identity and conflict around the maternal in her thinly disguised autobiographical novel *Una donna*. Yet, as Fanning demonstrates, that work can also be read as a challenging reconfiguration of the maternal which would echo through the novels of later writers; one which takes account of the intense physical pleasures and the strong pull of motherhood while firmly rejecting the role of the mother as it was understood at the time and drawing attention repeatedly to the threat to the self posed by maternity. If, in the mid-twentieth century, Fanning notes, writers tended towards oblique references to motherhood, if any, or negative representations of sacrifice and limitation, from the 1970s onwards there was a marked effort to reconceptualize the maternal and a particular interest in the mother–daughter relationship. As in Aleramo's novel, the corporeality of motherhood and its disruption to identity remained central concerns, but these are aspects which also open the way to literary and philosophical dimensions of motherhood, and a means of embracing otherness more widely.

Mary Jo Bona's chapter suggests that this interest in diverse representations of the maternal (as well as a strong interest in the mother–daughter relationship) has crossed the Atlantic to Italian diaspora communities. Her study focuses on experimental narratives by Italian-American authors Carole Maso, Mary Cappello and Alison Bechdel, all of which explore relationships between mothers and daughters, from the point of view of daughters who identify as lesbian. As Bona points out, literary Italian-American representations of mothers may have had some familiar tropes, but they also had sufficient context and nuance to move beyond stereotypical media representations of migrant groups. These recent writers have shifted further still from traditional representations of ethnicity, but, Bona suggests, an analysis of "heritage culture" in their novels throws light in particular on their reworkings and reimaginings of the mother–daughter relationship.

For all these writers, whether in Italy or in its diaspora, motherhood was a complex issue: it was certainly not reducible to a single meaning. For them, as for many politically active women, from first-wave feminists to the postwar parliamentary pioneers examined by Tambor, moreover, motherhood could have positive meanings. But it posed many dilemmas for women, and, as the chapters in this volume by Gabriella Gribaudi and Chiara Saraceno show, the realities for Italian mothers are, and have been, complex.

In her contribution Gribaudi compares the lived realities of three generations of Neapolitan women over the course of much of the twentieth century with the portraits of strong, overbearing wives and mothers (and their contrastingly weak and downtrodden husbands) in the well-known Neapolitan plays of Eduardo De Filippo. In some cases, she found, the women's lives do seem to echo the overdrawn characters of the theatrical representations but the realities which emerge from the oral testimonies she has used suggest a far more complex panorama—and one that changed markedly over different generations—than the stereotypical, simplistic image of gender relations of De Filippo's comedies.

Chiara Saraceno's chapter similarly explores lived realities. She focuses on the practicalities of life for modern Italian mothers and the constraints that make it increasingly difficult for Italian women to fulfil their desire for maternity, which include particularly high levels of youth unemployment and job insecurity, widely shared ideals of "good" motherhood and of children's needs, and limitations on access to reproductive technologies. As she argues, those who do become mothers face a further range of obstacles, such as the limitations of social policy and the consequent reliance on kin networks, the scarcity and unevenness of childcare provision, and problematic school timetables.

This complex situation facing mothers—or would-be mothers—is now much discussed in Italy, whether through publications, online blogs and discussion forums or more traditional media, largely instigated by women.[48] Indeed, as Marina d'Amelia commented at the Rome event (where Saraceno presented the paper on which her chapter for this volume is based), a novelty of recent times is that women now express a widespread "ambivalence towards maternity," and are prepared to say openly that motherhood brings "joy," but also "anxiety, difficulty and conflict."[49] This was evident in the contributions of other speakers at the same event (both on the platform, and in the audience). Journalist Alessandra Di Pietro, for example, talked about her own experience as a working mother who had never had a permanent employment contract: for her, the legal provision of maternity leave was of little use and this meant that she had to "make up motherhood as she went along," at times convinced that she was making her own decisions but aware, on reflection, that she was also "following deep-seated stereotypes." Trade unionist Lidia Obando drew attention to the crucial role played by immigrant domestic workers in their temporary "mothering" of many of Italy's children; these women often have to leave their own children behind in their countries of origin and struggle to gain full rights as citizens in Italy. Parliamentarian Livia Turco felt that her priorities and way of doing politics had been profoundly influenced by motherhood, but she too had experienced considerable difficulties as a government minister when also the mother of a young child. She had always been keen to be seen as both a mother and a politician, but she identified one of the main problems today for Italian women as a kind of "symbolic vacuum," in which there is still no positive way of representing the combination of motherhood and work.

Members of the audience in Rome put most emphasis in their contributions on practical issues like the limitations of state support and childcare provisions, and the problems that arise at work when a woman is pregnant or when she tries to return to work after having had a baby. As one member of the audience—the journalist Chiara Valentini—pointed out, it has become commonplace for women to try to hide pregnancies in the workplace and, she commented, Italy's very low birth rate is not a result of women wanting to work instead of having children, but because it has been very difficult, or in some cases impossible, to combine work with motherhood.[50] Another obstacle that was mentioned, though perhaps surprisingly briefly, was the highly unequal division of labour within the home and there was very little discussion of the role of fathers.

The Stereotype Today

Mammismo is, of course, a largely negative stereotype. In an analogous manner to the British mother-in-law joke, made famous in particular by comedians like Les Dawson and Bob Monkhouse (in which mothers-in-law are portrayed as overbearing, meddlesome, unattractive figures who

LA MAMMA: ITALIAN MOTHERS PAST AND PRESENT 19

threaten a husband's authority in the home by their disapproving attitude to their daughter's choice of husband), the term *mammismo* was coined as a way of blaming women for men's own failings.[51] Unlike the mother-in-law joke, which, although not totally gone, an onslaught of feminist critique has made seem simply old-fashioned, the idea of *mammismo* is still with us in the twenty-first century. Alvaro's neologism (together with the related terms *bamboccione* and *mammone*) has proved remarkably persistent and remains instantly recognizable (although not necessarily acceptable) to modern-day Italians.

Italy is, of course, much less a nation of housewives than it was in the postwar years, and the size of the Italian family has shrunk dramatically, but a number of factors have contributed to the persistence of the *mammismo* stereotype. One is that, as previously mentioned, the focus of the joke, and of more serious discussions, tends to be the son, rather than the mother herself. Thus, Italian feminists may not particularly like jocular references to "*la mamma*" but they have not targeted them in the way that British feminists have the mother-in-law joke. Furthermore, the stereotype might have faded away had it not seemed to resonate with certain aspects of present-day Italy's social realities. Italy does seem, indeed, to be a nation of *mammoni* where many adults of both sexes, but particularly men, continue to live with their parents until quite an advanced age (although, of course, Italy is far from the only European country where this is true). And the family, in twenty-first-century Italy, continues to be remarkably strong, linking Italians together with ties that are both emotional and practical. Within that family, mothers are, in many ways, still held in great esteem (although, as the discussion above demonstrated, this is often more a question of rhetoric than of concrete measures to support them in their maternal role). Herein may lie, as one of the members of the audience at our Rome event pointed out, one reason for women failing to really challenge the stereotype. She felt that in some ways *mammismo*-style over-mothering could, perversely, be seen as a response to machismo and male power, in that it seems to give women power, albeit a limited form of power restricted to the family and the home. Some mothers, including herself, she felt, are reluctant to relinquish this "traditionally Italian maternal power" over their children. The other members of the audience did not seem particularly keen to debate this perhaps uncomfortable question, but the pride that many Italian women have in their skill as mothers, and their strong identification with the role, is undoubtedly relevant.

20   P. MORRIS AND P. WILLSON

The persistence of the stereotype, however, cannot just be explained in this way, as a product of women's own choices, for the irony is, of course, that the stereotype warns of the danger to society of what might be called "over-mothering" in a situation where social policy and cultural and economic factors do nothing to combat this. On the contrary, they seem to conspire to make women focus all their energies on motherhood. And parenting (for which there is as yet no gender-neutral word in Italian) is still seen as women's work alone, to the extent that when a man takes on tasks that are traditionally seen as maternal (as a few young men are doing in Italy today) another, telling, neologism has appeared—*il mammo*, a term that literally translates as "male mother."[52]

NOTES

1. On Catholic views of motherhood and the maternal role since the late nineteenth century see, for example, Koch, "La madre di famiglia nell'esperienza cattolica."
2. Anna Bravo, "Madri fra oppressione ed emancipazione," p. 78. (This chapter was first published as "La nuova Italia: Madri fra oppressione ed emancipazione," in *Storia della maternità*, edited by Marina d'Amelia.)
3. The term "the golden cage of Italian youth" comes from Dalla Zuanna, "The Banquet of Aeolus," p. 144.
4. This term is often associated with Padoa-Schioppa although he was not, in fact, the first to use it. As Silvana Patriarca notes in her chapter in this volume, the term *bamboccione* was used by the novelist Ennio Flaiano as early as 1951.
5. As Luca Storti, Joselle Dagnes, and Javier González Díez have argued, this leads to "stereotyped views of the situation, which are based on little empirical evidence and are inadequate for understanding the country's problems" Storti et al., "Undisciplined, selfish big babies?" p. 51.
6. https://www.theguardian.com/lifeandstyle/2010/jan/20/italys-mamma-boys-cant-cut-ties. Interestingly, the reference to the stereotype only featured in the title: the article itself was a more serious one about how a man had been forced for financial reasons to return to live with his parents at the age of 36 and the difficulties he experienced in this situation. There continues to be an appetite for journalism on this subject, as witnessed by the episode of ITV's foreign current affairs programme *On Assignment*, "Italy's Mamma's Boys: The Curse of the Mammoni" (first aired 26 January 2016), which was partly inspired by the research being carried out for this project and for which Morris was an expert adviser.
7. De Rosa, "Il tuo lui è un mammone?" Numerous similar examples of various kinds can be found on Italian websites such as: http://27esimaora.

corriere.it/articolo/il-potere-delle-mamme-sui-figli-maschi-adulti/. Another good example is the book by Blini, *Mamma mia!*, a wacky and wide-ranging comic look at the stereotype and its supposed impact on modern Italian society.

8. Typical of this is, for example, Anon., "'Bamboccioni': Italia terza in classifica," p. 4. Italy's third place (mentioned in the title), the paper reported, resulted from the fact that, among European countries, both Slovakia and Croatia had more stay-at-home young adults (aged 18–34) than Italy. The Italian percentage reported was, nevertheless, a striking 65.8 per cent.

9. See http://www.telegraph.co.uk/men/relationships/10643710/Whats-the-opposite-of-Mammismo.html.

10. On the Jewish mother, see Antler, *You Never Call! You Never Write!* This stereotype emerged after the Second World War (p. 8) at roughly the same time as the Italian one.

11. Directed, written by, and starring Gianni di Gregorio. Released in English as *The Salt of Life*.

12. Leone, *Confessioni di un mammone italiano*.

13. Culicchia, *Ameni Inganni*. In this novel, it is Alberto who, driven by an almost pathological fear of relationships and commitment, chooses this lifestyle of eternal adolescence: indeed his mother encourages him to lead a more normal life. For a discussion of this work see Masenga, "The 'Delaying of Age' Novel" pp. 176–92. Masenga does argue, however, that in most of the "delaying of age" novels she has studied the protagonists identify mainly with their peers and there is "a strong opposition to familial and, more generally, adult figures, who are blamed for complying with the social system and, indeed, symbolizing it. The prolonged youth—or the delaying in defining themselves as adults—does not necessarily correspond to a desire to stay within the family of origin; on the contrary, it develops as a form of reaction to *mammismo*" (p. 82).

14. Benedetti, *The Tigress in the Snow*, p. 4.

15. For a discussion of how the dominant models of masculinity in Italy have changed over the course of the twentieth century up to the present day, see Sandro Bellassai, *L'invenzione della virilità*. Bellassai argues that the main motors of change have been feminism and the advent of the consumer society.

16. O'Rawe, *Stars and Masculinities*, p. 11. See also O'Rawe's discussion of the "crisis discourse" on pp. 4–5 and Sergio Rigoletto's criticism of "the binary logic underlying the way in which the axiom of masculinity in crisis in Italian cinema is predominantly framed," which "sets a normative male ideal in relation to which cinematic representations of men are to be measured" (*Masculinity and Italian Cinema*, p. 6). Bellassai, too, in the final chapter of *L'invenzione della virilità*, depicts the end of the century as a

period of crisis for masculinity. None of these works, however, directly consider the figure of the *bamboccione*.

17. Reich, *Beyond the Latin Lover*, p. xii. Natalie Fullwood has explored the idea of male failure in the films of the period more broadly in *Cinema, Gender and Everyday Space*. Neither Reich nor Fullwood, however, addresses the mother–son relationship when discussing masculinity.

18. Lippmann. *Public Opinion*. On stereotypes, their uses and misuses, and for some reflections on Lippmann's ideas, see Dyer, "The Role of Stereotypes."

19. Lippmann, *Public Opinion*, pp. 90–91.

20. Lippmann, *Public Opinion*, p. 90.

21. For a discussion of how psychologists have discussed stereotypes see Glăveanu, "Stereotypes Revised."

22. Patriarca, *Italian Vices*.

23. For the last twenty years the Motherhood Initiative for Research and Community Involvement (MIRCI), along with the *Journal of the Motherhood Initiative*, has been an important focus for a wide range of research on motherhood. See http://motherhoodinitiative.org/

24. Much has been written about this. See, for example, Sambuco, "Corporeal Bonds"; Benedetti, *The Tigress in the Snow*; Lazzari and Charnley (eds), *To Be or Not to Be a Mother*.

25. A pioneering work on the history of motherhood in Italy was d'Amelia (ed.), *Storia della maternità*. See also Fiume (ed.), *Madri. Storia di un ruolo sociale* (mostly about the early modern period).

26. See, for example, Filippini, *Generare, partorire, nascere*.

27. As Ann Taylor Allen wrote in 2002 (comments that are, arguably, still largely true today): "Despite the central importance of this theme [motherhood] to the history of women and of feminism, it has often been neglected by historians, who are usually most interested in women's entry into new areas such as politics, the professions, sports, and social life outside the family. Motherhood, many imply, was a 'traditional' role..." (Allen, *Feminism and Motherhood*, p. 2.)

28. As mentioned above, one of the more developed areas is that of masculinity and film.

29. D'Amelia, *La mamma*.

30. On "invented traditions," see Hobsbawm and Ranger (eds), *The Invention of Tradition*.

31. D'Amelia, *La mamma*, p. 15.

32. Alvaro, "Il mammismo," p. 184. Alvaro (1895–1956) was a southerner (born in San Luca in Reggio Calabria) from a modest background (his father was a primary school teacher). In addition to his work as a newspaper journalist (mainly in the periods before and after Fascism, given his anti-fascist politics) he wrote numerous novels and non-fiction works as

well as a few plays. On his life and work see, for example, Virdia, "Alvaro, Corrado."

33. Alvaro, "Il mammismo," p. 187.
34. Bravo, "Madri fra oppressione ed emancipazione," pp. 77–78.
35. For a discussion of this work (Fabio Cusin, *L'Italiano: Realtà e illusioni*. Rome: Atlantica Editrice, 1945) see Patriarca, *Italian Vices*, pp. 204–07 and her chapter in this volume.
36. Household structure and land tenure systems were, of course, extremely varied in Italy. Patrilocality was particularly prevalent in households that were "*appoderati*" (where the peasants lived on the land they tilled, like sharecroppers). On the structure of peasant families see, for example, Barbagli, *Sotto lo stesso tetto*; Manoukian, "La famiglia dei contadini."
37. Cavigioli, *Women of a Certain Age*, p. 40.
38. Patriarca, *Italian Vices*, p. 9. Much has been written on representations of southern Italy, both on the "orientalist gaze" of northern Italians towards it and on foreign views. See, for example, Schneider (ed.), *Italy's Southern Question*; Moe, *The View from Vesuvius*. On foreign travellers or residents who wrote about the South see, for example, Ouditt, *Impressions of Southern Italy*; Alù, *Beyond the Traveller's Gaze*.
39. Bravo, "Madri fra oppressione ed emancipazione," p. 114.
40. D'Agostino, "Forever Mamma's Boy," p. 28.
41. See also, Morris, "From Private to Public."
42. In a recent book, for example, Gabriella Gribaudi recounts how one group of Italian soldiers returning home after the defeat in Greece, on sighting the Italian coast, greeted it with the song "Mamma, Mamma son tanto felice perche ritorno da te" ("Mamma, I'm so happy that I'm coming back to you"; Gribaudi, *Combattenti sbandati prigionieri*, p. 109).
43. On this point see Bravo, "Simboli del materno." On how women's role in the Resistance has been remembered and commemorated more broadly see Perry Willson, "Saints and Heroines."
44. On the latter point, see also Bracke, *Women and the Reinvention of the Political*.
45. See also Glynn, *Women, Terrorism and Trauma*.
46. Updated versions of the contributions to the Edinburgh workshop (apart from Maddalena Tirabassi's paper) have been published as a "forum" article: Barocci et al., "Mothers and *Mammismo* in the Italian Diaspora." A fuller version of Adalgisa Giorgio's paper has appeared as Giorgio, "The Italian family, motherhood and Italianness in New Zealand."
47. Mary Contini is the director of what is arguably Scotland's best-known Italian delicatessen as well as a chef/restaurateur. Her numerous publications include two autobiographical cookbooks, addressed to her elder and younger daughters respectively, *Dear Francesca* and *Dear Olivia*.

48. There are now vast numbers of so-called "Mummy blogs." For a substantial bibliography and discussion of the way that mothers, as readers of blogs, use the "mammasphere" as a cultural site through which the identities and role of motherhood, and the mother–child relationship, are socially and digitally (re)constructed, see Orton-Johnson, "Mummy Blogs." Another increasingly common format is the maternal memoir. For a study of recent Italian memoirs, see Marina Bettaglio, "Maternal Memoirs."

49. See d'Amelia's comments on mothers, blogs and stereotypes in "Cambia il mestiere," also reported in Giovanna Pezzuoli, "La ribellione delle blogger."

50. Valentini is a well-known journalist who has written a great deal on issues related to women. One of her recent publications—*O i figli o il lavoro*—focuses particularly on questions relevant to this debate. See also Adalgisa Giorgio, "Motherhood and Work in Italy."

51. On the mother-in-law joke see Davies, "The English Mother-in-Law Joke." Davies, a sociologist, uses comparative data to argue that mother-in-law jokes are typical of societies where nuclear families are prevalent and they do not occur in patrilineal societies. She sees the mother-in-law joke as a means of creating distance to diffuse family situations, produced, she argues, by "a particular tension within the social ordering of kinship in nuclear families. The anomaly is the intrusion of the wife's mother into the life of a family supposed to be limited to husband, wife and dependent children" (p. 35). While this argument about the origins of the joke is a persuasive one, her conclusion that misogyny has nothing to do with it is less convincing.

52. "Il mammo" was, for example, the title of a sitcom about a male single parent, broadcast on the Italian television channel Canale 5 for three seasons (2004–7). See O'Rawe, *Stars and Masculinities*, for an interesting discussion of the figure of the *mammo* and the role of "new fathers" (or *padri materni*) in post-2000 Italian cinema (pp. 78–82). As she notes, there has been considerable sociological and media interest in the subject in recent years.

BIBLIOGRAPHY

Allen, Ann Taylor. *Feminism and Motherhood in Western Europe, 1890–1970: The Maternal Dilemma*. New York: Macmillan, 2005.

Alù, Giorgia. *Beyond the Traveller's Gaze. Expatriate Ladies Writing in Sicily (1848–1910)*. Oxford: Peter Lang, 2008.

Alvaro, Corrado, "Il mammismo." in *Il nostro tempo e la speranza. Saggi di vita contemporanea*. Milan: Bompiani, 1952.

Antler, Joyce. *You Never Call! You Never Write! A History of the Jewish Mother.* New York: Oxford University Press, 2008.

Anon. https://www.theguardian.com/lifeandstyle/2010/jan/20/italys-mamma-boys-cant-cut-ties *The Guardian*, 20 January 2010.

Anon. http://www.telegraph.co.uk/men/relationships/10643710/Whats-the-opposite-of-Mammismo.html

Anon. "'Bamboccioni', Italia terza in classifica." *Metro*, 22 April 2015.

Anon. "Italy's Mamma's Boys: The Curse of the Mammoni." *On Assignment* (ITV), first aired 26 January 2016. See http://www.itv.com/news/2016-01-26/italys-mammas-boys-the-curse-of-the-mammonis/

Barbagli, Marzio. *Sotto lo stesso tetto. Mutamenti della famiglia in Italia dal XV al XX secolo*, Bologna: Il Mulino, 1984.

Barocci, Silvia, Garroni, Maria Susanna, Giorgio, Adalgisa, Morris, Penelope, Ricatti, Francesco, Willson, Perry. "Mothers and *Mammismo* in the Italian Diaspora." *Altreitalie. International Journal of Studies on Italian Migrations in the World* no. 50 (Jan.–June 2015): pp. 143–163.

Bellassai, Sandro. *L'invenzione della virilità. Politica e immaginario maschile nell'Italia contemporanea.* Rome: Carocci, 2011.

Benedetti, Laura. *The Tigress in the Snow: Motherhood and Literature in Twentieth-Century Italy.* Toronto: University of Toronto Press, 2007.

Bettaglio, Marina. "Maternal Momoirs in Contemporary Italy." in *To Be or Not to Be a Mother: Choice, Refusal, Reluctance and Conflict. Motherhood and Female Identity in Italian Literature and Culture*, edited by Laura Lazzari and Joyce Charnley. Special issue of *Intervalla* 1 (2016).

Blini, Fabrizio. *Mamma mia! La figura della mamma come deterrente nello sviluppo culturale, sociale, ed economico dell'Italia moderna.* Milan: Baldini Castoldi Dalai Editore, 2007.

Bracke, Maud. *Women and the Reinvention of the Political: Feminism in Italy 1968–1983*, New York: Routledge, 2014.

Bravo, Anna. "Madri fra oppressione ed emancipazione." in Anna Bravo, Margherita Pelaia, Alessandra Pescarolo, Lucetta Scaraffia, *Storia sociale delle donne nell'Italia contemporanea.* Rome-Bari: Laterza, 2001.

Bravo, Anna. "Simboli del materno." in *Donne e uomini nelle guerre mondiali*, edited by Anna Bravo. Rome-Bari: Laterza, 1991.

Cavigioli, Rita. *Women of a Certain Age. Contemporary Italian Fictions of Female Ageing.* Madison: Fairleigh Dickinson University Press, 2005.

Contini, Mary. *Dear Francesca: An Italian Journey of Recipes Recounted with Love.* London: Ebury Press, 2002.

Contini, Mary. *Dear Olivia: An Italian Journey of Love and Courage.* London: Ebury Press, 2006.

Culicchia, Giuseppe. *Ameni Inganni.* Milan: Mondadori, 2011.

D'Agostino, Raeleen. "Forever Mamma's Boy." *Psychology Today*, March–April, 2008.

Dalla Zuanna, Gianpiero. "The Banquet of Aeolus: a familistic interpretation of Italy's lowest low fertility." *Demographic Research* 4, article 5, (2001): pp. 133–162.

D'Amelia, Marina. "Cambia il mestiere di mamma? Dai manuali novecenteschi alle mamme blogger." Paper delivered at the "Storia in Piazza" Festival on Sexual Identity, Genoa, 20 April, 2013. http://www.palazzoducale.genova.it/storia/2013/files/audio/449.mp3

D'Amelia, Marina. *La mamma*. Bologna: Il Mulino, 2005.

D'Amelia, Marina (ed.), *Storia della maternità*. Rome-Bari: Laterza, 1997.

Davies, Christie. "The English Mother-in-Law Joke and its Missing Relatives." *Israeli Journal of Humor Research* 2, n. 2 (2012): pp. 12–39.

De Céspedes, Alba. *Quaderno proibito*. Milan: Mondadori, 1952.

De Rosa, Laura. "Il tuo lui è un mammone?" *PourFemme*, 22.01.2015. http://coppia.pourfemme.it/articolo/il-tuo-lui-e-un-mammone-test/15161/

Dyer, Richard. "The Role of Stereotypes." in *Media Studies: A Reader*, 2nd Edition, edited by Paul Marris, Sue Thornham. Edinburgh: Edinburgh University Press, 1999.

Filippini, Nadia. *Generare, partorire, nascere. Una storia dall'antichità alla provetta*. Rome: Viella, 2017.

Fiume, Giovanna (ed.), *Madri. Storia di un ruolo sociale*. Venice: Marsilio, 1995.

Fullwood, Natalie. *Cinema, Gender and Everyday Space: Comedy, Italian Style*. Palgrave: New York, 2015.

Giorgio, Adalgisa. "Motherhood and work in Italy: A sociocultural perspective." *Journal of Romance Studies* 5, n. 3 (2015a): pp. 1–21.

Giorgio, Adalgisa. "The Italian family, motherhood and Italianness in New Zealand. The case of the Italian community of Wellington." *Women's Studies International Forum* 52 (September–October 2015b): pp. 53–62.

Glăveanu, Vlad. "Stereotypes Revised—Theoretical Models, Taxonomy and the Role of Stereotypes." *Europe's Journal of Psychology* 3, n. 3, (2007). Available at: http://ejop.psychopen.eu/article/view/409

Glynn, Ruth. *Women, Terrorism and Trauma in Italian Culture*. New York: Palgrave, 2013.

Gribaudi, Gabriella. *Combattenti, sbandati, prigionieri. Esperienze e memorie di reduci della seconda guerra mondiale*. Rome: Donzelli, 2016.

Koch, Francesca. "La madre di famiglia nell'esperienza cattolica." in *Storia della maternità*, edited by d'Amelia. Rome-Bari: Laterza, 1997.

Hobsbawm, Eric and Terence Ranger (eds). *The Invention of Tradition*. Cambridge and New York: Cambridge University Press, 1983.

Lazzari, Laura and Joyce Charnley (eds). *To Be or Not to Be a Mother: Choice, Refusal, Reluctance and Conflict. Motherhood and Female Identity in Italian Literature and Culture*, Special issue of *Intervalla* 1 (2016).

Lippmann, Walter. *Public Opinion*. New York: Macmillan, 1929 [1st published 1922].

Leone, David. *Confessioni di un mammone italiano*, Florence: Mauro Pagliai Editore, 2014.

Manoukian, Agopik. "La famigli dei contadini." in *La famiglia italiana dall'ottocento a oggi*, edited by Piero Melograni, Rome-Bari: Laterza, 1988.

Masenga, Ilaria. "The 'Delaying of Age' Novel in Contemporary Italian Literature (1980–2011)." PhD thesis, University of Exeter, April 2013.

Moe, Nelson. *The View from Vesuvius. Italian Culture and the Southern Question.* Berkeley: University of California Press, 2002.

Morris, Penelope. "From Private to Public: Alba de Céspedes' Agony Column in 1950s Italy." *Modern Italy* 9, (2007): pp. 11–20.

O'Rawe, Catherine. *Stars and Masculinities in Contemporary Italian Cinema.* Palgrave: New York, 2014.

Orton-Johnson, Kate. "Mummy Blogs and Representations of Motherhood: 'Bad mummies' and their readers," *Social Media + Society* 3, n. 2 (2017): pp. 1–10.

Ouditt, Sharon. *Impressions of Southern Italy: British Travel Writers from Henry Swinburne to Norman Douglas,* London: Routledge, 2013.

Patriarca, Silvana. *Italian Vices: Nation and Character from the Risorgimento to the Republic.* Cambridge: Cambridge University Press, 2010.

Pezzuoli, Giovanna. "La ribellione delle blogger agli stereotipi. Di mamme non ce n'è una sola..." *La 27ora*, 18 April 2013. http://27esimaora.corriere.it/articolo/la-ribellione-delle-blogger-agli-stereotipi-di-mamme-non-ce-ne-una-sola/

Reich, Jacqueline. *Beyond the Latin Lover: Marcello Mastroianni, Masculinity, and Italian Cinema.* Bloomington and Indianapolis: Indiana University Press, 2004.

Rigoletto, Sergio. *Masculinity and Italian Cinema: Sexual Politics, Social Conflict and Male Crisis in the 1970s.* Edinburgh: Edinburgh University Press, 2014.

Sambuco, Patrizia. *Corporeal Bonds: The Daughter–Mother Relationship in Twentieth-Century Italian Women's Writing.* Toronto: University of Toronto Press, 2012.

Schneider, Jane (ed.). *Italy's Southern Question: Orientalism in One Country.* Oxford: Berg, 1998.

Storti, Luca, Joselle Dagnes, and Javier González Díez. "Undisciplined, Selfish Big Babies? The Cultural Framing of the Italian Financial Crisis." *Modern Italy* 23, n. 1 (2018): pp. 51–67.

Valentini, Chiara, *O figli o il lavoro.* Milan: Feltrinelli, 2012.

Virdia, Ferdinando. "Alvaro, Corrado." *Dizionario biografico degli italiani*, vol. 2. Rome: Treccani, 1960, *ad vocem.*

Willson, Perry. "Saints and Heroines: Re-writing the History of Italian Women in the Resistance." in *Opposing Fascism*, edited by Tim Kirk, Anthony McElligott. Cambridge: Cambridge University Press, 1999.

CHAPTER 2

Mammismo/Momism: On the History and Uses of a Stereotype, c.1940s to the Present

Silvana Patriarca

As understood in contemporary Italian culture and deployed in social and political discourse, *mammismo* only partly has to do with the phenomenon of the overly protective mother and the living-at-home adult son, which has become the subject of jokes all over the world. In fact, it is often the signifier of something else, namely a troubling peculiarity that widens to a social and political disorder and allegedly sets the country apart from the idea of the advanced Europe to which it aspires to belong. Indeed, *mammismo* points to an "unnatural" situation of long-term dependency, if not prolonged subjection, of the male with respect to the female: a pathology that produces irresponsible and infantilized males, the "mama's boys," who in turn damage the quality of the polity. If the figure of the *mammone*, the dependent male, is the target of contempt and ridicule, *mammismo* seems a way of blaming the mother figure for the ills of society at large. But when and how did this idea emerge? And how has it been used in political and social discourse?

S. Patriarca (✉)
Fordham University, New York City, NY, USA
e-mail: patriarca@fordham.edu

© The Author(s) 2018
P. Morris, P. Willson (eds.), *La Mamma*,
Italian and Italian American Studies,
https://doi.org/10.1057/978-1-137-54256-4_2

In her history of the mother in modern Italian society, Marina d'Amelia pointed out the specific "psychological-political" context in which the term *mammismo* was coined. It was the Calabrian writer Corrado Alvaro who, in the early 1950s, first used this neologism as a synonym of another neologism, namely *maternismo*. By these terms Alvaro referred to Italian mothers' doting on their male offspring, a habit that had repercussions in society at large. D'Amelia primarily links the emergence of the idea to the trauma of the war and the needs of a postwar society in search of reassurance through the invention of "myths of cohesion." It was then that some intellectuals resorted to the archetype of the "Great Mediterranean Mother" to explain why motherhood was so important in Italian society. However, the stereotype of the Italian mother which crystallized at that time was the result of a long historical process of sedimentation of experiences, views and prescriptions about the role of mothers in Italian society which had started with the making of the "patriotic mother" in the Risorgimento.[1]

Building on d'Amelia's identification of the context in which the idea of *mammismo* originated, this chapter will discuss the way in which *mammismo*—by no means, as we will see, a purely Italian invention—and the connected idea of *civiltà materna* (maternal civilization) were articulated in a society which despised the feminine, but exalted the maternal and enforced a strict heterosexual norm. I will point out how these ideas expressed in gendered terms a discontent with the postwar political order, a discontent that existed both on the left and on the right of the political spectrum. The notion was in part over-determined since it was tied with older nationalist tropes which associated political and military weakness with effeminacy and strength with masculinity. When originally formulated, however, *mammismo* and maternal civilization were a vehicle for the expression of political discontent and criticism on the part of the liberal left. Yet the diffusion of the idea at a popular level occurred primarily thanks to the cinema, which made the figure of the "mama's boy" into an object of mockery and laughter, in contrast to the image of the mother, who may be portrayed as tyrannical or over-indulgent but is rarely made fun of in Italian culture.[2]

BLAMING WOMEN: MOTHERS AS SCAPEGOATS DURING AND AFTER THE SECOND WORLD WAR

The word *mammismo* may have been coined in Italy in the early 1950s, but it had a similar-sounding American antecedent: "momism." This term had appeared in the US about ten years earlier and had gained popularity in the early Cold War period. It was American novelist and essayist Philip Wylie who coined this word in a diatribe against American "moms" in his *Generation of Vipers*, a book that attacked many aspects of American society, including the "common man" worshipped by politicians. The volume went into twenty printings by 1955.[3] As Joyce Antler has observed, Wylie depicted the "middle-aged, middle-class American mother as a destructive and sinister tyrant who stifled, dominated, and manipulated her family— especially sons—and the entire nation. Mom became the scapegoat for a host of perceived national deficiencies."[4] She was blamed for undermining the nation at a moment when it most needed strong men to fight its many enemies. The idea of momism was further developed by military psychiatrist Edward Strecker in *Their Mothers' Sons* (1946) which identified the cause of homosexuality in this type of mother. In all these cases "unhealthy" or "deviant" masculinity was made to derive from "moms" and connected to political anxieties in society at large.

A similar set of assumptions about the social consequences of (bad) motherhood was also at work in the emergence of the Italian idea of *mammismo*, even though with significantly different meanings and implications, not to mention a quite different historical-societal context. While American momism emerged during the war, Italian *mammismo* was a product of its aftermath. During the Second World War the propaganda of the Republic of Salò—the rump fascist state established in northern Italy after the fall of Fascism—blamed Italian women for not conforming to the idea of the self-sacrificing mother and wife who, they claimed, had prevailed during the previous world war.[5] In this new war, the fascist press complained, mothers were literally hiding their sons in their mattresses so that they would not be recruited by the army of Mussolini's puppet state. Of course, this ludicrous attempt to displace responsibility onto women for a war started and lost by men[6] contrasted with a reality that saw women engaged in all sorts of survival activities and even in military action, especially after the disbanding of the army that followed the armistice of 8 September 1943, and the beginning of the Resistance. Their behaviour, if anything, reflected the unpopularity that by then the fascist war had acquired among all strata of Italian society, even those which had supported Fascism throughout the dictatorship and had not opposed Mussolini when he entered the war in June 1940 believing that it would be a quick affair ending in victory.

But the left too was not generous with women: partisans often forbad those who had participated in the Resistance from marching in the victory parades that celebrated the liberation of Italy. The image of the woman who betrays the nation by having sexual relations with the enemy was not just pervasive among nationalists and conservatives, but appeared also in early Resistance narratives such as Italo Calvino's *The Path to the Spiders' Nests*. A strong backlash against women took place after the war in a heavily male-dominated society eager to return to normalcy.[7] This also meant that women were thrown out of well-paid jobs so that men could take their place, and considering the very limited purge that took place against the Fascists, the men in question could easily be former Fascists.[8]

Fascism had represented an aggressive attempt to "re-virilize" the nation by reshaping Italian masculinity in a militarized and militaristic way and by reasserting traditional gender roles at a time when they were being questioned by feminists. Necessarily the military defeat in the Second World War made the trope of the effeminacy of Italian men—which had tormented Risorgimento patriots—resurface with a vengeance.[9] The poor military reputation of the Italians reached a new low in the eyes of foreign soldiers, Germans and Allies alike, who looked down with contempt at the defeated people.[10] The "mama's boy" may be seen as a new instance of the feminization trope at a time when the nationalist dreams of virility appeared to have definitively dissolved.

If a major military defeat, followed by foreign occupation, gave rise to a deep sense of crisis and frustration among Italian men, only partially balanced by fighting in the Resistance, the frustration was further fed, especially on the left, by the beginning of the Cold War. Then Italy became a dependent/client of the US, lacking any autonomous foreign policy, and was "invaded" by American products and models. This was a situation of de facto limited sovereignty that could not but strengthen perceptions of national feminization. Intertwined with the evolving international situation, a domestic political event also contributed to this set of negative self-perceptions, namely the results of the elections of April 1948 that sealed the overwhelming victory of the Christian Democratic party and of its supporters, the US and the Catholic Church, with the latter engaged at the time in an effort to "re-Christianize" Italian society through the promotion of the cult of the Virgin Mary.

A casting in gendered terms of the crisis of Italian society during the war and in the postwar years can be found in several writings of the inventor of *mammismo*, Corrado Alvaro, especially in his diaries which the writer filled with observations on the social behaviour and attitudes of the Italians to serve as a source of ideas and possible subjects for his fiction pieces and journalism. His eyes were particularly focused on women. Women's behaviour served as an indicator of the corruption and disintegration (*disgregazione*) of Italian society. Alvaro was inclined to broad misogynist generalizations on the essence of being female such as the following: "woman who in herself has no shape [*è informe*] wants to be created and invented in love by man."[11] Women were materialistic, "unpoetic and passive," and obsessed with love.

In his diary entries from the late 1930s and early 1940s, Alvaro's insistence on female "materialism" was clearly tied to the feelings of humiliation provoked by the defeat and associated with the Allied occupation.[12] Comparing the Germans and Americans as occupiers, he noted that some Italians, in spite of their suffering under the Germans, almost longed for the latter because they had something in common with them, namely scarcity, while the wealthy Americans looked down insolently on the Italians.[13] Their contempt was particularly visible in the "colonial" attitudes they displayed in their treatment of Italian women: they had sex with these women and at times even married them only to dump them when they went back home.[14] The fact that many women (at times pushed by Italian men) eagerly exchanged sex for money with Allied soldiers, including black soldiers, led Alvaro to sobering considerations about Italian, and in particular southern, society.[15]

As American hegemony continued in the postwar years and Christian Democracy won a landslide victory in the elections of 1948, Alvaro, who at the time espoused strongly anti-clerical views, noted how that election was a "victory mainly of women," who had thereby delivered the country to the rule of priests.[16] The fears that some on the left had shared about extending political rights to women had, after all, proven true. Women, and with them many men too of course, had voted on the side of conservatism, of "low politics," instead of ideals: these were Alvaro's disconsolate conclusions. Overall anxieties about the weakening of a distinctive national identity and the loss of an alleged "Italian humanity" in connection with the Americanization of Europe permeated the entries in Alvaro's journals.[17]

The article on *mammismo* that Alvaro published in 1951 expanded on these negative images of the female by focusing in particular on the mother figure. For this writer Italy was a backward society still dominated by instinct, and thus still close to animal/biological behaviour. While modern societies raised their children with an understanding of the collective to which they belonged, a sense of being a collectivity was not at all strong among Italians, a result of the way Italian women spoiled their male children. Italian men grew up learning individual ways of coping with life, they relied on cunning and insolence, they had an exaggerated sense of their own rights and no sense of a higher order to which they should submit. Italy was a "society of men raised by their mothers as if they were protagonists."[18] This is what Alvaro called the "*mammismo* complex."[19] It dominated a society that at the same time wasted its men by not providing sufficient means of subsistence or by sending them to fight pointless wars, as Italy had been doing in the past half century.

These critical views did not make much of an impact in a society in which in 1954 the jury of the most popular song contest in the country, the Festival of Sanremo, gave first prize to "Tutte le mamme," a very sentimental song dedicated to the beauty and sweetness of all mothers. Two years earlier (the very same year that Alvaro's piece appeared in an essay collection), popular Neapolitan writer Giuseppe Marotta published a collection of short stories entitled *Le madri*, which exalted to an extreme degree the self-sacrificing spirit of mothers and especially their adoration for their children.[20] Significantly, Marotta exalted the figure of the mother as opposed to "the woman," which he equated to a concentrate of vanity, ignorance, and lack of patriotism, underlining how easily women had thrown themselves into the arms of all the foreigners who had been occupying the peninsula in recent years. Not by chance, several of the fictional mothers in his short stories were single women swept along by instinctual love for their offspring born out of wedlock, and thus made into "normal women" by motherhood.

If we go back to American momism and compare it to the features of *mammismo*, it appears clearly that while the former was a gendered reaction to war anxieties and the perception, as well as the reality, of the stronger position of women in American society, *mammismo* had more to do with the crisis provoked by the war defeat and the anxieties generated by the new postwar order. Moreover, while Wylie lambasted the tyrannical mother figure, Alvaro lamented the effects of the over-indulgent *mamma* who spoiled her male offspring. More importantly, the domineering mother figure lambasted by Wylie was construed as a contingent and thus temporary phenomenon, not as an anthropological and trans-historical characteristic of the whole society. This, however, was exactly the case of Italian *mammismo*, which constructed the maternal as an eternal phenomenon and a defining trait of Italian society.

"Great Mothers" and "*Civiltà Materna*": Italian Society in the Light of (Pop-) Psychology

In spite of his statements, Alvaro does not stand out as a particularly misogynist writer in postwar Italy; in fact in his work he also showed a keen sensitivity to the suffering of women, especially those of the lower classes.[21] Moreover, his views on women's passivity were quite common in the context of the 1940s, a period when even a feminist like Simone de Beauvoir had a rather ambivalent perception of women, making all life events connected to the female body into "figures of pure facticity," to use Toril Moi's expression, the opposite of transcending activities.[22] For the most part Alvaro spoke the language of his time and deployed the dominant metaphors of the culture in which he lived.

Some of Alvaro's ideas about the negative influence of the mother in Italian families and its impact on society can already be found in one of the texts that, immediately after the collapse of Fascism, offered reflections on the Italian "character" in the light of the dictatorship: Fabio Cusin's *L'italiano. Realtà e illusioni* published in 1945. For Cusin, a Triestine historian close to the Action Party, the family was the original incubator and locus of many of the problems of Italian society which had led to fascist authoritarianism. Families were dominated by "animal-like" ties and Italian men inherited from their mothers their "feminine traits," namely their emotionalism and sentimentality. In Cusin's view, the "animal" love between mother and son shaped men in a way that made them unable to sublimate their own animal instincts. Hence the "psychic infantilism" of Italian men. In this world, the lack of character education led to all sorts of political pathologies: thus "[t]he domineering child [...] will be the faction man of tomorrow, the brigand of the past, the anarchist and the demagogue of our times."[23]

Cusin's Triestine background may have predisposed him to this sort of psychological analysis, although his approach was in part still shaped by ideas about the psychology of peoples that had been circulating in European culture since the late nineteenth century from the pens of writers such as Gustave Le Bon. However, in contrast to Alvaro, who never seemed to refer explicitly to the discourse of psychology, Cusin was the expression of an emerging tendency to psychologize Italian society. Albeit not completely novel,[24] this tendency gained some strength in the 1950s with the spread of depth psychology and in particular of the Jungian archetype of the "great mother," understood as an a-priori form organizing human

36   S. PATRIARCA

existence, one particularly widespread in Mediterranean societies (hence the "great Mediterranean mother").[25] Like Freud, Jung shared the male bias of the psychology and psychoanalysis of his time and conceived of woman in essentialist terms, attributing to her nature unconsciousness and passivity.[26] As a female archetype, the "great mother" had two sides: one protective and tolerant, the other seductive and engulfing. Even though possessing some stereotypical female traits, the figure was not devoid of some analytical complexity.[27]

It was a Jungian psychologist who left Germany for Italy in 1936 and who became the founder of the Italian Association of Psychology, Ernst Bernhard, who contributed to making the great mother popular in the Italian "high" culture of the 1950s and 1960s. Among his patients and friends were well known writers and artists such as Natalia Ginzburg and Federico Fellini. Bernhard interpreted the "mystery of the Italian soul" in light of this archetype, which in his view dominated Italian life through the excessive role of the mother figure in the family.[28] This overwhelming presence, he felt, led to many neuroses among children as well as to the extremely passionate character of Italian men. Like Jung, along with the negative side of the archetype Bernhard saw also the good side, claiming that the latter gave Italian society a "beneficial human warmth." This was a society where tolerance and compassion were widespread—and one may notice here how the idea is intertwined with and contributes to the "*brava gente*" stereotype (the idea that Italians were a "good-hearted" people) which became the dominant narrative about Italian national identity at end of the Second World War, easily absolving the Italians from their responsibility in the war and the Holocaust. Significantly, Bernhard read Fascism as a "patriarchal attempt at overtaking" the dominance of the maternal, an attack which was eventually defeated.[29] For the German psychologist the influence of the great mother did not operate on its own, however, but was strengthened by the strong presence of the Catholic Church, a loving and at the same time punishing/domineering force. In this discourse the Catholic Church also tended to be gendered as female.

In his analysis of the evils of American society Wylie too had relied on psychological theories. As he himself recognized: "Most of the observations and criticisms in the book derive from the applications of the theories of 'dynamic psychology'—that is from a use of the psychological insights of Sigmund Freud and Carl Jung."[30] Even more than Freud's psychology, Jung's was applied to the understanding of the characteristics of whole societies. In the interwar period Jung commented on the state of the

"European psyche" which he believed was unbalanced due to the "mental masculinization" which women were undergoing.[31] Moreover, his notions of archetypes and collective unconscious, when applied to the psychology of nations and ethnic communities, ended up essentializing them,[32] or, to be more precise, ended up adding a new layer of meaning to already existing ideas of difference.

Articulated in the liberal monthly *Tempo presente* in December 1961, Bernhard's views elicited quite different responses. The first came from the writer and theologian Sergio Quinzio who, in a brief and dismissive note, found many faults in the reasoning as well as in the evidence of Bernhard. To each of Bernhard's generalizations he opposed a counter-example and to counter Bernhard's stereotypes about the Italians, he added his own. The Italians' sexual problems could be explained by their traditional sexual morality and their "great instinctual and passionate nature" which was not particularly Italian since it could be found among various other peoples who had a strong patriarchal tradition (and lived in warm climates) such as the Arabs. Quinzio even questioned Bernhard's sample and surmised that his patients were members of the elites who had developed "psychic imbalances" (*"squilibri psichici"*) due to their hasty adoption of foreign lifestyles. The conclusion of the theologian was that ordinary Italians were nothing like those imagined by Bernhard, a conclusion that falls within the traditional discourse of the Catholic Church: at least since the beginning of the Church–state conflict in Italy, churchmen always claimed to know better than anyone else who the "real" Italians were.[33]

The second and very different response came from Antonio Gambino, a journalist of liberal convictions who at the time was a contributor to the weekly magazine *L'Espresso* and was to become one of the founders of the daily newspaper *Repubblica* in 1976.[34] Gambino thought that there was much truth in Bernhard's ideas: in fact, the latter had been even too indulgent (*benevolo*) towards the Italians and their defects.[35] From this remark, Gambino proceeded to develop the great mother hypothesis into the theory of "maternal civilization," stressing the negative political consequences of "a collective mentality dominated by maternal values." Italian popular culture was full of references to the model of the mother who operated without moral and juridical principles, exclusively following the instinct of the "blood tie." Among his examples of this mentality, Gambino referred to Eduardo De Filippo's most famous play, *Filumena Marturano* (1946),[36] which featured a former prostitute who tricked a long-time former lover into marrying her, thus giving a father to her three children, only one of whom was his. The behaviour of Filumena, and the approval it received in the play and in Italian society (the play was such a great success that it was made into a film in 1950, a TV series in 1962, and into another film in 1964), were for Gambino an example of the maternal mentality which does not recognize collective norms enshrined in the legal system.[37]

Like Alvaro and Cusin, Gambino also believed that the dominance of maternal values in the family brought about anarchy in the wider society in the sense that it produced individuals who had no respect for the law and formal authority. In turn the lack of principles and even of a capacity for objective evaluation led to the development of prejudices and superstitions. In this analysis, Italy's political stagnation, *trasformismo*, and Machiavellianism were all products of this tendency, which was also at the origin of a lack of faith in the capacity to change through action (that is, fatalism) and even of *qualunquismo*, namely a fundamentally conservative distrust of politics and politicians ("they are all the same"). In other words, the maternal became a "category *passe-partout*" to explain vastly diverse political problems in Italian society.[38] Maternal civilization produced individuals dominated by sceptical, anarchic and amoral attitudes, and it was Catholicism in particular—Gambino added—that fostered these traits through its central institution, namely confession, which stifled the development of a well-rooted sense of responsibility by allowing individuals to easily get rid of any sense of guilt.

In Gambino's idea of maternal civilization, the ambivalence and complexity of Jung's and Bernhard's great mother was considerably reduced and simplified. Similarly, Italian commentators at the time seemed to see only the stifling side of the great mother: "Italy is a suffocating mother" proclaimed a *Corriere della Sera* review of a 1965 French travelogue by Dominique Fernandez entitled *Mère méditerrannée* (the book title played on the assonance between the French *mère* meaning mother, and *mer* meaning sea). The author was a prolific French writer who declared in fact his attraction for this mother figure, which he also saw as endowed with the characteristics of both sexes. He stressed his love for what he called "the exuberant Madre Mediterranea, the most Italian source of compassion and tenderness,"[39] but also a force capable of being hard and challenging with her children, of moulding them into strong men (he was talking of the Sardinians in particular). This more complex meaning was lost on the Italian reviewer who, like many Italians, did not share the exoticism that foreigners tended to associate with the peninsula and the Mediterranean region.

The debate on maternal civilization did not seem to move beyond the pages of the journal which published Gambino's essay, but the idea may call to mind the "amoral familism" syndrome identified by American political scientist Edward C. Banfield in his study of a village in Lucania in the second half of the 1950s, a period when social scientists were trying to understand the bases of functioning (and non-functioning) democracies. What Banfield meant by amoral familism—the exclusive care of one's family interests at the expense of those of the collectivity—pointed to a connection to be drawn between the "private" sphere of the family and the public sphere of power. But Banfield's amoral familism depended as much on men as it did on women: it was an ethos that originated from various factors among which the most important were poverty, the predominance of the nuclear family, and especially a type of education that was too indulgent with children and unable to instil solid moral principles. Indeed, Banfield saw both parents—and it would seem the father even more than the mother—as responsible for bringing up selfish children.[40]

In his 1962 elaboration of the idea of maternal civilization Antonio Gambino did not refer to Banfield's study. However, he incorporated the idea of amoral familism—made into the ethos of the whole society—in a volume he published several years later, in 1998, in the middle of another critical period of Italian history. Here, in contrast to the American scholar, he maintained that it was not the family itself that was the origin of the problem, but the family dominated by the maternal figure, the mother-centred family.[41] In this later book, Gambino linked even more pathologies of Italian society and politics to the dominance of the maternal, thus truly making it the universal, good-for-everything explanation: from the quarrelsomeness of individual Italians, to the widespread political corruption, from the irresponsibility of the elites, to the lack of historical memory and even terrorism, pollution, and the fragility of the feeling of national belonging and national loyalty (in which he included even the decline of the birth rate). All these issues were manifestations of a weak or missing paternal principle and thus of a lack of respect for ethics and the law in a society dominated by the familial-maternal principle.[42]

Both ideas of maternal civilization and amoral familism were controversial and did not have much of an impact at the time of their appearance and it is only in recent years that amoral familism (rather than maternal civilization) has become an important component of the self-representation

40   S. PATRIARCA

of Italian society—at least in some intellectual circles.[43] In the 1960s Italian intellectuals subscribed primarily to Catholic or Marxist (or both) paradigms and distrusted culturalist and psychological readings of social and political phenomena. In contrast, the idea of *mammismo* was to have a much more successful career as it was picked up by the mass culture industry.

THE USES OF A STEREOTYPE: *MAMMISMO* AT THE MOVIES AND IN POLITICAL DISCOURSE

In the 1950s the term *mammismo* was slow to take hold and, as late as 1958, a journalist of the daily newspaper *La Stampa* still appeared to believe that the term came from the US: summarizing the findings of the American magazine *Look* on the "state of the American male" the Italian newspaper stressed how the latter was increasingly controlled by women who dominated men psychologically in a "technique" called *mammismo*, evidently a translation of momism. Demanding mothers and controlling wives pushed men to work long hours to satisfy their desire for money and amusements, and made it difficult for them to chase skirts, a process resulting in men getting tired, passive, anxious and desensitized (the *Look* article actually used the term "impotent"). Since the state of the US supposedly showed Italy its most likely future, Italians needed to know what to expect in order to avoid repeating the same "mistakes."[44]

But more than through newspapers and magazine articles, it was through mass culture, and in particular through the cinema, that *mammismo* entered the realm of enduring stereotypical representations in Italian society. In this popular version of the notion, it is the *mammone* or "mama's boy" that is the centre of attention and the object of derision, the "overgrown boy" that novelist Ennio Flaiano also called a "*mammarolo*" (Roman dialect term for *mammone*) or "*bamboccione di casa*" (big home-loving baby) as he drew his picture in his writings and film scripts.[45] In Federico Fellini's first major success, *I vitelloni* (co-scripted by Flaiano in 1953), Alberto Sordi played one such character, as he did in several other comedies of the 1950s, enduringly inscribing the figure of the *mammone* in the imaginary of post-1945 Italy. As the prototypical weak and cowardly male, this type usually lives in a family dominated by women and is unable to impose himself in the outside world, the public sphere in which men define themselves in distinctive gender terms. The protagonist of Luigi Zampa's film *Un eroe dei nostri tempi* (1955) provides another splendid representation of this character. But the mama's boy can also be at the same time an opportunistic exploiter of his female relatives, as is the case with the character played by Alberto Sordi in *I vitelloni*.[46]

The dyad of the strong mother-weak son acquired a more pathological air in later years. A film of 1965, Nanny Loy's *Made in Italy*, consisting of a series of satirical sketches on the "customs" of the Italians, featured an episode with the popular actor Peppino de Filippo playing a 60-year-old man still living and working with his very controlling mother, both usurers. He never gets married because of his mother's opposition and acquires all her negative traits. In another popular satire on the "vices" of the average Italian, which appeared in 1977, an episode entitled "Mammina e mammone" (Mammy and mamma's boy) brought again to the screen the pathological couple: the overly domineering/protective mother and the no longer youthful but totally dependent son, played by Ugo Tognazzi. Dressed in an eccentric fashion, the son follows the old mother everywhere she goes and carries the trash that she tells him to collect. The two wander the streets of Rome until they return to their hovel, which is completely filled with the stuff they must have gathered over the years.[47] Particularly in the latter film, the dependent man is completely ridiculed and feminized. The ridicule to which weak men were exposed in these comedies confirms the patriarchal tendencies of most Italian cinema in those years.[48]

In the 1970s a strong and suffocating mother came also to be associated with the inhibition of "normal" sexuality. Several comedies made in these years feature figures of weak and impotent men who are the quintessential product of tyrannical mothers. Films such as *Di mamma non ce n'è una sola* (There's More Than One Mother, 1973), *Alla mia cara mamma nel giorno del suo compleanno* (To My Dear Mother On Her Birthday, 1974), *Per amare Ofelia* (To Love Ophelia, 1974) foregrounded men unable to detach themselves from their mothers, and mothers unwilling to let their sons free. These mama's boys are portrayed as members of the social elite, exhibiting the mannerisms stereotypically associated with homosexual men. Liberation, sexual and otherwise, comes in the shape of a disinhibited female of lower-class extraction (a former sex worker, a domestic servant) who finally leads the male protagonist to experience the joys of "normal" sex. An easy pretext for showing lots of female flesh, these films were also a vehicle for the reassertion of the heterosexual norm in a period in which the breaking of old sexual taboos was becoming more widespread, especially among young people.[49]

If originally the diagnosis of *mammismo* as a pathology of Italian society came from intellectuals located on the liberal left of the political spectrum, in its subsequent transformation into a mass culture stereotype, no longer part of a more complex analysis, the idea moved around easily in different quarters. This is perhaps only to be expected. In this more simplistic version, the misogynist component of the idea tended to take over and become all dominant, especially when inflected on the right of the political spectrum. It came also to be constantly associated with those allegedly "Italian" traits deprecated by conservatives and the nationalist right, such as *viltà* (cowardliness) and *mollezza* (feebleness). It popped up, for example, in the prose of the conservative opinion maker Indro Montanelli when he railed against Italian mothers who opposed sending their sons to the first Gulf War of 1990: "When they gather together to go into the streets [...] [mothers] become the plague of the Country, the breeding ground of all its weaknesses, cowardice and corruptions [...] Of this '*mammona*' Italy Christian Democracy is the perfect example."[50] The same tropes appeared in the commentaries of neo-right commentator Maurizio Veneziani during the political transition of the early 1990s, after the fall of the "first republic," when he invited his readers to get rid of that "cowardly and *mammista* Italy" in order to pursue the transformation of Italian society in neoliberal ways.[51]

But the figure of the mama's boy also lurked behind the term *bamboccioni* used by the centre-left Minister of the Economy and Finance Tommaso Padoa-Schioppa in 2007 to refer to the young adults still living at home with their parents. In his view these young people needed to be encouraged to leave and become more responsible and independent. This was certainly a worthy goal. Yet, unfortunately, living at home was and is not a matter of free choice for most young people in a country where the rate of youth unemployment has been hitting record highs for several years.[52]

CONCLUSIONS

I have argued that the origins of *mammismo* as an idea and as a stereotype are complex and must be placed in a transnational context, in the privileged relationship that Italian culture developed with the new postwar hegemon, the United States. Both *mammismo* and its more sophisticated sibling *civiltà materna* (maternal civilization) were originally the expression of a gendered criticism of Italian institutions and of a political discontent which was situated mainly on the liberal left of the political spectrum: in this discourse *mammismo* was denounced as an archaism that impeded the modernization of Italian society. Afterwards, as a stereotype in mass commercial culture, *mammismo* extended its range of uses and meanings in society at large and across the political spectrum. Today it is taken for granted as a component of the idea of Italian national "character," and references to it have become cross-cultural.

These ideas relied on a kind of psycho-anthropological gaze applied to the observation of one's culture and undoubtedly made some intuitive sense. However, they ignored history and especially the autonomy and agency of fathers in the family. In the cultural determinism of *civiltà materna* men come out as strangely deprived of any real responsibility, they do not seem to take part fully in the drama that is occurring around them, as if their presence in the family and in society does not really matter. If it is the mother's influence that—since time immemorial—has shaped everything in the family, how can one blame men? What Gambino and others failed to see was that the "maternal" in Italian society was itself a product of the continuing patriarchal arrangements of that society and not an archaic trait originating in time immemorial.[53]

This was the patriarchal society that in the postwar period continued to dump the burden of parenting on mothers, making them entirely responsible for the care and education of their children. Fathers were often absent, spending most of their time outside the home at work or socializing with their friends, but they still maintained a position of "authority and correction" in the family.[54] Moreover, and more importantly, the Catholic clergy—that is a group of unmarried men who call themselves "fathers"—constantly emphasized women's maternal obligations, letting fathers off the hook. As Pius XII stressed in a speech of 1957, mothers were expected to sacrifice all to their families: "[the mother's] fundamental principle should be her abnegation and her continuous sacrifice; without forgetting that her duties towards the small society [the family] must come before all her social obligations."[55]

This quotation from the head of the Catholic Church reminds us that the maternal in Italy is also at the same time a Christian, or, to be more precise, a Catholic construction. To look at the role of gender in this Italian construction and in the actual power relations supporting it implies recognizing the specificity of Italian patriarchy and, in particular, its articulation with the dominant religion of the country. As the historical anthropologist Luisa Accati has argued, in a Catholic society such as Italy where for centuries the Church has imposed its powerful cultural symbols, Catholicism exercises its hegemony over the maternal, represented by the powerful symbol of the Virgin Mary, the mother of Christ. In Catholic symbolism the mother–son dyad is greatly privileged at the expense of the wife–husband dyad.[56] Thus sons, especially some celibate ones such as clergymen, have more power (at a symbolic level, at least) than husbands. The weakness of husbands/fathers—and more generally of civil authorities—follows not from the excessive power of women, but from the excessive power of certain men.

It is this symbolic power configuration that Accati invites us to attend to if we want to understand the anthropological roots of certain troubling traits of Italian politics. Behind a "great mother" there is often a powerful kind of "mama's boy" in the shape of a priest. The gendered character of the *mammismo* trope and its underlying misogyny should thus not lead us to dismiss the issues raised by some of the critical observers of Italian society whom we have discussed in the previous pages. Some of them pointed out real and persistent problems in Italian society such as the weakness of civil authorities, particularly when they have to enforce the law against the interests of the powerful. The Berlusconi years—another troubled "*ventennio*" of sorts in modern Italian history—have shown this dramatically well.

NOTES

1. D'Amelia, *La mamma*. Alvaro's article actually first appeared in the Turin daily newspaper *La Nuova Stampa* in 1951 with the title "Rose di maggio", and was subsequently reprinted in a more extended version and with the title "Il mammismo" in his collection of essays *Il nostro tempo e la speranza*.
2. This absence of mockery towards the mother figure contrasts remarkably with the stereotype of the Jewish mother studied by Antler, *You Never Write!*
3. Wylie, *Generations of Vipers*.
4. Antler, *You Never Write!*, p. 74. Momism had also an impact in American film: see Chopra-Gant, "Hollywood's 'Moms' and Postwar America."
5. Gabrielli, "Le nostre donne."
6. Even in an anti-fascist, neo-realist film such as *Rome Open City* (1945) the figure of the collaborator is displaced onto a woman, Marina, who loves luxury and has an affair with a Nazi woman.
7. See Mafai, *Pane nero*, ch. 11.

MAMMISMO/MOMISM: ON THE HISTORY AND USES... 45

8. At times, women protesting the loss of their jobs noted this occurrence: see for example the letter written by a "committee of working women in Palermo" who in May 1945 stressed how they had to suffer the burden of the war and then lost their jobs to benefit some war returnees who had formerly been *manganellatori* (fascist thugs): see Archivio Centrale dello Stato.

9. I elaborate on this trope in my *Italian Vices.*

10. Buchanan, "Good morning, pupil!"

11. Alvaro, *Ultimo diario (1948–1956),* p. 31 (the year of this entry is 1948).

12. Alvaro, *Quasi una vita,* p. 243 (the year is 1940).

13. Alvaro, *Quasi una vita,* p. 340 (the year is 1944; I am quoting from the 1959 edition).

14. Alvaro, *Quasi una vita,* p. 432 (1947).

15. Alvaro, *Quasi una vita,* p. 403 (1947). Anxiety about interracial sex is evident in this and other entries.

16. Alvaro, *Ultimo diario,* p. 27 (1948).

17. Alvaro, *Ultimo diario,* p. 32 (1948), p. 33 (1949).

18. Alvaro, "Il mammismo," p. 187.

19. Alvaro, "Il mammismo," p. 186.

20. Marotta, *Le madri.* On this work see also Benedetti, *The Tigress in the Snow,* p. 76.

21. See in particular some of the stories collected in *Gente in Aspromonte.*

22. Moi, *Simone de Beauvoir,* p. 154. On the ambivalent relationship of de Beauvoir to the female see Moi, *Simone de Beauvoir,* ch. 6.

23. Cusin, *L'italiano.*

24. Some signs of it were present even earlier in anti-fascist milieus trying to explain the victory of Fascism: see for example the analysis of Borgese, *Goliath: The March of Fascism.* Borgese saw the dominance of the family in Italian society as the result of the loss of liberty and independence at the end of the Middle Ages. The family was dominated in a tyrannical (but overt) way by the father, but this tyranny was "balanced" by the (covert) tyranny of the wife (p. 49). The tyranny of the family group in society was in turn seen as a breeding ground for political tyranny (p. 88).

25. Erich Neumann, a student of Jung and an important art historian, was also a vehicle for the diffusion of these ideas in Italy: see his beautifully illustrated *The Great Mother.*

26. Passerini, *Europe in Love,* p. 96.

27. For a sampling of Jung's views of the feminine archetype see Jung, *Aspects of the Feminine.*

28. Bernhard, "Il complesso della Grande Madre."

29. Bernhard, "Il complesso."

30. Wylie, *Generations,* p. xvii.

46 S. PATRIARCA

31. Jung, "Woman in Europe" (1927) discussed by Passerini, *Europe in Love*, pp. 93–96.
32. Passerini, *Europe in Love*, p. 99.
33. Quinzio, "La Grande Madre mediterranea." On the Catholic Church's idea of the Italian character see Logan, "The Clericalist Counterpoint." Another positive take on the great mother can be found in the film review by Elisabetta Ferrarelli, "Retorica del mammismo."
34. Gambino (1926–2009) was originally from Sicily but spent all his life in Rome: see his obituary in *La Repubblica* of 3 May 2009 (Ajello, "Addio ad Antonio Gambino"). The obituary underlines how Gambino had a strong passion for psychoanalysis, particularly Jung's.
35. Gambino, "La civiltà materna."
36. Discussed by Gabriella Gribaudi in a later chapter in this volume.
37. Ironically the play represents a strong woman of the Neapolitan lower classes, hardly an example of traditional motherhood: see Fischer, "Strong Women and Nontraditional Mothers."
38. I am borrowing the term from La Rovere, *L'eredità del fascismo*, p. 17.
39. Fernandez, *Mère Méditérranée*, p. 149.
40. Banfield, *The Moral Basis of a Backward Society*, pp. 150–52.
41. Gambino, *Inventario italiano*, p. 63.
42. Even then Gambino continued to rely on views about femininity and the maternal that derived from Jungian psychology and even from nineteenth-century German classicist Johann Jacob Bachofen, who saw matriarchy as an archaic form of civilization preceding the more evolved (albeit less harmonious) patriarchal culture and equating it "with a condition of homogeneity, materiality, and harmony with nature, a primitive social order embodying a lost happiness ... The emergence of civilization was understood in terms of a development from an archaic, chthonian feminine sphere of undifferentiated unity to a patriarchal culture governed by 'higher spiritual laws'": see Felski, *The Gender of Modernity*, p. 51. At the same time Gambino claimed that he was aware that Italian society was patriarchal and that he only spoke of maternal values, not of a matriarchy.
43. On the currency of this idea in contemporary Italy see Alessi, "Famiglia, famiglie e identità italiana."
44. [l.b.] "Il matriarcato conviene?" *Look* magazine in fact published a series of three articles devoted to the state of the American male: the first (referred to by the Italian journalist), which had the title "The American Male: Why Do Women Dominate Him?" appeared in the issue of 4 February 1958, pp. 77–80. The other two appeared in the 18 February and 4 March issues respectively.
45. Flaiano, *Diario notturno*, pp. 391–92. The terms appear in notes that he wrote in 1951. On Flaiano see also Trubiano, *Ennio Flaiano and His Italy*.

MAMMISMO/MOMISM: ON THE HISTORY AND USES...   47

46. On Sordi's characters as representing a caricature of the "mama's boy" see also Ferrarelli, "Retorica del mammismo," p. 728.
47. The episode is in *I nuovi mostri* directed by Dino Risi, Ettore Scola and Mario Monicelli (1977). There is an English version of the film entitled *Viva Italia!*
48. On the patriarchy reproduced in Italian cinema see Cottino-Jones, *Women, Desire, and Power in Italian Cinema.*
49. For a critical review of these films see Bergogna, "Tre registi 'contestano' il mammismo."
50. Montanelli, "Eventualmente." On Montanelli see also my *Italian Vices*, ch. 8.
51. Veneziani, "Uccidiamo finalmente Alberto Sordi."
52. On the issue of youth unemployment and the infelicitous term used by Padoa-Schioppa see Diamanti, "La falsa leggenda dei ragazzi bamboccioni."
53. On the maternal as a patriarchal or Christian construction see Kaplan, *Motherhood and Representation.*
54. See Bravo, "Madri fra oppressione ed emancipazione," p. 111. The article discusses working-class families of the 1930s, but this model persisted also after the war, especially in lower-class families. Laura Benedetti (*The Tigress in the Snow*, p. 81) has noted the absent father theme in Elsa Morante's postwar fiction, which contrasted with the constant presence of mothers trapped in irrational and instinctual roles.
55. From a radio speech by Pius XII broadcast on 11 May 1957, quoted by Koch in "La madre di famiglia nell'esperienza sociale cattolica," p. 239.
56. Accati, "Il marito della Santa," subsequently expanded in *Il mostro e la bella*. Accati's interpretation is brilliant, even though the issue of variation over time would require more attention.

BIBLIOGRAPHY

ARCHIVAL DOCUMENTS

Archivio Centrale dello Stato, Ministero dell'Interno, Direzione Generale di Pubblica Sicurezza, Divisione Affari Riservati e Generali 1944–46, busta 117.

PUBLISHED SOURCES

Accati, Luisa. "Il marito della Santa. Ruolo paterno, ruolo materno e politica italiana." *Meridiana* 13 (1992): pp. 79–104.

48   S. PATRIARCA

Accati, Luisa. *Il mostro e la bella. Padre e madre nell'educazione cattolica dei senti-menti.* Milan: Cortina, 1998; English transl.: *Beauty and the Monster. Discursive and Figurative Representations of the Parental Couple from Giotto to Tiepolo.* Florence: European Press Academic Publishing, 2006.

Ajello, Nello. "Addio ad Antonio Gambino così raccontava la sua Europa," *La Repubblica*, May 3, 2009 (accessed online).

Alessi, Giorgia. "Famiglia, famiglie e identità italiana," *Storica* 55 (2013).

Alvaro, Corrado. *Gente in Aspromonte.* Milan: Garzanti, 1955.

Alvaro, Corrado. "Il mammismo," in Corrado Alvaro, *Il nostro tempo e la spe-ranza. Saggi di vita contemporanea.* Milan-Rome: Bompiani, 1952, pp. 183–190.

Alvaro, Corrado. "Rose di maggio." *La Nuova Stampa*, May 19, 1951.

Alvaro, Corrado. *Ultimo diario (1948–1956)*, 3rd edn. Milan: Bompiani, 1966; orig. 1959.

Alvaro, Corrado. *Quasi una vita. Giornale di uno scrittore.* Milan: Bompiani, 1994; orig. 1956, re-edited in 1959.

Antler, Joyce. *You Never Write! You Never Call! A History of the Jewish Mother.* New York: Oxford University Press, 2007.

Banfield, Edward C. *The Moral Basis of a Backward Society.* Glencoe, IL: The Free Press, 1958.

Benedetti, Laura. *The Tigress in the Snow. Motherhood and Literature in Twentieth-Century Italy.* Toronto: University of Toronto Press, 2007.

Bergogna, L. "Tre registi 'contestano' il mammismo all'Italiana." *La Stampa*, 10 March, 1974 (accessed online on May 14, 2014).

Bernhard, Ernst. "Il complesso della Grande Madre. Problemi e possibilità della psicologia analitica in Italia," *Tempo presente*, 6 (1961): pp. 885–889.

Borgese, Giuseppe Antonio. *Goliath: The March of Fascism.* New York, Viking Press, 1937.

Bravo, Anna. "Madri fra oppressione ed emancipazione." In Anna Bravo, Margherita Pelaia, Alessandra Pescarolo and Lucetta Scaraffia, *Storia sociale delle donne nell'Italia contemporanea.* Rome-Bari: Laterza, 2001.

Buchanan, Andrew, "'Good morning, pupil!' American Representations of Italianness and the Occupation of Italy, 1943–45," *Journal of Contemporary History* 43, n. 2 (2008): pp. 217–240.

Chopra-Gant, Mike. "Hollywood's 'Moms' and Postwar America." In *Motherhood Misconceived: Representing the Maternal in US Films*, edited by Heather Addison, Mary Kate Goodwin-Kelly and Elaine Roth, pp. 125–137. Albany: State University of New York, 2009.

Cottino-Jones, Marga. *Women, Desire, and Power in Italian Cinema.* New York: Palgrave Macmillan, 2010.

Cusin, Fabio. *L'italiano. Realtà e illusioni.* Rome: Atlantica, 1945.

MAMMISMO/MOMISM: ON THE HISTORY AND USES... 49

d'Amelia, Marina. *La mamma.* Bologna: Il Mulino, 2005.
Diamanti, Ilvo, "La falsa leggenda dei ragazzi bamboccioni," in *La Repubblica*, 13 February 2012. http://www.repubblica.it/politica/2012/02/13/news/ leggenda_bamboccioni_diamanti-29782504/ last accessed on 6 January, 2016.
Felski, Rita. *The Gender of Modernity.* Cambridge, MA and London, UK: Harvard University Press, 1995.
Fernandez, Dominique. *Mère Méditérranée.* Paris: Grasset, 1965.
Ferrarelli, E. "Retorica del mammismo," *Tempo presente*, 7 (1962): pp. 727–729.
Fischer, Donatella. "Strong Women and Nontraditional Mothers: The Female Figure in *Napoli milionaria!* and *Filumena Marturano* by Eduardo De Filippo." In *Women in Italy, 1945–1960: An Interdisciplinary Study*, edited by Penelope Morris, pp. 211–223. New York and Houndmills: Palgrave Macmillan, 2006.
Flaiano, Ennio. *Diario notturno.* in *Opere*, vol. 2, Milan: Mondadori, 1994; orig. 1956.
Gabrielli, A. "Le nostre donne," *Repubblica* (Florence edition), 11 March 1944, quoted in Dianella Gagliani, "Il fascismo italiano e la femminilizzazione del mito dell'esperienza della guerra." In *Il sacrificio*, edited by Renata Ago, pp. 113–140. Rome: Biblink, 2004.
Gambino, Antonio. "La civiltà materna," *Tempo presente*, 7, n. 4–5 (1962): pp. 328–337.
Gambino, Antonio. *Inventario italiano. Costumi e mentalità di un paese materno.* Turin: Einaudi, 1998.
Jung, Carl Gustav. *Aspects of the Feminine.* Princeton, NJ: Princeton University Press, 1982.
Kaplan, E. Ann. *Motherhood and Representation: The Mother in Popular Culture and Melodrama.* London: Routledge, 1992.
Koch, Francesca. "La madre di famiglia nell'esperienza sociale cattolica." In *Storia della maternità*, edited by Marina d'Amelia. Rome-Bari: Laterza, 1997.
La Rovere, Luca. *L'eredità del fascismo. Gli intellettuali, i giovani e la transizione al postfascismo 1943–1948.* Turin: Bollati Boringhieri, 2008.
[l.b.] "Il matriarcato conviene?," *La Stampa*, 14 February 1958 (accessed on May 14, 2014).
Logan, Oliver. "The Clericalist Counterpoint: Corruption and Character in *La civiltà cattolica* (1850–c.1950)," paper presented at the Association for the Study of Modern Italy conference on The Italian "Character," London, December 2011.
Mafai, Miriam. *Pane nero. Donne e vita quotidiana nella Seconda Guerra Mondiale.* Milan: Mondadori, 1987.
Marotta, Giuseppe. *Le madri. Storie.* Milan: Bompiani, 1957; orig. 1952.

50   S. PATRIARCA

Moi, Toril. *Simone de Beauvoir. The Making of an Intellectual Woman*. Cambridge, MA and Oxford, UK: Blackwell, 1994.

Montanelli, Indro. "Eventualmente," in Indro Montanelli, *La stecca nel coro 1971–1994. Una battaglia contro il mio tempo*. Milan: Rizzoli, 1994, pp. 440–441 (orig. *Il Giornale* 15 August 1990).

Neumann, Erich. *The Great Mother: An Analysis of the Archetype*. New York: Pantheon Books, 1955.

Patriarca, Silvana. *Italian Vices: Nation and Character from the Risorgimento to the Republic*. Cambridge, UK: Cambridge University Press, 2010.

Quinzio, S. "La Grande Madre mediterranea," *Tempo presente*, 7 (1962): pp. 140–141.

Trubiano, Marisa S. *Ennio Flaiano and His Italy. Postcards from a Changing World*. Madison and Teaneck: Farleigh Dickinson University Press, 2010.

Veneziani, M. "Uccidiamo finalmente Alberto Sordi, non l'attore, ma la sua, la nostra viltà," *Il Giornale*, July 6, 1994.

Wylie, Philip. *Generations of Vipers*. Normal, IL: Dalkey Archive Press, 1996.

CHAPTER 3

Mothers, Workers, Citizens: Teresa Noce and the Parliamentary Politics of Motherhood

Molly Tambor

There is a meme circulating on the internet consisting of a montage of photographs of Italian MEP (Member of the European Parliament) Licia Ronzulli with her daughter. In each photo Ronzulli is shown debating or voting in the European Parliament; over the years she does this with her baby in a carrier against her chest, then a toddler held in her lap, and finally as a young girl who imitates her mother's action in writing notes and voting. Ronzulli has attracted both praise and criticism for her gesture; she maintains that it is the best way to remind citizens and other politicians of the need to support more rights for working women's ability to achieve a work–life balance.[1] This member of Forza Italia and good friend of Silvio Berlusconi garnered praise even from those of opposing political viewpoints for making use of the European Union rule allowing women to bring their children to work, which she called "not a political gesture, but a maternal one."[2] There is a complexly layered image at work in this series of photos: as this woman who is quite literally a representative represents herself as a mother, and as a mother who specifically represents

M. Tambor (✉)
Long Island University, Brookville, NY, USA
e-mail: Molly.Tambor@liu.edu

© The Author(s) 2018
P. Morris, P. Willson (eds.), *La Mamma*,
Italian and Italian American Studies,
https://doi.org/10.1057/978-1-137-54256-4_3

51

other women as mothers, guides her daughter in the process of democratic participation and self-representation. Yet the comments section of *The Guardian* article in which she was quoted contains more criticism than praise, as many readers complain that mothers and children should "stay at home and not bother anybody else." The image of the maternal here both serves to empower Ronzulli and the women she represents, and to limit the identities women can powerfully inhabit, while making women primarily responsible for the care of children and the ongoing health of the family politic. Given Italian mistrust of the state and blaming of mothers for many of Italy's political and economic woes, privileging the maternal identity of femininity is a relatively fraught enterprise.

It does not take a professional historian to discern in these photos the way that Ronzulli's cradling of an infant, a child whose gesture imitating her mother's voting can also be read as a Madonna and child raising a hand in benediction, is an echo of a long tradition of exalting the maternal in Italy. But the echoes of one specific moment are quite arresting. In 1948–50 the Communist (PCI, Partito comunista italiano) MP Teresa Noce and her Christian Democrat (DC, Democrazia cristiana) counterpart Maria Federici led a campaign to pass a comprehensive law for the rights of working mothers. Delegations of pregnant women and mothers carrying their babies repeatedly descended on the offices of their elected representatives to demonstrate in favour of the law's passage. Like Ronzulli they were insisting on the visibility and presence of motherhood in the public sphere, as part of the work that women perform both inside and outside the home. And like Ronzulli they were making use of the traditional authority of the Italian mother within the family to claim an authoritative political voice outside it. In one notable incident while the bill was bogged down in committee with competing amendments, Noce recounted that a delegation of women from Bergamo visited Minister of Labour Amintore Fanfani's parliamentary office in Rome. He apparently instructed his secretary to inform the women he was not available and more or less hid in his office for hours; but they waited outside the building until he finally had no choice but to leave for the day. They administered a very public scolding, during which Fanfani hung his head and submitted to their claims like a good son, promising to move the bill more quickly through committee so it could be put to a general vote.[3] Noce recounted this episode as a humorous and triumphant one, but, while the mothers' delegation may have seen it as a victory for women's rights, it now appears as a foreshadowing of the stereotypical relationship of dominating mothers

MOTHERS, WORKERS, CITIZENS: TERESA NOCE AND THE PARLIAMENTARY... 53

and browbeaten sons on which the trope of *mammismo* blames the weaknesses and failures of the Italian state.

Throughout this campaign for women's rights, Noce, Federici and the other female MPs of Italy's first republican Parliament represented themselves and their newly enfranchised female constituents primarily as mothers—and as martyrs. All the elected female candidates had been in the Resistance, an act of self-sacrifice for the liberty of the nation's sons and daughters. All frequently left their own children to travel around the country for political demonstrations, recruitment for women's organizations, party rallies, and other forms of dedication to politics and national renewal as an enactment of passion. Communist women in particular did not hesitate to take on the label "Red Saints" in their efforts to reconcile and unite Italians. In an earlier work I reconstructed the collective political biography of this cohort of women, Italy's first nationally elected politicians; I called them a "lost wave" of feminists.[4] Here I will attempt to re-examine a specific segment of their activism through the lens of maternal symbolism. How did the image of "*la mamma*" operate in their self-representation and their political campaigning? How much, and in what ways, was Italian women's newly gained citizenship created as the rights and duties of mothers?

These MPs asserted through their self-portrayal that Italy's mothers were the nation's best guarantee of a return to "normalcy" after twenty-plus years of war and Fascism, and the contribution they made to reconstructing Italian society and politics demanded that women-as-mothers be recognized with full rights and full participation in the public sphere. But, like Ronzulli, their successful use of a maternalist discourse for women's rights had a negative aspect as well. Claiming responsibility can mean accepting the burden of blame. And choosing to exalt mothers may garner support across the political spectrum, but only because that exaltation means different things to different people.

According to Marina d'Amelia, the concept of *mammismo* can be traced to the immediate postwar period; she finds its first usage in 1952. Silvana Patriarca, in her contribution to this volume, explores how this idea expanded in subsequent years into a blaming stereotype that not only belittled Italian mothers but also condemned their role in creating an Italian masculinity frozen in arrested development, so that men remain dependent, emasculated, and therefore incapable of restoring morality and vigour to Italian social life and political culture as well.[5] Yet if this periodization is correct, the pathologizing of Italian mothers was simultaneous with a moment in which activist women were successfully using maternalist discourse to win real rights. Perhaps this is a coincidence, but it is one which bears analysis. These competing discourses about the meaning of maternity were clearly touching upon some very important questions about (re)making Italy and (re)making Italians. What was at stake in the struggle over different implicit definitions of motherhood and femininity in these exchanges? *Mammismo* was building on tradition, but its specificity had to do, as Patriarca argues, with a perceived "unnatural" condition of long-term dependency which was a political fear quite specific to the post-fascist, Cold War context. The efforts of women activists suggest that the anxiety surrounding mothers is also a sign of a moment of change and ferment in gender roles. The women of the early parliaments rarely articulated their goals as feminist or progressive or, least of all, transgressive. They presented them as necessary reforms to reinforce family values, implement the Constitution, and shore up Italy's democratic legitimacy. They were trying to assuage anxiety but, I would argue, there was a great deal of challenge to and reform of gender roles smuggled in through this search for non-ideological consensus.

The influx of women to Parliament and political leadership did not last; after the end of the third legislature of 1958–63 the numbers of female MPs dropped precipitously and did not regain similar levels until the late 1980s. *Mammismo* may therefore have been one of the signs that men, restored to what they saw as their legitimate leadership of public and economic life, were seeking to reclaim their primacy and close the window of women's moment of protagonism in rehabilitating Italy in the family of democratic nations. This chapter thus presents, through the story of the campaign for the 1950 law for the protection of working mothers, both a portrait of successful uses of maternalist politics for women's rights and a case study of the ambivalent consequences of politicizing maternity.

WOMEN'S CITIZENSHIP AND POSTWAR PROJECTS OF RECONSTRUCTION

As in the immediate post-First World War and interwar period, after the Second World War traumatized European societies sought to reconstruct the sexual order along with other forms of stability.[6] Despite the motivation that the war and postwar may have offered Italian men for a backlash against women, however, this time women would not retreat from new rights in politics and new roles in public. The trope of the Italian mother,

MOTHERS, WORKERS, CITIZENS: TERESA NOCE AND THE PARLIAMENTARY... 55

though under attack from some quarters, paradoxically served women's rights activists in a positive and effective way as they sought to reconcile Italians to women's suffrage, women's equal citizenship as proclaimed by the new Constitution, and women's role in the marketplace as both workers and, as reconstruction progressed, leaders of the transition to a consumer economy.

Women achieved the right to vote in the immediate aftermath of the war, and exercised it for the first time in the 1946 elections and referendum which transformed Italy into a republic.[7] Most Italian men too, after more than two decades of war and the fascist regime, were novice voters and democratic citizens in this period. It is especially interesting that women had this powerful opportunity to call for women's rights within a context where the defeat of Fascism had stripped Italian men of their political legitimacy and masculine confidence, so that women could argue they could be a bulwark of democracy by building mass political participation and by restoring the proper gender and family order in Italy that would redeem it with regard to the international family of democratic nations. Despite the way that Italian men would use the Resistance to claim they had redeemed their own nation, the Anglo-Americans tended to be rather dismissive of Italian masculinity. The urgency of a democratic rebirth for Italy in this moment encouraged both a national and an international discourse that portrayed women as necessary participants, even leaders, in restoring morality and dignity not only to the process of reuniting families in a peaceful society, but to the public sphere as well. American journalist Anne O'Hare McCormick articulated this view in her *New York Times* article "Bulldozer and the Woman with a Broom," in which she argued that it would be women who would perform the housecleaning of a Europe suffering from the chaos and destruction of total war.[8] But the Americans did not view Italian women as completely autonomous and fully prepared democratic nation builders. Italian women, viewed as mothers, were also a properly dependent group who could serve as junior partners to be mentored in the Cold War alliance. The Young Women's Christian Association, for example, publicized its campaign to raise funds for Italian reconstruction with a photograph of a mother entering a voting booth with her baby in her arms. The caption read, "This mother is casting her first ballot ... a new privilege for Italian women. She needs YWCA guidance in democracy."[9] Italian women did, however, respond energetically to the call to participatory democracy, creating their own agenda to a great extent by forming organizations that made this a period of mass

56 M. TAMBOR

activism in women's associationism. The two major associations in this period were the left-sponsored Unione Donne Italiane (UDI, the Union of Italian Women) and the Catholic Centro Italiano Femminile (CIF, the Female Italian Centre). In the first elections of the postwar period the major campaign both groups engaged in was to educate and guide Italian women as new voters and citizens who could guarantee the birth and nurturing of democracy.[10]

In this same 1946 election the members of the Constituent Assembly were chosen, 21 of whom were women. These pioneering female politicians came largely from the two emerging mass parties, the PCI and DC, which represented the increasing bipolarization of Cold War politics. However, the women shared a formative politicization in their anti-fascist backgrounds, as leaders of the Resistance, and of the national women's organizations. Together they cooperated across ideological lines to include in the new Constitution multiple guarantees of women's equality in rights, at work, and in the family.[11] Already in the Constitution's articles, however, a contradiction emerged between guaranteeing all citizens equality and promising to protect the family and women's special role within it. Socialist leader Angelina Merlin argued successfully for the inclusion in Article 3 of sex as one of the forms of difference that could not form a basis for discrimination; at the same time Teresa Noce helped articulate the wording of Article 37, which first states that working women must have the same rights and equal pay as working men, but then goes on to require that working conditions must allow the woman "to fulfil her essential familial role and assure special and adequate protection to the mother and child."[12] Along with Noce and Merlin, DC member and then-president of CIF Maria Federici, and PCI member Teresa Mattei negotiated at length over this definition of women's role in the family as "essential." Federici wanted the words to be plural, "essential functions," referring in her definition to both familial and maternal roles; Mattei wanted to emphasize the protection of the working mother as opposed to the state's protection of all mothers; and Merlin disagreed with the very use of the word "essential," which she argued was limiting and portrayed women as essential only within the domestic sphere of the family as opposed to the rights she felt should be guaranteed to women throughout society without any false distinction between private and public participation.[13] Many articles were debated in relation to the proper understanding of the state's relationship to the family, including, not least, the debate over whether to include the Lateran Accords, which made Catholicism

MOTHERS, WORKERS, CITIZENS: TERESA NOCE AND THE PARLIAMENTARY... 57

Italy's official state religion. These eventually became Article 7. The contradictory relationship between legal guarantees of women's equality, constitutional promises of special protection for particular social and economic roles, and the state's recognition of the "sacred" status of the family as the central institution of a Catholic society was thus established at the very founding of Italy's republic.

Following the ratification of the new Constitution, in the first general election of Members of Parliament in 1948, the trend of especially targeting women voters continued as the mass parties sought out numerous female candidates and campaigned with messages of family unity, stability and a new politics that would redeem Italy in the family of democratic nations. Forty-four women entered Parliament's first legislature from 1948 to 1953 and, once there, again cooperated in passing a string of women's rights laws which implemented the guarantees of the Constitution. In this, and subsequent legislatures, the state regulation of prostitution was ended and state-run brothels closed; civil service careers previously closed to women were opened to all; parents were guaranteed equal jurisdiction over family decisions and children born out of wedlock were guaranteed recognition; by the 1970s the Family Code had been revised and both divorce and abortion were legalized by referendum.[14]

Notably the first of this series of laws was the law for the protection of working mothers known commonly as the "Noce law" after its main author and sponsor, Teresa Noce, already famous by her battle name "Estella" for her long-time communist militancy, participation in the Spanish Civil War, and her Resistance activity, which resulted in her internment in—and survival of—the women's concentration camp at Ravensbruck.[15] She proposed the law in 1948, and, after some revision and amendment, it was passed in 1950. The law requires obligatory yet generously paid maternity leave for most categories of working women, as well as requiring time off for nursing and caring for young infants, and the provision by employers of nursing rooms and child care centres. It is exemplary of the ambivalence around the figure of the "*mamma*" among Italians at the time. All could agree she was important; not all agreed she should work outside the home, and few felt comfortable discussing her outside the context of religiously sanctioned marriage. Women activists may have already been discussing legalizing divorce and promoting the idea that women should have only "children we want, when we want them," but male party leaders quashed such controversial topics as unsuitable for mass mainstream politics.[16] Nonetheless Noce and her colleagues opened the path to such conversations with this law as a wedge issue. In addition, the campaign for the law was marked by extensive union organizing among female textile workers, local celebrations of public assistance for maternity and childcare, and grassroots activism by coordinated delegations of pregnant constituents visiting their elected representatives to urge support for the bill in Parliament. In that sense, the 1950 law is exemplary of the success women's rights activists had in mobilizing the trope of the maternal in the service of women's rights and political participation.

THE RESISTANCE AS "*MATERNAGE DI MASSA*": HOW WOMEN BECAME KEY TO DEMOCRATIZATION AND DEFASCISTIZATION

In the context of the postwar, with Italy's precarious position both politically and materially, there were many good reasons to address the question of women's entry into full citizenship through the discourses of motherhood. The effects and uses of the maternal image are complex and sometimes contradictory; in this case, I argue, the image of the mother helped the public to accept women's new, more visible roles as worker and citizen as a source of confidence and optimism in this period of moral anxiety.

Anna Bravo is perhaps the most notable voice among feminist historians of the Resistance to emphasize the importance of maternal symbolism in female partisans' own testimonies of their participation; and how the symbolism continued in the memory politics of the Resistance. Coining the term "*maternage di massa*" ("mass mothering") to describe the ways that women saved escaping POWs (prisoners of war) and deserting soldiers after Italy's 8 September 1943 change in Second World War alliances, she then expanded this description of women's Resistance activity to show that women were involved on a mass scale if one defines the Resistance as a civil movement and not only an armed one. Further, she analysed how the figure of the mother could draw on Catholic traditions of sacrifice and redemption to perform the work of making the Resistance into a national myth of Italians' authentic identity as an anti-fascist, democratic people. Perry Willson, in reviewing this historiography, points out that this scholarship demonstrates how the maternal register was useful on a broad level since it was uncontroversial, showed women in an asexual, non-transgressive light as just doing the nurturing that is naturally feminine. It also

MOTHERS, WORKERS, CITIZENS: TERESA NOCE AND THE PARLIAMENTARY... 59

helped "avoid problems of national guilt" so that "on one level the Resistance could be seen as a kind of recuperation of Italian masculinity."[17] But Willson goes on to discuss other research which opens up more complicated forms of narrating the female experience of Resistance: women often recounted their participation as mothers to emphasize their active agency and growing politicization, and they also often represented themselves not only as mothers, but as sisters—and as fighters, leaders, and increasingly as protagonists of their own lives.[18]

Thus, during the transition to peacetime and democracy, women politicians used their Resistance credentials to establish their legitimacy as national leaders, repackaging that experience as a reassuring, nurturing one and claiming to be nothing more threatening than mothers seeking to protect their families. Even women who had until recently been "professional revolutionaries" (the title of one of Noce's autobiographies) now took care to be photographed with babes in arms. "You have many children, you are fat and you have long hair. A woman's leader has to be that way," commented Marisa Rodano, somewhat acerbically.[19] One of the 44 women elected to the first Parliament, founding member and soon to be president of UDI, and leader, with her husband, of a movement to reconcile Catholics and the Communist Party, Rodano had been an important member of the Roman Resistance. Yet it was apparently her identity as wife and mother of five children that legitimated her public role, or made it more acceptable. Still the protagonism, courage and autonomy they had experienced in the Resistance were not lost values in the postwar period. The call for peace, for the rebuilding of families and national life, was not a return to the past. Women's new status as equal citizens meant that the content of maternal symbolism was necessarily changed, and charged with new kinds of responsibilities and challenges. Popular Front election posters showed happy, healthy babies held in loving parents' arms as the family unit turned together towards bright new days; Christian Democrat posters showed mothers standing in front of frightened children, arms outspread to protect them from the evils of Communism; women's organizations admonished women to be the guardians of peace in an atomic age with pietà-like images of mourning mothers cradling their threatened or damaged children.[20]

Noce's own public persona was not a perfect fit for this imagery. A long-time militant and proud proletarian, she was infamously yet proudly argumentative, hot-tempered and independent-minded. She was not Rodano's long-haired pretty woman, jokingly taking on critics of her

60 M. TAMBOR

appearance by always being the first to call herself ugly. Nicknames, some self-chosen, included "Madonna Tempesta," "*testa dura*," "*brutto muso*" and "*Brutta, povera, e comunista*" ("Our Lady of the Hellstorm," "hard-head," "ugly snout," and "ugly, poor, and Communist"). Yet she was also a famous Resistance heroine, a highly successful union organizer—she was the president of FIOT, the Federazione Italiana Operaie Tessili (Italian Federation of Textile Workers, a women's union)—and a member of the Central Committee of the PCI, in addition to being elected to the Constituent Assembly and the first three legislatures of Parliament. None of this, however, prevented her from portraying herself as naturally conforming to an idealized, if unsentimental, maternal role as she emphasized, above all, her fierce devotion and self-sacrifice as a mother: for her own two sons, and in her mission to represent and protect all Italian mothers.[21]

Like Noce, this cohort of women also articulated, in their autobiographies and in their activism, the rights of women in roles other than the maternal. Still, the *mamma* was much in evidence in these self-presentations: professional ambition, intellectual prowess or empowered sexuality were hardly visible at all in their public discourse on femininity. For women MPs, the potential reconciliation of the sexual order along with the bolstering of a new democratic political order made the privileging of maternal aspects of Italian femininity and women's citizenship the best rhetorical strategy.

Motherhood as a Balm for Catholic and Cold War Anxieties

Cold War anxieties did produce "mother-bashing"; for example in the United States mothers who stayed at home and spoiled or "smothered" their kids were held responsible by sociologists and psychologists of the era for homosexuality and other disorders of their children.[22] As Patriarca points out, much of the motivation for the blaming stereotype of *mammismo* had its source in anxieties about Italian masculinity; and these anxieties were not unfounded, since a certain racist undermining of Italian virility was common among American Cold Warriors. Kaeten Mistry and Alessandro Brogi, for example, have highlighted how George Kennan worried that "dagoes" would not be capable of an autonomous choice of democracy, since Italian men were notoriously weak, cunning and lacking in the integrity characterizing the superior masculinity of Anglo-Americans.

Fiorello LaGuardia, mayor of New York and himself a beloved incarnation of Italo-American identity, complained that among millions of Italians no man could be found with "balls big enough" to be a credible leader.[23] On the domestic front Sandro Bellassai has explored the sense of threatened masculinity that accompanied opposition to women's activism in the mass parties and to women MPs' proposals for new laws such as Merlin's campaign to close state-regulated brothels.[24] This relative vacuum in masculine power in the early postwar years in Italy encouraged a discourse whereby mothers were called upon by Atlantic allies and by the Catholic Church, to uphold the dignity of family and to help guard against the rise of Communism.

In October 1945 Pope Pius XII gave a speech to the members of CIF declaring the Church's support of women's suffrage and equal rights. Yet he emphasized that women's role was as the defenders of the boundary between the private, traditional world of the *casa* (home) and the threatening, chaotic change occurring in the *mondo* (world). Women's participation in politics was obviously an important part of the Church's strategy for combating Communism and the spread of materialist American-style modernity. Therefore women were called upon specifically as mothers, "whose task it was to bring the men of the family back to the faith" where every suffering woman becomes a mother and every man transforms back into a good son.[25] In later speeches Pope Pius XII continued his calls to women as his helpmeets in "win[ning] married people over to a service of motherhood."[26]

The response from Catholic women militants was welcoming of the invitation to political participation, yet critical of the new stance and its opposition of *casa* and *mondo*. "Woman is the home, and the home is the world," Christian Democrat and Catholic women's leader Angela Maria Guidi Cingolani argued in an article published in the Catholic journal *Il Popolo* in 1945, "and the participation of women in political life is justified by her indisputable duty to make her mission as spouse and mother as effective as possible."[27] Cingolani was famous for having been the first woman to speak in an Italian legislative session: in October 1945 she had given a speech in the Consulta (interim unelected legislative body acting before the first elections). At that time she had recognized the importance of women's new presence in political life with a joke that was both a reassurance and a rebuke: "Don't be afraid that women's contribution will be a return to matriarchy, if such a thing ever existed. We know better than to aspire to that; but even if we did, we certainly couldn't do any worse than you men have done!"[28] This barbed remark both exploited and exploded a whole set of gendered assumptions, for if women had indeed been confined only to the private sphere of nurturing and were not responsible for Italy's fascist past of violence, aggression and poor government then the blame sat squarely on male heads, including those in the room who wished to see themselves and Italy exonerated for such deeds. Conversely, women could more credibly promise to bring only peace, solidarity and rebirth to public life as they had to the private sphere. Cingolani and her peers accepted the identification of women with maternity, but posed that identity as expansive rather than limiting, and with no boundary between private and public. They affirmed that all Italian citizens were in need of mothers' care, and that the whole world had become women's home to claim.

Gender and the concept of the maternal were deployed in this period both to redefine and to shore up the social and political order. The difficult transition elicited deeply ambivalent feelings towards women as workers and as mothers; yet it was necessary that women should participate in the public sphere to defascistize and to legitimize Italy during the Cold War. Women were both blamed for men's inability to find jobs and return to "normal" peacetime life, and at the same time called upon to become protagonists in building a new peaceful family and social order. The vivacious debate between and among Catholic and Communist women about women's labour—outside the home and in the home—and about the social and political value of motherhood was thus downplayed in public as women MPs cooperated to pass women's rights laws under an umbrella justification of protecting mothers' ability to fulfil their duties—not only to their individual children, but to the nation as a whole.

The Right to Work and Mothering as Social Labour

Despite the cooperation at the parliamentary level for women's rights, there was conflict between the Catholic and communist ideals of women's role at work and in the family. In the PCI the dominant analysis was the emancipationist line, that liberation and equality in society would be achieved by a working class rise to power. In consequence women should be encouraged to work for pay outside the home so that both male and female proletarians would win equality together. Because PCI secretary Togliatti had immediately championed this interpretation in his first postwar speeches to party women's groups, it was also known as the "*linea togliattiana"* (Togliatti's policy). Sometimes reductivist in simplistically equating women's rights with the right to work, in the more nuanced analysis of female activists it became a tool to force the party to support their initiatives in favour of guaranteeing women's constitutional rights to equal education, job access, and adequate working conditions and equal pay.[29]

Catholics were more ambivalent about women's role as workers. A survey of 100,000 housewives undertaken by CIF in 1949 had shown that 90 per cent reported they were content not to work outside the home. To many women, jobs outside the home were not liberating but a sign of poverty and, more importantly, a further claim on their already precious time. CIF leaders argued that keeping house, raising children, providing fresh and nutritional food, and managing a family budget and schedule was already full-time work with an important economic and social value. Women, they asserted, aspired instead to better housing with indoor plumbing, labour-saving domestic appliances and a secure family income, perhaps with state subsidies.[30] Elisabetta Vezzosi has argued that while the numbers of housewives without external paid employment appeared to rise in the 1950s, the census figures from 1951 and 1961 may mask the fact that many women who identified themselves to census-takers as housewives were in reality agricultural workers in a family concern, or piece-rate workers at home. She points out that the status of housewife was seen as denoting a higher quality of life and independence than such work statuses would.[31] For the Catholics, therefore, representing the interests of women and protecting maternity was more focused on the idea of re-valuing the unpaid labour of women; CIF's most energetic campaigns in the postwar were for "housewives' pensions."[32]

The idea of protecting mothers' special function did cross party lines, however, and both groups substantially agreed that women performed a great deal of unpaid labour which ought to be recognized as having social and economic value for society as a whole. Teresa Noce presented obligatory maternity leave as a boon to working mothers and a limit on bullying employers, not an unfair limit discriminating against ambitious women. In this sense, while the *legge Noce* was an innovation for social citizenship in Italy, it was a continuation rather than a rethinking of a much longer legacy, both fascist and pre-fascist, of protective approaches to women's work. Not only did the title use the word *tutela* (tutelage or protection), but much of the language of the debate and the public campaign was characterized by the repeated rhetoric of "protection" of motherhood, of infants, of maternity and maternal "honour" (this last connoted as her sexual propriety, her modesty and her good reputation). This language demonstrates not only the ideological foundation in the protective ideas of Liberal feminists and fascist-era creators of ONMI (Opera nazionale maternità e infanzia, National Organization for Maternity and Infancy) but also the desire to displace the more controversial discussions of women's autonomy, women's work and women's liberation that the subject could have called forth.[33] Nonetheless, the bill's language and provisions depicted mothers as citizens who had the right to choose how and when to work, and how and when to have children. The emphasis was less on the vulnerability of female reproductive systems to the dangers of labour and more on the entitlement of women to become and remain both workers and mothers simultaneously. Further, the target of the law was not the family but the individual. Women deserved this right not as a way to shore up the family unit but as an earned recompense for the good they did for society and the economy; the underlying idea was that motherhood was a social contribution and that being a working mother was a form of public, even political, participation.[34] This was therefore a new use of older maternalist and protective arguments, one which heralded the building of an Italian welfare state and the cementing of social citizenship through claims about women's health and women's work as a larger obligation of the state to its citizens.

How many women did work for pay in postwar Italy, and how many of them were mothers? Italy did not experience the rising consumption of the "economic miracle" right away; during the campaign for the 1950 law most Italians still faced hunger, scarcity of housing stock, and the displacement and separation of families that had been a consequence of the regime's struggles for autarchy and of total war. While the fascist regime had tried to limit women's work, its rules had not changed the profitability to employers of women's lower pay in the northern textile and tobacco factories, for instance, or the long tradition of total family participation in agricultural work. And of course the war had meant that women had no choice but to replace men in multiple roles in civil society. All this, in addition to the less quantifiable effect of women's participation in the Resistance on women's sense of autonomy and their politicization, meant that anyone who proclaimed the expectation or ideal of a nation of middle-class housewives was not reflecting the lived experience of the majority. Official statistics counted around 6.5 million working women, or about 26 per cent of the total female population throughout the 1950s. But some scholars argue that as much as 70 per cent of the workforce in the grey and black markets was female, meaning women's work was largely unreported; probably 40–48 per cent of women worked, a rate in line with other similarly developed countries.[35] The birth rate was quicker to respond to new circumstances, which the Fascists had pushed in demographic campaigns without much success, but which rose quickly in the postwar. Though Italy did not have as notable a "baby boom" as other countries, the population did rise by 17 per cent between 1950 and 1970, and the infant mortality rate fell sharply, from 63.8 to 29.6 per thousand births in the same period. Many women having babies were necessarily also represented in the 40–48 per cent figure of working women, and more of those women were living in the cities.[36] The role of working mother was therefore a more visible one by 1950, and this role directly challenged and disrupted the ideology of separate spheres, necessitating state involvement in guaranteeing women's citizenship and welfare rights.[37] Women MPs could count on a great deal of resonance among many ordinary Italians for a law that promised, by reinforcing motherhood, to heal and protect the family from both the damage of the recent war and dictatorial regime, and the current troubling changes of reconstruction and modernization.

Grassroots campaigning strongly employed this newly resonant maternal symbolism. Both UDI and CIF organized signature collections, special articles in their newsletters, donations, rallies, and speeches at local festivals and political events across the country. In Ferrara on the day of the Festa della Stampa Democratica (Festival for the Democratic Press, a PCI-sponsored rally-cum-entertainment) in autumn 1948, the regional chapter of UDI sponsored an allegorical float in the festival's parade with, on one side, "a miserable kitchen with poor sad babies, and on the other happy and well-fed babies in a daycare centre, illustrated with slogans and the text of Article 31 [of the Constitution]—it was met with sympathy and enthusiasm."[38] CIF leaders responded with a competitive brio, challenging their members to "bigger demonstrations, festivals, awards, and gift give-aways, tying the laws to the particular requests of women in each specific place ... day care, a preschool, a clinic, a school."[39] Maternity was thus represented as properly situated in the larger community, and the domestic space not as a cosy little refuge but as an isolated "miserable kitchen." It was the welfare state, with women participating in it fully, that could guarantee well-fed, healthy, happy families—this was the image promulgated by both Communists and Catholics in 1948–50.

The Proposal in Debate and Legislation

In June 1950 the Chamber of Deputies debated the law for the protection of working mothers in the general assembly. Female MPs emphasized above all that women's multiple contributions to society and the family were already work; work that must be supported and rewarded by a grateful nation of Italians who loved and venerated their mothers. They reminded their colleagues of the text of Article 37 in the Constitution: "The working woman has the same rights, and, for equal work, equal pay to the working man. Working conditions must allow her to fulfil her essential familial function and must assure to the mother and her child a special and adequate protection." In Federici's speech she asserted, "I repeat, we were forced to make this law … the substantial question has been to study a provision which, by Constitutional terms, it was obligatory to study."[40] This rhetorical strategy was not entirely successful, as male MPs like DC member Carlo Repossi returned the discourse to the "respect, the love, the devotion due to the working mother," and argued that such devotion could only be satisfied by arriving one day "at the point that the head of the family earns enough for the entire family so that the mother is never forced to work, but can stay at home and raise her own children; the law it is necessary to create is the one that finally creates the family salary [for men] so that the woman may be truly liberated economically and attend above all to her duties as mother."[41] He argued additionally that the costs of providing nursing and daycare centres would be too onerous for employers and that mothers might not even use them since they would fear for their and their infants' health in winter when they would have to travel from home to the workplace for care; these tender concerns for the health of mothers and their babies were echoed by others, with more and less medicalized language and referral to experts. In a short intervention Noce repeated that those very experts had been consulted in the writing of the bill, but that in the end this was "a law for Italian mothers by Italian mothers."[42]

By 14 July the debate had descended into more acrid conflict; an amendment was proposed to insert the word "*coniugate*" (married) in the sentence in Article 11 requiring child care centres and nursing rooms in places of work with more than 50 women. DC deputy De Maria argued in favour, saying, "We want to formulate a law that defends maternity, but which defends it in its true and proper form, a form which creates a halo around a woman's head and makes her worthy of veneration on the part of men." Noce, who, after a complicated relationship with PCI leader and notorious womanizer Luigi Longo ending in his covert annulment of their marriage, was herself effectively an unmarried mother by this point, angrily called out "All motherhood is sacred!" The amendment succeeded, though in a compromise which lowered the number of married women required to activate the requirement to 30 and with the deputies agreed that once the facilities were activated, any mother would have the right to make use of them.[43] The lengthy and wide-ranging debate over the law contradicts the sense of the cooperating women MPs that they could avoid controversy over women's rights by focusing on the ideals of the mother and the Constitution. It reveals the strong reluctance to view the subject of Noce's law as the individual woman citizen and the enduring assumption that women were only public subjects and bearers of rights when properly collocated within the web of a respectable patriarch-led family structure. Despite their victories in passing numerous laws for women in the postwar period, women MPs faced this difficulty repeatedly in their efforts to popularize and legislate women's citizenship rights; the laws they proposed in this liberatory vein suffered amendments and revisions that diluted their ability to separate women from the role of mother-within-the-family.

With this bitter exchange the debate was nearly over; the final law passed on 26 August 1950. It required maternity leave for varying periods by category of work (hard labour stopped six months before delivery and industrial work three months before, agricultural work eight weeks before, and six weeks for other categories), but in no case less than six weeks before the due date and eight weeks after delivery. Women were guaranteed 80 per cent of their full pay, financed through a national health insurance mutual fund, and guaranteed their return to the same position for a full year. Upon return, working mothers were given a year with paid daily breaks amounting to two hours for nursing and infant care. Any workplace employing at least 30 married women under the age of 50 was required to have a nursing room and childcare.

CONCLUSION

The law Noce and Federici fought so hard for with their female colleagues and grassroots activists went largely unenforced, has been revised several times over the years, and has had mixed results for the employment rates of women and their equality in the workplace. It attempted a new approach

68   M. TAMBOR

to the tradition of the feminist use of the figure of the mother to establish an authoritative public role for women, but this strategy had major drawbacks as it has been vulnerable to other, less empowering models of maternity. Sadly, the latter trend has continued. Recent studies have shown that maternity leave, even and perhaps especially generous policies like those Noce championed, can have the contradictory effect of reducing the number of women in the workforce and reducing the ratio of women's pay to men's pay for those who do work.[44] It is only when parental leave policies do not make individual employers pay for the benefits directly, and when policies are offered and enforced in a gender neutral way, that they actually equalize men's and women's workforce participation and income, and successfully create a work–life balance for parents. In Italy this pattern has held true: the immediate result of the Noce law was that many employers simply did not comply with the law, while others either hired fewer women altogether or required them to sign the so-called "*clausola di nubilato*," a pre-signed letter of resignation by which a woman agreed that she would lose her job upon marriage—the assumption being that maternity leave would always closely follow upon a woman's marriage. Attempts to close such loopholes and implement the constitutional guarantees to remove obstacles to women's equality that women like Lina Merlin had helped write thus led them to new campaigns, such as Merlin's struggle to get the law passed that outlawed the *clausola di nubilato* in 1963.[45] Even so, in the long term women in Italy have had a comparatively low participation rate in the official workforce relative to other similarly developed countries, and have tended to cluster in part-time jobs and precarious, temporary contracts when they do work outside the home. And the stereotypical expectations of women fulfilling their "essential family functions" remain in the norms that hold women responsible for home cleanliness, hands-on mothering, and labour-intensive shopping and cooking for fresh made-from-scratch meals. Noce at one point complained, "If we were to begin making the men wash diapers they would understand the weight of these problems, which are not just women's problems, and the laws would be enforced. Especially if the women were, as they ought to be, in the majority in town councils and neighbourhood committees, in all the organisms of political power."[46]

Still, the stereotype of *mammismo* was clearly not uncontested in the 1950s. Before Alvaro coined the term in 1952 women politicians had already accustomed Italians to a different, far more positive model of motherhood, much like the one used by earlier feminists to claim that maternal virtues benefited all of society. Indeed, it may have been the competition between positive and negative views of motherhood as a political role that has most strongly influenced Italian political culture. Postwar women activists championed participatory, direct democracy as the cure for authoritarian forms of government, but this could have contributed to ordinary Italians' distrust of the state. Mariuccia Salvati has suggested that such aims led to "an excess of 'anti-formalism' *vis-à-vis* democracy," which resulted in a "prevailing sense of distance, passivity, and even contempt toward the national state."[47] Was this one of the drawbacks of elevating motherhood to "sacred" status? Noce claimed to have no regrets; and Licia Ronzulli is still repeating her "maternal gesture." It seems that maternal symbolism continues to work in ambiguous and contradictory ways for female workers and mothers—and perhaps for all Italian citizens.

NOTES

1. "In pictures: MEP Licia Ronzulli's daughter Vittoria in Strasbourg parliament," http://www.telegraph.co.uk/news/picturegalleries/worldnews/10461357/In-pictures-MEP-Licia-Ronzullis-daughter-Vittoria-in-Strasbourg-parliament.html.
2. Ronzulli quoted in Jane Martinson, "A High Five to Licia Ronzulli for Her Stance on Children in the Workplace," *The Guardian*, 24 October 2012. http://www.theguardian.com/commentisfree/2012/oct/24/high-five-licia-ronzulli-children-workplace.
3. Noce, *Rivoluzionaria professionale*, p. 409.
4. Tambor, *The Lost Wave*; see also Tambor, "Red Saints." My treatment of citizenship as gendered and as composed of rights and duties (or privileges and obligations), in which women have more often achieved citizenship conceived as duty, is indebted in particular to Linda Kerber, *No Constitutional Right to Be Ladies*. See also Canning, *Gender History in Practice*.
5. D'Amelia, *La mamma*.
6. Important works analysing the "war between the sexes" of this period include Higonnet et al., eds., *Behind the Lines*; Hagemann and Schüler-Springorum (eds), *Home/Front*; Roberts, *Civilization without Sexes*; and de Grazia, *How Fascism Ruled Women*; see also Canning, *Gender History in Practice*, pp. 42–59.
7. The decree granting women the right to vote was the Decreto legislativo luogotenenziale n. 23 del 1 febbraio 1945, "Estensione alle donne del

70   M. TAMBOR

diritto di voto," passed by the Bonomi government. See Rossi-Doria, *Diventare cittadine*, pp. 20–26; Gaiotti de Biase, "The Impact of Women's Political and Social Activity in Postwar Italy," p. 221.

8. O'Hare McCormick, "Bulldozer and the Woman with a Broom," *New York Times*, 29 March 1945.

9. Quoted in Laville, *Cold War Women*, p. 56.

10. Pojmann, *Italian Women and International Cold War Politics*. See also Gabrielli, *Il club delle virtuose*; Michetti et al., *Udi: laboratorio di politica delle donne*; Ascoli, "L'Udi tra emancipazione e liberazione"; Taricone, *Il Centro italiano femminile*; Dau Novelli, *Donne del nostro tempo*.

11. Federici, "L'Evoluzione socio-giuridica della donna alla costituente," p. 122; Addis Saba et al., *Alle origini della Repubblica: Donne e Costituente*.

12. Costitutuzione della Repubblica Italiana, Art. 37.

13. Noce et al., "Relazioni su Garanzie economico-sociali per l'assistenza della famiglia." The texts of these four women's speeches during the 10 May 1947 assembly meeting are reproduced under the chapter title "Titolo III: Rapporti economici (Discussione artt. 30–34)" in Morelli, *Le donne della Costituente*, pp. 126–37. See also Morelli, "Le madri della Costituzione," p. 401.

14. Tambor, *The Lost Wave*; Odorisio et al., *Donna o cosa?*; Sarogni, *La donna italiana*; Taricone and De Leo, *Le donne in Italia: Diritti civili e politici*.

15. Noce, *Rivoluzionaria professionale*; Noce, *Vivere in piedi*.

16. On the struggle of the women's associations to achieve autonomy from male dominance that treated them as mere auxiliaries to party and Vatican lines, see Tambor, *The Lost Wave*, pp. 40–44; Pojmann, *Italian Women and International Cold War Politics*; Sanfilippo, *Pane, amore e politica*; Spano and Camarlinghi, *La questione femminile nella politica del P.C.I.*, p. 203; Ferrari, "Contested Foundations."

17. Willson, "Saints and Heroines," p. 195. For the concept of "*maternage di massa*," see Bravo and Bruzzone, *In guerra senza armi*, pp. 66–76; Bravo, "Guerra e mutamenti nelle strutture di genere."

18. Willson, "Saints and Heroines"; see also Tambor, *Lost Wave*, pp. 32–38 and notes.

19. "Hai molti figli, sei grassa e hai i capelli lunghi. Una dirigente delle donne dev'essere così," cited in Mafai, *L'apprendistato della politica*, p. 147. See also Casalini, *Famiglie comuniste*.

20. Ombra, *Donne manifeste*, pp. 46, 129; Ventresca, *From Fascism to Democracy*, pp. 210–11.

21. See her memoirs: Noce, *Rivoluzionaria professionale*; Noce, *Vivere in piedi*. See also Boneschi, *Di testa loro*, p. 167.

22. Ladd-Taylor, "Mother-Worship/Mother-Blame," p. 663.

23. Mistry, *The United States, Italy and the Origins of Cold War*, pp. 98–104; Brogi, *A Question of Self-Esteem*, pp. 26–29.
24. Bellassai, *La legge del desiderio*; Bellassai, *La morale comunista*.
25. Scaraffia, "'Christianity Has Liberated Her," p. 276.
26. Pope Pius XII, "Address to Midwives on the Nature of Their Profession," http://www.catholicculture.org/culture/library/view.cfm?id=3462&CF ID=103675889&CFTOKEN=26566144. The pope gave the speech in essentially the same form to the Italian Catholic Union of Midwives 29 October 1951, and 26 November 1951 to the National Congress of the Family Front and the Association of Large Families, National Catholic Welfare Conference, Washington, DC.
27. "La donna è la casa, e la casa è il mondo … e la partecipazione della donna alla vita politica si giustifica in quanto ha il compito precipuo di render più efficace la sua stessa missione di sposa e di madre." Mafai, *L'apprendistato della politica*, p. 111.
28. *Atti Parlamentari*. Consulta Nazionale, Assemblea Plenaria, VI. Seduta di 1 ottobre 1945, p. 121.
29. Gaiotti de Biase, "The Impact of Women's Political and Social Activity," p. 229; Mafai, *L'apprendistato della politica*, pp. 66–67. The most famous of Togliatti's expositions of the PCI's link between emancipation and democracy was made to the first women's conference of his party in June 1945: see Palmiro Togliatti, "L'emancipazione della donna."
30. Judt, *Postwar*, p. 338 n12, points out that in 1957 less than 2 per cent of Italian households had refrigerators. See also Willson, *Women in Twentieth-Century Italy*, p. 121.
31. Bini et al., "Genere, consumi, comportamenti negli anni cinquanta," pp. 8–9.
32. On housewives' pensions, see Taricone, *Il Centro italiano femminile*, pp. 99–117; Pojmann, *Italian Women and International Cold War Politics*, pp. 46–47.
33. On the history of this protective line of thought, and how social citizenship was characteristically presented as the justifying base of political citizenship for women by maternalism, see Bock and Thane, *Maternity and Gender Policies*; Koven and Michel, *Mothers of a New World*.
34. Willson, *Women in Twentieth-Century Italy*, pp. 105, 112–13; Bravo, "Simboli del materno"; Buttafuoco, "Motherhood as a political strategy."
35. Weber, "Italy," pp. 191–92; Piccone Stella, *La prima generazione*, table p. 98; Meyer, *Sex and Power*, p. 40.
36. Judt, *Postwar*, p. 330; Willson, *Women in Twentieth-Century Italy*, pp. 120–22.
37. Canning, *Gender History in Practice*, pp. 81ff.

72   M. TAMBOR

38. UDI, Maternità 1948/1, Udi centro, "Campagna per la tutela della maternità, relazione regione per regione," 25 settembre 1948. On festivals and other practices of Italy's political subcultures, see Gundle, *Between Hollywood and Moscow*.
39. "Tutela delle lavoratrici madri," *Bollettino di attività del Cif*, no. 18, June 1948, special insert; quoted in Pojmann, *Italian Women and International Cold War Politics*, pp. 59–60, n. 54, 55.
40. *Atti parlamentari*, seduta antimeridiana 27 giugno 1950, p. 20093.
41. Ibid., pp. 20080, 20084.
42. Ibid., pp. 20092–93, 20086.
43. Ibid., p. 20889.
44. See, for example, Claire Cain Miller, "When Family-Friendly Policies Backfire," *New York Times*, 26 May 2015. Revisions and additional laws included the following: in 1954 Maria Maddalena Rossi proposed a bill extending protection of working mothers to farm families; in October 1955 Adele Bei tried to impose the universal enforcement of the Noce law on all employers; and in 1958 a law was passed which regulated work and leave for piece-workers at home. In 1971 law number 1204 of 30 December, "*Tutela delle lavoratrici madri*," extended maternity benefits to all Italian working women and extended the leave that could be taken to a full year, and law number 1044 of 6 December 1971 created a national network of public daycare/preschool centres, leading to the final dissolution of ONMI in 1975. In 1977, Tina Anselmi pushed through a law that affirmed the direct responsibility of fathers as primary caregivers and provided for alternation of absences between father and mother to care for a child. Spano and Camarlinghi, *La questione femminile nella politica del P.C.I.*, pp. 188–89; Selvaggio, *Desiderio e diritto di cittadinanza*, p. 47; Michetti et al., *Udi: laboratorio di politica delle donne*, p. 223; Gaiotti de Biase, *Questione femminile e femminismo*, p. 58. On the continuing defiance of these laws, see Boneschi, *Santa pazienza*, p. 333.
45. Taricone, *Il Centro italiano femminile*, p. 157. The law which addressed this problem was *Legge 9 gennaio 1963*, n. 7 "*Divieto di licenziamento delle lavoratrici per causa di matrimonio*."
46. Noce, *Rivoluzionaria professionale*, preface, pp. 47–48.
47. Salvati, "Behind the Cold War," pp. 564–65.

BIBLIOGRAPHY

"In pictures: MEP Licia Ronzulli's daughter Vittoria in Strasbourg parliament," http://www.telegraph.co.uk/news/picturegalleries/worldnews/10461357/In-pictures-MEP-Licia-Ronzullis-daughter-Vittoria-in-Strasbourg-parliament.html

MOTHERS, WORKERS, CITIZENS: TERESA NOCE AND THE PARLIAMENTARY... 73

Addis Saba, Marina, Mimmo de Leo, and Fiorenza Taricone, eds. *Alle origini della Repubblica. Donne e Costituente*. Rome: Consiglio dei ministri, Commissione nazionale per le pari opportunità, Dipartimento per l'informazione e l'editoria, 1996.

Ascoli, Giulietta. "L'Udi tra emancipazione e liberazione (1943–1964)." In *La questione femminile in Italia dal '900 ad oggi*, edited by Nadia Fusini, Mariella Gramaglia, Lidia Menapace et al. Milan: Franco Angeli Editore, 1977, pp. 109–159.

Bellassai, Sandro. *La legge del desiderio. Il progetto Merlin e l'Italia degli anni Cinquanta*. Rome: Carocci, 2006.

———. *La morale comunista: Pubblico e privato nella rappresentazione del PCI (1947–1956)*. Rome: Carocci, 2000.

Bini, Elisabetta, Enrica Capussotti, Giulietta Stefani, and Elisabetta Vezzosi. "Genere, consumi, comportamenti negli anni cinquanta Italia e Stati Uniti a confronto," *Italia Contemporanea* n. 224 (September 2001): pp. 1–17.

Bock, Gisela and Pat Thane, eds. *Maternity and Gender Policies. Women in the Rise of the European Welfare States 1880s–1950s*. London and New York: Routledge, 1991.

Boneschi, Marta. *Di testa loro. Dieci italiane che hanno fatto il novecento*. Milan: Mondadori, 2002.

———. *Santa pazienza. La storia delle donne italiane dal dopoguerra a oggi*. Milan: Mondadori, 1998.

Bravo, Anna. "Guerra e mutamenti nelle strutture di genere," *Italia contemporanea*, n. 195 (June 1994): pp. 367–74.

Bravo, Anna and Anna Maria Bruzzone. *In guerra senza armi. Storie di donne. 1940–1945*. Rome: Laterza, 1995.

Bravo, Anna. "Simboli del materno," in *Donne e uomini nelle guerre mondiali*. edited by Anna Bravo. Roma-Bari: Laterza, 1991.

Brogi, Alessandro. *A Question of Self-Esteem. The United States and the Cold War Choices in France and Italy 1944–1958*. Westport, CT and London: Praeger, 2002.

Buttafuoco, Annarita. "Motherhood as a political strategy: the role of the Italian women's movement in the creation of the Cassa Nazionale di Maternità", in *Maternity and Gender Policies. Women and the Rise of the European Welfare States, 1880s–1950s*. edited by Gisela Bock and Pat Thane. London: Routledge, 1991.

Canning, Kathleen. *Gender History in Practice: Historical Perspectives on Bodies, Class, and Citizenship*. Ithaca, NY: Cornell University Press, 2006.

Casalini, Maria. *Famiglie comuniste. Ideologie e vita quotidiana nell'Italia degli anni cinquanta*. Bologna: Il Mulino, 2010.

d'Amelia, Marina. *La mamma*. Bologna: Il Mulino, 2005.

74 M. TAMBOR

Dau Novelli, Cecilia, ed. *Donne del nostro tempo. Il Centro Italiano Femminile. (1945–1995)*. Rome: Edizioni Studium, 1995.

de Grazia, Victoria. *How Fascism Ruled Women: Italy 1922–1945*. Berkeley: University of California Press, 1992.

Federici, Maria. "L'Evoluzione socio-giuridica della donna alla costituente," in *Le donne nel Parlamento della repubblica dalla Consulta alla VII Legislatura*, edited by Anna Miserocchi, Beniamino Altezza, Daniela Chiassi, Mario Mammuccari. Viterbo: Fondazione Cesira Fiori, Union printing, 1989.

Ferrari, Chiara. "Contested Foundations: Postmodern Feminism and the Case of the Union of Italian Women," *Signs* 33, 3 (Spring 2008): pp. 569–94.

Gabrielli, Patrizia. *Il club delle virtuose. Udi e Cif nelle Marche dall'antifascismo alla guerra fredda*. Ancona: Il lavoro editoriale, 2000.

Gaiotti de Biase, Paola. "The Impact of Women's Political and Social Activity in Postwar Italy," in *The Formation of the Italian Republic*, edited by Frank Coppa and Margherita Repetto-Alaia. New York: Peter Lang, 1993.

———. *Questione femminile e femminismo: nella storia della repubblica*. Brescia: Morcelliana, 1979.

Gundle, Stephen. *Between Hollywood and Moscow: The Italian Communists and the Challenge of Mass Culture, 1943–1991*. Durham, NC: Duke University Press, 2000.

Hagemann, Karen and Stefanie Schüler-Springorum, eds. *Home/Front: The Military, War, and Gender in Twentieth Century Germany*. Oxford: Berg, 2002.

Higonnet, Margaret R., Jane Jenson, Sonya Michel, and Margaret Collins Weitz, eds. *Behind the Lines: Gender and the Two World Wars*. New Haven: Yale University Press, 1987.

Judt, Tony. *Postwar: A History of Europe since 1945*. New York: Penguin, 2005.

Kerber, Linda. *No Constitutional Right to Be Ladies: Women and the Obligations of Citizenship*. New York: Hill and Wang, 1998.

Koven, Seth and Sonya Michel, eds. *Mothers of a New World: Maternalist Politics and the Origins of Welfare States*. New York: Routledge, 1993.

Ladd-Taylor, Molly. "Mother-Worship/Mother-Blame: Politics and Welfare in an Uncertain Age," in *Maternal Theory. Essential Readings*. edited by Andrea O'Reilly, Toronto: Demeter Press, 2007, pp. 660–667.

Laville, Helen. *Cold War Women: The International Activities of American Women's Organizations*. Manchester: Manchester Univeristy Press, 2009.

Mafai, Miriam. *L'apprendistato della politica. Le donne italiane nel dopoguerra*. Rome: Editori Riuniti, 1979.

Martinson, Jane. "A high five to Licia Ronzulli for her stance on children in the workplace," *The Guardian*, October 24, 2012. http://www.theguardian.com/commentisfree/2012/oct/24/high-five-licia-ronzulli-children-workplace

Meyer, Donald. *Sex and Power: The Rise of Women in America, Russia, Sweden, and Italy*, 2nd edn. Middletown: Wesleyan University Press, 1989.

MOTHERS, WORKERS, CITIZENS: TERESA NOCE AND THE PARLIAMENTARY... 75

Michetti, Maria, Margherita Repetto and Luciana Viviani. *Udi: laboratorio di politica delle donne. Idee e materiali per una storia*, 2a edizione. Soveria Mannelli: Rubbettino Editore, 1998.

Mistry, Kaeten. *The United States, Italy and the Origins of Cold War. Waging Political Warfare, 1945–1950*. Cambridge: Cambridge University Press, 2014.

Morelli, Maria Teresa Antonia, ed. *Le donne della Costituente*. Rome-Bari: Laterza, 2007.

———. "Le madri della Costituzione," in *La Costituzione Repubblicana. Fondamenti, principi e valori, tra attualità e prospettive*, edited by Cesare Mirabelli Milan: Edizione Ares, 2010, pp. 393–417.

Noce, Teresa, Lina Merlin and Michele Guia, "Relazioni su Garanzie economico-sociali per l'assistenza della famiglia," Archivio dell'Assemblea Costituente, Gruppo di serie 006, Commissione per la Costituzione, Serie 003, Relazioni, studi e ricerche (27-08-1946/13-02-1947) busta 74 sottofascicolo 3.

Noce, Teresa. *Rivoluzionaria professionale*. Milano: La Pietra, Bompiani, 1974.

———. *Vivere in piedi*. Milano: Gabriele Mazzotta, 1978.

Odorisio, Maria Linda, Anna Rossa Doria, Lucetta Scaraffia and Monica Turi. *Donna o cosa? Cronistoria dei movimenti femminili in Italia dal Risorgimento a oggi*. Turin: Edizioni Milva, 1986.

O'Hare McCormick, Anne. "Bulldozer and the Woman with a Broom," *New York Times*, March 29, 1945.

Ombra, Marisa, ed. *Donne manifeste: L'Udi attraverso i suoi manifesti, 1944–2004*. Milan: Il Saggiatore, 2005.

Piccone Stella, Simonetta. *La prima generazione. Ragazzi e ragazze nel miracolo economico italiano*. Milan: Franco Angeli, 1993.

Pojmann, Wendy. *Italian Women and International Cold War Politics, 1944–1968*. New York: Fordham University Press, 2013.

Roberts, Mary Louise. *Civilization without Sexes: Reconstructing Gender in Postwar France, 1917–1927*. Chicago: University of Chicago Press, 1994.

Rossi-Doria, Anna. *Diventare cittadine. Il voto alle donne in Italia*. Florence: Giunti Gruppo Editoriale, 1996.

Salvati, Mariuccia. "Behind the Cold War: Rethinking the Left, the State and Civil Society in Italy (1940s–1970s)," *Journal of Modern Italian Studies* 8, n. 4 (2003): pp. 556–577.

Sanfilippo, Anna Laura. *Pane, amore e politica. Le comuniste in provincia di Latina dopo la Liberazione (1944–1956)*. Rome: Ediesse, 2013.

Sarogni, Emilia. *La donna italiana. Il lungo cammino verso i diritti, 1861–1994*. Parma: Pratiche Editrice, 1995.

Scaraffia, Lucetta. "'Christianity Has Liberated Her and Placed Her Alongside Man in the Family': From 1850 to 1988 (*Mulieris Dignitatem*)," in *Women and Faith: Catholic Religious Life in Italy from Late Antiquity to the Present*, edited by Lucetta Scaraffia and Gabriella Zarri. Cambridge: Harvard University Press, 1999.

76 M. TAMBOR

Selvaggio, Maria Antonietta. *Desiderio e diritto di cittadinanza: Le italiane e il voto. Atti del convegno Napoli 6–7 dicembre 1995.* Palermo: La Luna, 1997.

Spano, Nadia and Fiamma Camarlinghi. *La questione femminile nella politica del P.C.I. 1921–1963.* Rome: Edizioni Donne e Politica, 1972.

Tambor, Molly. *The Lost Wave: Women and Democracy in Postwar Italy.* New York: Oxford University Press, 2014.

————. "Red Saints: Gendering the Cold War, Italy 1943–1953," *Cold War History* 10: n. 3 (2010): pp. 429–456.

Taricone, Fiorenza. *Il Centro italiano femminile. Dalle origini agli anni Settanta.* Milan: Franco Angeli, 2001.

Taricone, Fiorenza and Mimmo de Leo, eds. *Le donne in Italia. Diritti civili e politici.* Napoli: Liguori Editore, 1992.

Togliatti, Palmiro, "L'emancipazione della donna," reproduced in *Donne Comuniste. Antologia di scritti e discorsi,* edited by Graziella Falconi. Rome: Claudio Salemi, 1989, pp. 52–80.

Ventresca, Robert. *From Fascism to Democracy: Culture and Politics in the Italian Election of 1948.* Toronto: University of Toronto Press, 2004.

Weber, Maria. "Italy," in *The Politics of the Second Electorate: Women and Public Participation: Britain, USA, Canada, Australia, France, Spain, West Germany, Italy, Sweden, Finland, Eastern Europe, USSR, Japan,* edited by Joni Lovenduski and Jill Hills. Boston: Routledge and Kegan Paul, 1981.

Willson, Perry. "Saints and Heroines: Re-writing the History of Italian Women in the Resistance," in *Opposing Fascism: Community, Authority and Resistance in Europe,* edited by Tim Kirk and Anthony McElligott. Cambridge: Cambridge University Press, 1999.

————. *Women in Twentieth-Century Italy.* London: Palgrave Macmillan, 2010.

CHAPTER 4

Problems and Prescriptions: Motherhood and *Mammismo* in Postwar Italian Advice Columns and Fiction

Penelope Morris

With the disruptions and displacements of war and reconstruction, subsequent Cold War divisions and the development of a modern consumer society, the period following the Second World War was one of vast upheaval in Italian society. Women were at the centre of national debates at the time. In their new roles as voters, politicians, activists and prime consumers, they were at the vanguard of social change, but provoked anxiety among the more conservative sections of society, who preferred instead to emphasize the importance of wives and mothers as guarantors of the family and tradition; a bulwark against the "threats" of both modernism and individualism. It was in this atmosphere of contention surrounding women and motherhood, that, in the early 1950s, as Marina d'Amelia notes, the term *mammismo* was coined by Corrado Alvaro, encapsulating the idea that women, as mothers, should be made scapegoats for the recent and current failings of Italy.[1] The stereotype was, however, one among a number of competing—but also overlapping—maternal discourses circulating at the time and emanating from, for example, both the

P. Morris (✉)
School of Modern Languages and Cultures, University of Glasgow, Glasgow, UK
e-mail: penelope.morris@glasgow.ac.uk

© The Author(s) 2018
P. Morris, P. Willson (eds.), *La Mamma*,
Italian and Italian American Studies,
https://doi.org/10.1057/978-1-137-54256-4_4

77

left and right of the political spectrum, from the Catholic Church and from advocates of women's rights.[2]

One of the challenges facing the researcher is to understand not only the ways in which motherhood has been constructed discursively in the public sphere, predominantly by men, but also how these discourses have been received, processed, reproduced or utilized, by women. Advice columns offer a particularly fruitful source for exploring both, and for investigating the (perceived) issues facing mothers and the versions of ideal motherhood that predominated in 1950s Italy. They constitute, I argue, a discursive space in which normative prescriptions come up against the anxieties and practicalities of everyday, "private" lives, exposing the fault lines in ideologies and, in some cases, offering a vision of a different kind of society.

This chapter focuses on the advice columns of four very different weekly magazines, representing major streams of thought at the time: *Grazia*, a popular women's magazine which dated back to before the war; *Famiglia cristiana*, a Catholic family magazine; *Noi donne*, a women's magazine closely allied to the Communist Party; and *Epoca*, a self-consciously modern family illustrated weekly. It examines the contrasting ways in which they approach the maternal and the stereotype of *mammismo* in particular. As will be suggested, it is the advice column of Alba de Céspedes in the magazine *Epoca* that provides, in many ways, the most nuanced and insightful treatment of motherhood. As de Céspedes was also a best-selling writer whose novels focused on the intimate worlds of contemporary women, including issues surrounding motherhood, she effectively had a "double voice" in public on these matters. An analysis of these two voices reveals what she chose not, or was not able, to say about motherhood in her column, and a depth of feeling and criticism only hinted at in her journalism.

Magazines and Advice Columns in Postwar Italy

The huge growth in popularity of magazines was a notable feature of the cultural industries in postwar Italy, with pre-existing publications revamping their formats and increasing circulation, and other new, family-oriented news weeklies appearing for the first time, putting Italy, where there had traditionally been relatively few readers, in the lead in Europe for magazine circulation figures.[3] Consumer objects in themselves, they provided a window onto new fashions and leisure pursuits, and commentaries on

PROBLEMS AND PRESCRIPTIONS: MOTHERHOOD AND *MAMMISMO...*   79

subjects such as the latest current affairs or the lives of the famous. Naturally the magazines varied widely, depending on the target readership and the publisher, as well as any political or, in some cases, religious orientation. However, a tendency that can be discerned in all of them was the attempt to reconcile modernity and tradition. In a rapidly changing society, such publications—including communist and Catholic magazines— aimed to present themselves as part of a modern, forward-looking world. Yet, at the same time, if to varying degrees, they insisted on an essentially conservative understanding of cultural mores, particularly with regard to the family, gender roles and sexual conduct.[4]

The magazines all encouraged interchange with readers. Most magazines, and some newspapers, had at least one advice column. The burgeoning of this format in the 1950s suggests that they were increasingly popular with readers. With the seismic shifts of this decade, many Italians found themselves in situations to which they were unaccustomed or in which they perceived that society's rules were changing. Usually associated with sentimental and relationship problems, and with the historically negative connotations of both the "feminine" and the "popular," in fact the columns varied widely. While all may have been read as a form of entertainment—sometimes as a kind of commodification of distress—at the same time there were columns which addressed a broad range of topics and often included the very serious treatment of issues central to the political discourse of the day and to an understanding of the relationship between private and public worlds.[5]

Recently there has been some attention paid to advice columns in academic studies, but there remains a great deal of unmined material.[6] Advice columns do not, of course, provide unmediated access to the views and intimate lives of "ordinary Italians." The question of authenticity always arises and any analysis must take into account the historical and socio-cultural context of the magazine and its readership, as well as the persona of the adviser and their posited relationship with the readers. Nevertheless, there are many examples of what appear to be genuine exchanges[7] and in all cases they give a strong indication of the kind of societal problems and issues that the magazine editors or columnists identified as most pressing or most interesting to readers. They also offer a means of exploring the kind of solutions that could be envisaged at the time and an insight into areas of contention or ambiguity.

In her 2006 study of wives and mothers in 1950s Italy, Rebecca West contrasts the "unreality" of the idealized prescriptions of domestic manuals

80   P. MORRIS

(which all insist on what, following Cavarero, she calls the "whatness" of the female role), with the relative "reality" of the individual experiences (the "who-ness") explored and detailed in fictional works.[8] Advice columns operated in a different context again. In their implication of direct interaction with readers, they had to perform a balancing act between the ideals and prescriptions of advisers, editors and the ideologies they subscribed to, and the real, everyday and current concerns, prejudices and beliefs of readers. In this way, advice columns created a unique, if mediated, space for the discussion of intimate concerns in a public forum.[9] This is particularly relevant for Italy in the 1950s and early 1960s, which offered few other sources of advice outside the family other than the family doctor or local priest.

Advice columns in Italy in the 1950s also constitute a forum which is notable for the significant participation of women—whether as readers or columnists—so that, very unusually for the sources available for the period, and long before the "mummy blog" of recent times, mothers themselves were addressed and were raising issues about their own role in society.[10] At the same time, such columns were not, as popularly characterized, confined to women's magazines and a female readership, but also involved men—as readers, editors and advisers—in what might be seen as the distinctly "feminine" realms of the family, relationships and emotions.[11]

SIGNORA QUICKLY AND DONNA LETIZIA IN *GRAZIA*

The women's magazine *Grazia*, first published in 1938, underwent a process of renewal in the postwar period. It increased its range of content and overall quality, but retained a largely conservative and moralistic outlook, according to which Italian women were essentially wives, mothers and home-makers. It was aimed at a relatively educated, middle-class readership, though demanded rather less of its readers than the other magazines discussed here. In the 1950s, there were two long-running advice columns (although at times more than two): Donna Letizia's "Saper vivere" (How to Live) and Signora Quickly's "Ditelo pure a me" (Do Tell Me). Donna Letizia, whose real name was Colette Rosselli, became extremely well known in Italy as an arbiter of good taste, as did the guide to good manners inspired by her column, published first in 1960 and reprinted many times.[12] In the 1950s, her column was mainly a guide to social etiquette and only occasionally answered questions that would more familiarly be found in an advice column.

The second column, though much less well known now, ranged over many different issues, including motherhood. Signora Quickly's "Ditelo pure a me" was actually penned by a middle-aged man, the playwright and screenwriter Dino Falconi (1902–90), but this was much less well known than the identity of Donna Letizia. Signora Quickly is overtly a pseudonym—taken from Shakespeare's *Merry Wives of Windsor*—but the fiction of a female adviser is maintained throughout.[13] Signora Quickly styles herself as middle-aged and married with no children. She continually refers to herself as a mother figure to her readers however, addressing them as "my child" or "my dear." There are letters from some older readers who are mothers of teenage or grown-up children—but for the most part the correspondents are teenagers themselves or young women. Indeed, Signora Quickly derives her authority, such as it is, from her seniority and her adopted familial role. "In some ways I think of myself," she says, "as the mother of all my little friends at *Grazia*."[14]

Signora Quickly puts forward a very clear line on motherhood and brooks little variation. Any reluctance to become a mother on the part of her younger readers is severely criticized. Maternity is seen as the inevitable destiny of women, as "natural": "Don't you think that women were created to become mothers? And if that's how it is, what's the point in all this talk of freedom?"[15] Motherhood is presented as essentially selfless and "synonymous with sacrifice, in fact it becomes sublime through sacrifice."[16] It is, Quickly says, the pinnacle of female achievement: the birth of a child is when a woman becomes "the ark, the tabernacle, the altar of the family."[17] The pseudo-religious language used here is far from incidental of course, recalling as it does the Catholic Church's veneration of motherhood, and of the Virgin Mary in particular.

However, while citing the idealized figure at the centre of the family, the column also attempts to deal with some of the everyday difficulties of its readers. When mothers do write in, the question that most often appears is how much freedom to allow their daughters. In response, it is almost an obsession with the column that mothers must safeguard their daughter's morality—that is, in practice, their virginity and consequent marriageability. It is perhaps not surprising that the focus should be on the mother–daughter relationship, as men are in a sense external to the female environment posited by a women's magazine. However, it is also clear from Signora Quickly's answers that it is mothers, not fathers, who bear the responsibility for the education of their children and indeed the blame if things go wrong. There is also very little mention of sons, who apparently cause few problems; but of course when it came to sexual propriety in a society which applied double standards to male and female behaviour, then it was true that at least in this respect mothers did not have to pay the same attention to sons. As for the daughters, while it might seem that Signora Quickly was simply insisting on traditional Catholic morality, in fact the picture was rather more complex. Protecting a daughter's reputation was also a means to an end, as one of a mother's main responsibilities was to ensure that her daughter married. It is made clear in the column that mothers should impose discipline, but also encourage daughters make themselves appealing and effectively available to men. This advice takes on very different connotations for any reader aware that Signora Quickly is actually a man.

As for daughters' attitudes to mothers, on the other hand, complaints are not accepted at all. Their problems are dismissed and there are references to the "natural" understanding that exists between mothers and daughters, which in practice means acquiescence, for, as Signora Quickly asserts, "mothers are never wrong."[18] The situation changes, however, when a woman marries and has children. From that point on, she belongs to a "separate, little nucleus" and her allegiance must always be to her husband.[19] In fact, Signora Quickly goes further on a number of occasions and suggests that a wife should also be prepared to act as a mother to her husband. "Our husbands," she comments in 1950, "are often also our sons and it's not just a joke of nature that maternity has its origins in love."[20] Some years later, she advises a reader on how she should deal with her husband: "this is exactly what you must force yourself to be with him at the moment, a mother, a tender, understanding, wise and consoling little mother [*mammina*]."[21] Such an assertion could be seen as a foreshadowing of the notion of *mammismo*, perhaps proposing that all relationships with men can ultimately be reduced to this kind of infantilization. However, both responses above were provoked by a wife asking how to deal with an unfaithful husband and, as elsewhere in this column, "mothering" husbands has far more to do with double standards, with minimizing the responsibility of the husband for his infidelity and with putting the onus on the wife to maintain the relationship: "Show tolerance towards him. As you would tolerate the whims and naughtiness of your children."[22]

In general, the column does not explore the idea that mothers have a particularly significant relationship with their sons, except as implied in one recurring theme: the question of the relationship between a daughter-in-law

PROBLEMS AND PRESCRIPTIONS: MOTHERHOOD AND *MAMMISMO*... 83

and a mother-in-law. This does come up frequently and in both advice columns in *Grazia* there is the assumption that the relationship is always fraught. In all cases, the mother's attachment to the son goes unquestioned and the problem is presented as one that exists specifically between the two women. The etiquette of dealing with mothers-in-law appears quite frequently in Donna Letizia's column. The daughter-in-law must be on her guard; when advising a reader on how to dress when meeting her future mother-in-law for the first time she warns that "future mothers-in-law can see through everything, her piercing look will spot a safety pin through three layers of material."[23] She counsels caution; it is better not to try to have too close a relationship, she advises.[24] Or, as Signora Quickly warns, "Mothers-in-law, when they put their minds to it, are real calamities."[25]

This difficult relationship is seen as an increasingly common problem, but one that has a very practical source in the cohabitation of a young couple and their parents-in-law. Indeed, Signora Quickly remarks, one of the secrets of married life is to avoid such a situation.[26] When it does happen, it is understandable, Signora Quickly suggests in 1956, that the mother-in-law is not happy:

> What do you expect? That these elderly mothers [madri di famiglia], who are often authentic "heads of the family" [capi di famiglia] should adapt to acting almost as maids for the wives of their sons, just because they had the imprudence or carelessness to get married before they could afford their own home?[27]

Thus the conflict between the generations is presented as a power struggle within the home, where the daughter represents a challenge to the mother-in-law's status. Of course, this is highly simplistic, suggesting that the roles available are either "head" or "maid," with apparently no room for negotiation or compromise. Conversely, the relationship between mother and son, or indeed between son and mother-in-law, seems to be of little interest to Signora Quickly or her readers. There is no mention here of mothers "spoiling" their sons, but in any case, given that wives are encouraged to be indulgent in a motherly way towards their husbands, it seems hardly likely that a "*mammone*" would be criticized.

So mothers are venerated in *Grazia*, and assumed to have responsibility and natural authority, but with this comes the assumption that they will always put the rest of the family first and that their self-sacrificial, ever-giving form of mothering will, where necessary, also apply to husbands. Motherhood

84 P. MORRIS

is seen as a series of essential qualities and feelings—the "joy" of motherhood is taken as given[28]—but also a role that must be performed correctly, to the extent that when a woman does not conform to the traditional ideal, she is told that she can no longer be considered a real mother.[29]

The stereotype of the formidable, problematic mother-in-law appears reasonably often and casual references to the "terrible mother-in-law" suggest it was seen as a fact of contemporary life.[30] However, there is no suggestion in either column that mothers over-indulge their sons or that there is a crisis in masculinity in the way expressed by Alvaro or by the "inept" male protagonists (*"inetti"*) of films of the period.[31] Dino Falconi does not seem to have been beset by such worries, or at least not ones he wished to air in a women's magazine through his alter ego. There is also no real criticism of the mother-in-law in this respect; she is seen as part of an older generation who does things differently and naturally wants to hold onto the power she has within the family. Nor is there any sense that this is an issue that should be addressed by society as a whole. Rather, it is understood as a problem for the daughter-in-law as an individual and she has to find ways of living with it.

PADRE ATANASIO IN *FAMIGLIA CRISTIANA*

Famiglia cristiana first appeared in 1931, published by the Società San Paolo. In the mid-1950s it increased its circulation hugely, having adopted the format of an illustrated weekly, and became one of the most popular publications in Italy.[32] Originally aimed primarily at women, after the Second World War the magazine extended its target readership to the whole family. Forgacs and Gundle note that in the postwar period it "represented a popular version of the most advanced Catholic thinking" and "offered a vision of modernization that combined aspects of American-style consumerism with established customs and values."[33] *Famiglia cristiana*'s advice column, "Cerchiamo insieme" (Let's seek together) was run throughout the 1950s by Padre Atanasio, a priest and, in a sense, the only professional advice-giver under consideration here. The image of motherhood that emerges from the column is, as might be expected, in line with the teachings of the Church in that period and shows little sign of the modernity of other aspects of the publication. Although there are responses which emphasize the joint responsibility of parents for their offspring,[34] most often it is the selfless mother who is identified as crucial for the well-being of children. Where a father is unfaithful, abusive or absent, the mother is reminded that she should sacrifice her own needs and happiness for the sake of the family and for a higher reward. Turning, as he often does, to readers in general, he implores:

> You, good mothers and faithful wives, continue in faith to offer up your daily suffering to the Lord. Nothing is more precious than your tears, your cries and your anguish! Think how the Madonna suffered! [...] You'll be in paradise after your death...

and even in this life, "you'll have the consolation of carrying out the will of God, of seeing your husband ask the Lord and you for pardon." Your children, he tells them, will remember you with "veneration" and "grateful admiration."[35]

Likewise, there is the utmost clarity when the mother's needs are set against those of the unborn child. When a reader suggests that a mother who has sacrificed herself to try to save her baby (who died anyway) has effectively committed suicide, the response is unequivocal:

> It's simple: her duty as a mother is precisely to make sure that the child she has carried for nine months is born. You can't have the luxury of starting a maternity and then breaking it off when it's no longer convenient. Every mother knows that when she is preparing to have a child, in the best of circumstances she will suffer a lot and in the worst she'll lose her life.[36]

In this column too, a common theme is the way that mothers are exhorted to protect the "virtue" of their daughters and blamed for its loss. To a letter from a young woman who has apparently had sex before marriage, Padre Atanasio replies "What a terrible responsibility mothers like yours have [...] You can at least cry with her and feel the remorse for how much she could have foreseen, avoided or prevented!"[37] The frequency of such letters suggests that the sexual conduct of young people was one of the main preoccupations of the columnist and magazine editors, and indeed that one of the main aims of the column was precisely to remind mothers of their "duty" towards their daughters in preventing such behaviour. On the other hand, Padre Atanasio is considerably more forgiving than Signora Quickly towards the struggles of readers who have already "sinned."

In following the Catholic Church's vision of motherhood closely, Padre Atanasio's point of view is in many ways simpler and less ambiguous than

86   P. MORRIS

that of *Grazia*'s advice columns. Nevertheless, by its very nature, an advice column offers a very particular way of conveying the Church's teachings. As a "problem page" it inevitably draws attention to sinners and possible sins, and seems designed to act as a dire warning to its readers, reminding women in particular of their responsibilities, and of the many problems that arise when they are neglected. Yet at the same time, as in *Grazia*, this sits rather uncomfortably with the equally strong conviction that mothers are, by their very nature, saint-like.

Renata Viganò and Giuliana dal Pozzo in *Noi donne*

Motherhood is an important theme throughout the 1950s in the women's magazine, *Noi donne*, culminating, in 1957, in an investigation into maternity which ran over six issues, each dealing with a different topic.[38] The subject is also given considerable space in its advice column. Theoretically open to all readers, the magazine was aimed above all at women on the left and produced by the left-wing UDI (Unione Donne Italiane).[39] Although not explicitly a communist publication, it was closely allied to the PCI (Partito comunista italiano). Overall, it aimed to present a progressive, alternative view of womanhood and motherhood, a counterpoint to the values of the Catholic Church, and to other conservative forces dominant in Italian society at the time, that is, primarily the Christian Democrat party, but also some on the left.[40] One prominent aspect of this was the magazine's openly sympathetic attitude towards teenage, unmarried mothers. While such figures were condemned by *Grazia*, and pitied by *Famiglia cristiana*, *Noi donne*'s columnists were consistent in maintaining that there was no shame in having a child out of wedlock, either for the mother or the child. Rather than obsessing with the potentially disastrous consequences for women of illicit sexual activity, *Noi donne* was more interested in countering the stigma facing women who were already unmarried mothers and in providing practical support.[41]

As far as other aspects of motherhood are concerned, however, the views expressed in *Noi donne*'s advice column changed quite significantly over the course of the decade, with the magazine adopting a stronger, more consistent and more independent line when Giuliana dal Pozzo took over both as editor and as adviser for the magazine's problem page in the mid-1950s.[42] From 1951 to 1955, the adviser was the ex-partisan, Renata Viganò, the well-known author of the best-selling Resistance novel, *L'Agnese va a morire*, published in 1949. In her column, "Fermo posta"

(Poste Restante), she supported the magazine's line on teenage mothers, but at times displayed some decidedly conventional understandings of family roles and morality. Similar to Signora Quickly, she assumes the generational and familial authority of a mother in her column.[43] Her "maternalistic" attitude implies a society in which younger generations still obey their elders, and she often tells teenagers that they must listen to their mothers. Moreover, in the advice she offers, women must ultimately bow to their husbands' wishes. Addressing a reader whose husband is an alcoholic, she tells her to "put up with it, be good," and think of her children: "I understand that I'm asking you to make an endless sacrifice, but that's how life is, especially for wives and for mothers feeling concern and affection for their husbands and children."[44] This combination of left-wing activism and conventional ideas on motherhood chimes entirely with her 1949 novel in which the middle-aged, peasant protagonist becomes "*mamma* Agnese" to the young partisans, and offers a reassuringly non-threatening version of female politicization.[45]

From 1955, however, *Noi donne* began to campaign much more openly for women's rights and the introduction of a divorce law.[46] When Giuliana dal Pozzo took over in 1956, she emphasized an equal relationship with readers: as she put it a couple of years later, "ours is a publication based on dialogue and reciprocal trust."[47] This collaborative approach is also suggested by the choice of title for her advice column: "Parliamone insieme" (Let's talk about it together). Dal Pozzo directly challenges the kind of wifely and motherly "tolerance" preached elsewhere, stressing the need for honesty within marriages and family relationships. In December 1956, for example, she appeals to mothers to be frank and clear in advising daughters and not to depend on threats and scaremongering.[48] Conversely, when a 15-year-old complains that her mother insists she should stay at home and sew, rather than attend political meetings, Giuliana dal Pozzo agrees that the mother is mistaken, but she urges the daughter to be patient and not to be unhappy and to think instead about "how much solitude, how much pressure due to prejudice, how many painful sacrifices your mother must have suffered in order to think in this way."[49] In encouraging reconciliation between two members of a family, dal Pozzo is also showing an understanding of the trauma and discrimination that the previous generation of women had endured and an insight into the way that this was being revisited on their children. In the rapidly changing society of the 1950s, with the emergence of a separate youth culture, dal Pozzo expresses scepticism towards the apparently innate "good sense" that justified maternal authority—and indeed the authority of the maternalistic advice columnist—yet she recognized too that mothering is inevitably also the passing on of values and habits and that both generations needed to be involved in an act of negotiation.

One of the main themes of *Noi donne* is women and work: the types of work women did, their working conditions and attitudes towards female labour. Responding to a mother who fears she is not "normal" for missing her children at work all week, but feeling anxious and agitated when at home with them, dal Pozzo counters that she is in fact entirely "normal." Those who do not want women to work, she says, play on mothers' desires to be with their children, yet motherly love does not just mean attachment to children, "but also a capacity for understanding, self-improvement, facing up to situations with intelligence, overcoming despondency, solving difficulties, calming nerves and working through your own tiredness."[50] In the future, she says, children will understand what it means to have a mother who can help them face the problems she herself faced and, in the meantime, she can still be the "dearest mother in the world," even if it is only one day a week. What dal Pozzo does consider abnormal, however, are the excessive hours demanded of mothers and the lack of nurseries and schools where children are properly cared for. In this way dal Pozzo insists on the dignity of working women and the need for better support, but, as is typical of the magazine, there is still an underlying suggestion that motherhood remains the principal concern for women.

When it comes to protecting daughters in particular, there is none of the scaremongering regarding their morals and protecting virginity, but dal Pozzo is much more explicit about the dangers of abuse of girls, by relatives and others, saying that she gets many letters on the subject, and imploring mothers—again seen as having primary responsibility—to be as vigilant as possible.[51] The question of abortion is also raised, as a problem that is pressing but has no immediate answer. As for cohabitation with in-laws, it is mentioned in the column and is judged as ill-advised. However, it is not seen to the same extent in terms of the relationship between the daughter-in-law and the mother-in-law, and the *mammismo* stereotype—and the "spoiled" or emasculated son—is not a feature of the magazine.

Advice columns by their nature focus on the individual's problems and the solutions that are offered often depend entirely on the individual and the choices that s/he makes. In *Noi donne* in the latter half of the decade, however, the biggest contrast with magazines such as *Grazia* and *Famiglia cristiana*, and indeed with some of Viganò's replies, is that a far greater emphasis is put on the need for society to change: the need for legislative reform and better social provision for maternity leave and childcare, and for a change in attitudes towards women who do not fit the idealized model of the perfect, married mother at home with her children. At the same time, the frequent letters from readers explaining the dire straits in which they find themselves, and for which dal Pozzo has no immediate remedy, draw attention to the very difficult realities of life for many of *Noi donne*'s readers.

ALBA DE CÉSPEDES AND "DALLA PARTE DI LEI" IN *EPOCA*

Epoca was published by Mondadori and first appeared in 1950. Influenced by the American magazine *Life*, it aimed to be thoroughly modern, while avoiding offending conservative and Catholic sensibilities. As Forgacs and Gundle observe, "the most innovative aspect [of the content] of the early issues was their declared emphasis on representing and reflecting the lives of ordinary Italians."[52] In keeping with this, prominence was given to dialogue with readers and to letters columns such as that of the novelist Alba de Céspedes, "Dalla parte di lei" (Her Side of Things).[53] Despite the name, which was actually taken from the title of her 1949 novel,[54] letters from both men and women appeared in the column (like *Famiglia cristiana*, but unlike the two women's magazines) and the range of subjects included, but also went well beyond, those of an emotional or intimate nature most usually associated with advice columns. In writing to de Céspedes, readers were corresponding with a prominent intellectual figure, whose best-selling novels were characterized by acute social commentary and strong female protagonists.[55]

Like the other advice columns discussed in this chapter, the questions and answers in "Dalla parte di lei" bear witness to a profound sense of a society in flux. Readers' letters express uncertainty about how to behave appropriately and deal with changing ideas about youth, the family, and relationships between men and women. De Céspedes' answers, which often quote from writers and philosophers, are more detailed and more carefully crafted than those found in the other columns. Although of relatively high social standing, as a famous novelist previously married to a count, de Céspedes' assumed relationship with her readers is similar to the egalitarian approach taken in *Noi donne*. While humorous on occasion, it certainly has none of the condescension that characterizes Signora

Quickly's answers. Like dal Pozzo, de Céspedes uses her column to argue for a different society, particularly for women, but she distances herself from any political (or religious) alignment. Indeed, as I have argued elsewhere, taken together, de Céspedes' answers can be seen as a genuine attempt to create a kind of compendium of lay morals and independent, practical advice for a world in which the old certainties no longer held sway.[56]

Like other roles in society, that of the mother was changing and it was important, de Céspedes asserts, to keep up with the times. She has considerable sympathy for both the older and the younger generations, but insists on the need to adjust expectations and behaviours. "Don't define yourself as an 'old-style' mother," she tells Luisa B T, "you have to live in your own time and face up to its problems courageously."[57] Many mothers, she comments in a later issue, "want to bring up their daughters following customs that belonged to their own times and which are different from those of today's generation"; they are scornful about "modern" ideas, as if they are somehow living outside the modern world.[58] Instead, she points out, it is not just scientists or philosophers who are creating this world and its modern habits, but precisely mothers themselves. When buying a fridge, having a perm, drinking an espresso in a bar, sending a telegram, they, more than anyone, "are no longer living in the times in which they were born."[59]

De Céspedes does not, however, underestimate the challenges that face women living in this "decade poised between two societies," in which expectations vary widely and many traditional attitudes persist.[60] Nevertheless, it is young women, she suggests, who need to "establish the transition from one tradition to another" in a time when:

> men still expect their wives to be beautiful dolls, ingenuous brides, meek housewives and mothers, but also companions who can work alongside them, who can discuss all those problems that were once forbidden subjects for women, who can give intellectual guidance to their children and in whom he can find all the love that he would previously have shared with a number of different women, and all the understanding and solidarity previously provided by friends.[61]

These new challenges could leave both sexes dissatisfied with each other. In the first year of her column, for example, de Céspedes detects an awareness of the kind of crisis in masculinity that is mentioned elsewhere

PROBLEMS AND PRESCRIPTIONS: MOTHERHOOD AND *MAMMISMO*... 91

in this volume but does not appear in the columns analysed so far. She notes that:

> Many women complain that men today are different from the way that they were, they don't have a sense of responsibility, they are weak, uncertain, dissolute, work only for economic gain, they don't have the kind of ambitions their fathers had. This is an indication of the way that the roles of fathers, mothers, spouses are changing; instead of pining for the past, we have to recognize that the roles of today have equal value, even if they appear in a new form. Customs usually evolve slowly, but recent wars [...] have made this evolution so rapid that we've been left disoriented. Our generation has the difficult task of adapting to these changes.[62]

Men could also be dissatisfied. In September 1952, "Silvio" and "Mario Ferrario," write in, the first complaining about "women's progress" and the second admiring the battle which women are fighting but unsure of the results, disconcerted that the women he meets are not like his mother. De Céspedes counters that "the image of the mother sewing for her own children must now be substituted by the mother who sits at a loom in a factory in order to be able to buy the ready-made clothes that her children need" and that this new kind of mother deserves just as much respect. "The birth rate shows that women are not ignoring what is considered to be their principal task," she says (a situation that would soon change of course) and she is far more moved by a woman who returns from work with medicine or a toy she has bought with money she has earned and then does the housework and helps with homework, than by a mother singing nursery rhymes to her children.[63]

Indeed, in a similar vein to Giuliana dal Pozzo in *Noi donne*, de Céspedes maintains that not only should mothers not be criticized for working, they should be positively encouraged to find work outside the home. If for some women it was in any case an economic necessity, for all women it could offer the possibility of self-fulfilment, dignity and greater independence. Indeed, it is a solution she often proposes to women caught in loveless marriages, faced with the impossibility of divorce and the social disgrace and practical difficulties—for women with no financial means of their own—of separation.

De Céspedes is also concerned, like dal Pozzo, about the stigma that surrounds both single mothers and their children. Similarly—but more assertively than in *Noi donne*—she advises that where a household cannot

92   P. MORRIS

be harmonious, there is no reason why parents should not resort to separation, annulment or divorce (in the rare cases where this was possible). It is wrong, to her way of thinking, for a mother to sacrifice herself for her children, as this only creates, in a phrase that echoes Aleramo's novel written half a century earlier, "a continuous succession of sacrificed creatures."[64] Moreover, she argues later that year, parents should not underestimate the wisdom of their own offspring: "children of today [...] are very skilled in understanding family difficulties and discuss them with friends who are suffering the same problems."[65]

In this way, de Céspedes recognizes a range of different kinds of motherhood and the rights of all members of the family to have their views taken into account, without, however, privileging those of the father as would have happened historically. The egalitarian, "modern" form of marriage she advocates means that one form of "mothering" she certainly does not approve of is that of the wife towards the husband: when "Emilia" suggests that women could often do more to stop men straying by treating them like children, de Céspedes objects that such a notion belongs to a previous generation and to a time when women were effectively slaves who had to resort to flirting and dissimulation. Directly challenging the kind of assumptions made by Signora Quickly in *Grazia*, de Céspedes asserts that such "humiliating expedients" should be rejected, and that "men should be neither tyrants nor babies."[66]

So, while presenting a new ideal to aspire to, "Dalla parte di lei" also takes full account of the very narrow definition of motherhood that prevailed in Italian society at the time, highlighting the challenges, and sometimes desperate realities, faced by women attempting to separate from their husbands or choosing between single motherhood, and society's condemnation, or many years irrevocably tied to a loveless marriage; a choice, as de Céspedes puts it, "between two humiliations."[67] She does suggest that "by their nature, [women] are inclined to express themselves completely through love and motherhood."[68] This has to be understood in context however. For de Céspedes, love is never trivial and she also recognizes that not all women wish to be mothers and that work can be just as, or more, important.

It could seem that a column which exposed the discrimination endemic in Italian society and insisted on a much wider definition of mothering beyond the narrow prescriptions of the Church or "tradition," might give little space to the stereotype of *mammismo*, with its sexist assumptions and rhetoric of blame. However, the overbearing mother and over-indulged son do indeed find their way into this advice column, and not just as a series of prejudices to be dismissed.

What in other magazines is either a caricature or a real problem for a cohabiting daughter-in-law receives a much fuller treatment here. Economic constraints are certainly part of the picture. In 1955, de Céspedes includes letters from "E.C." and "A. Costanzo" in order to illustrate "one of the most agonizing problems of our poor, overpopulated country," saying that she could have added "many others which recount the story of marriages which have foundered due to cohabitation with in-laws and parents, denying a young married couple the freedom they need."[69] Instead, she asserts, all families have a right to their own home, however modest, and all couples have the right to sleep separately from their children. Where that is not possible, couples should wait, because while it may work in a few cases:

> dozens of letters bear witness to struggles and rivalries between mothers-in-law and daughters-in-law: the one inevitably remains mistress of her own home and imposes her own experience and her own habits, while the other wants to be able to be mistress of her home and to continue in her own habits—which are an expression moreover of her own character—and also to make mistakes, just as everyone makes mistakes when they are setting out and learning.[70]

In such situations, she says, couples are forced into a platonic relationship and feel bitter and irritable, which can also lead to psychological problems.

The problem goes beyond the question of forced cohabitation however. Unlike the other columns, the effect on sons of a certain type of mothering also features. De Céspedes' single answer to a collection of five letters in 1954 is worth considering in some detail.[71] All focus on the excessive control exercised by some mothers. De Céspedes explains that she has grouped them together because "in fact there are mothers who, through their unknowing selfishness, end up bringing about exactly the situations that they had tried to avoid." By keeping their offspring away from friends and from relationships with their own age group, they engender a "dangerous state of mind" in young people which can lead them to stop taking care of themselves, to mistrust themselves and others or to carrying out sudden and frightening acts of rebellion. "Parents cannot be 'friends' of their children, because they have a relationship which inspires different emotions from those of friendship," and the self-denial of mothers is positively harmful:

> The mother who deprives herself of everything for the sake of her children—of friendships, reading, pastimes—then demands the same in return, doesn't realize that she is asking for something that is contrary to their age and their nature which will make them inhibited and affected.

Young people need to meet others who are indifferent towards them and to encounter different views in order to find out who they are:

> If, as they emerge from the affectionate attention of their mothers, from the indulgence, admiration and sympathy that meets every act, desire, virtue or vice, within the walls of their own homes [...] we deprive them of the difficulties that they have the duty—and I would even say the right—to face, by raising them in a world that is cocooned and illusory, the result will be that when, through marriage or when we die, they are obliged to face up to them, they won't have the resources to do so with ease.

"Such an unhealthy attachment is more harmful, I would say, than indifference," de Céspedes continues, and, as a result, if some find it difficult to find their way in life, others will find it completely impossible:

> particularly as they'll suffer the pain of mistaking maternal selfishness for altruism; they'll be oppressed by an unjustified sense of guilt which will prevent them from confiding in friends and loving a girl, fearing that they will betray an attachment that has nothing to do with the new feelings they have for others.

It should be noted that throughout this answer there is considerable slippage: there is apparently the intention at the outset not to specify gender, but in the course of the answer parents become mothers, and the reference to "loving a girl," in a context in which she was extremely unlikely to be referring to same-sex relationships,[72] clearly also pins the argument about the effects of parenting of this type on a male child. Indeed, it becomes clear from this and other answers that it is mothers in particular who suffocate their children in this way.

It also becomes clear that this is not just a matter of over-zealous and over-cautious parenting, but a situation brought about by the circumstances in which women find themselves. "This often happens," de Céspedes suggests, "to mothers who are widows or are neglected by their husbands," who turn then to their son for all their needs for love when he can only supply one kind of love. "They are the same mothers who, later, will prevent their offspring from moving away or taking a work trip that could be advantageous for their career or who will become rivals to daughters-in-law or sons-in-law." When we oblige children to do without their own lives, friends and secrets, she says:

> we demonstrate that their attachment to us is more important, in fact, than their own lives. And ultimately we even damage the memory of us that they will have after our deaths: since it is easy to create a myth around the memory of those who knew how to sacrifice the egoism of their own love for the sake of our lives, but not those who end up destroying lives through their selfishness[73]

Thus it is clear that for Alba de Céspedes, a kind of *mammismo* does exist, even if she never uses the actual term, but it is a consequence, at least in part, of the appalling lives that some women have to live and particularly the desolation of a loveless marriage. In this context, the only role in which such women can have recognition or control, or any sense of pleasure, is that of the overbearing or selfish mother, dressed up as self-sacrifice. As she had noted in 1952:

> The mother loves the son and, often, especially if she is a widow or victim of her husband's indifference, she unconsciously transfers all her accumulated and repressed feelings into her love for her son. In this way, by dominating her son, she enjoys the pleasure of dominating men. So, as the son leaves adolescence behind and becomes independent, the mother suffers and fights back.[74]

For de Céspedes, this is all part of a society in which women were obliged to marry for financial security, for decency (if pregnant) or for social status, but in which divorce was not an option and in which the need and desire for love was trivialized but was actually fundamental. It was, moreover, a society in which work for women was vital, not just for financial independence but to provide the kind of individual fulfilment which motherhood could not necessarily supply.[75] As far as de Céspedes was concerned, this behaviour in women is certainly not something instinctive or integral to them—and there is no sense here of it being a national trait— but rather the result of a particular set of cultural circumstances, brought

96 P. MORRIS

about by the patriarchal structures of Italian society. The focus is also very much on the mothers; while, as seen above, there is some reference to the effects on sons (and on both sexes), de Céspedes does not use her column to explore it in great detail.

It was the nature of *Epoca*, and particularly of de Céspedes' advice column, that an emphasis should be put on solutions to problems, on the progress of society and on improving opportunities for women. Part of the point of such a column was to empower readers (both male and female) to feel that they could change their own lives and those of others. As commodities, magazines in the 1950s were also selling a "modern" lifestyle and a certain optimism was inherent to that. It is striking then, that in the novel published around the same time, her other "public voice" as it were, de Céspedes chose to present both a bleaker picture of the situation of mothers and a much more negative portrait of the weak and "over-mothered" man.

In *Quaderno proibito*, published in 1952, the protagonist, Valeria, is a lower middle-class housewife and mother of two university-age children in postwar Italy. She starts to write a secret diary one day—the first-person narrative of the novel—and gradually realizes, with a creeping horror she can scarcely admit even to herself, that the life she had always believed to be happy and fulfilled is quite the opposite. She reflects that her personality has been entirely subsumed by her various roles—her children and also husband call her Mammà, to her mother she is still Bebè and at work she is Cossati—and that she is no longer Valeria to anyone. She is beset with financial worries and painfully aware that her family's social standing is no longer that of her mother's generation, or of her school friends who are not obliged to work. She is every inch the selfless, self-sacrificing mother, constantly exhausted by her dual burden but never questioning the lack of help from her family, nor their assumption that her office work is of no significance beyond the money it brings to the family.

The male characters are far more negative portrayals of masculinity than anything that appears in de Céspedes' advice column. Valeria's son, Riccardo, studying for a university degree though with little sign of progress, is waited on hand and foot by his mother, while haranguing his sister about "decent" behaviour, boasting about his submissive girlfriend, and making vague plans to find fortune in Argentina. Her husband, Michele, is a disappointed dreamer; while pinning his hopes on what is apparently a third-rate and possibly obscene film script, he hates his job in a bank, earns little, takes his wife and her labour entirely for granted, assuming she is too old (at 43) to expect any other kind of attention, and spends his life entirely focused on his own thoughts and fears of an impending third world war. Both men blame others for their misfortunes and entirely lack the courage and energy to take life on. Her daughter, Mirella, by contrast, is clever, motivated, has completed her law degree and is doing a job she loves, working with barristers. She is more sensitive to her mother's situation but there are frequent clashes between them because of her relationship with a separated man (motivated by love) and desire to lead an independent life.

Even though the four of them live as a separate unit, both grandmothers are an oppressive presence. Valeria's own mother sits in a darkened room, surrounded symbolically by portraits of her aristocratic ancestors, producing endless pieces of embroidery that no one wants, reminding her daughter that a woman must never be idle. Seen rarely in the novel, though demanding regular visits, she is a constant presence in Valeria's thoughts, regulating her behaviour and suppressing her desires for a different, freer and more fulfilling life. Her husband, Valeria's father, has practically no character at all. Having lost all sense of purpose once he retired, he is described as having effectively died from that moment. Michele's mother, on the other hand, is actually dead but exists as a photograph in their bedroom (of all places), and is regarded by her son as a "saint," the perfect "*mamma*" whose regular gifts of perfect tortellini seemed designed to throw into relief Valeria's own deficiencies as a housewife and mother.

Realizing how empty her life is—that her "days are squalid and her nights are solitary,"[76] and how little she believes in the values she once stood by, Valeria is tempted by the prospect of an affair and a trip to Venice with her boss. She draws back when she finds out that her son's girlfriend is pregnant and his grand plans to move to Argentina have been abandoned. Instead the novel ends at the point where the young couple will move into the family home, Valeria will give up work and any prospect of a different life, burning her diary and planning to become precisely the kind of traditional mother-in-law that she had to endure to a daughter-inlaw whose ignorance and submissiveness she reviles and whom she taunts with her own perfect tortellini and with stories of the excellent marriage that Riccardo could have made. The only cause for optimism is the independent-minded, and far-from-maternal Mirella, whom Valeria, in a moment of enlightenment encourages to escape, recognizing in bleak desperation that it is too late for herself: she can only act as a bridge to the future for the younger generations.

Conclusion

The advice columns in *Grazia* and *Famiglia cristiana* are concerned with maintaining the status quo, with preserving conservative attitudes to motherhood and its responsibilities, and dampening down any desire for change. In *Grazia*, Signora Quickly is a voice of authority, for all of her "affectionate" asides, and readers are given short shrift if they propose problems that suggest behaviour that is immoral or unconventional; indeed, such attitudes are clearly set up to be knocked down. Above all the mother must hold together marriages and the family and protect their daughters' virtue. The column in *Famiglia cristiana* is very similar in practice and equally patriarchal in attitude, but unsurprisingly has none of Signora Quickly's rather equivocal advice around the availability of daughters. It is always clear that Church doctrine inspires the answers rather than the mix of moralizing and attention to public reputation that transpires from "Ditelo pure a me." Both, however, display the anxieties and ambiguities inherent to a vision of motherhood that sees women as both saints and sinners.

The columns in *Noi donne* and *Epoca*, on the other hand, are far more concerned with dialogue, with finding solutions that would be of some comfort to readers and with challenging misogyny and inequality. In reality there is often little that could be offered in response to the kind of problems many mothers were facing, other than sympathy, but simply raising the issues and calling for the "modernization" of Italy and a change in attitudes and laws, could in itself be understood as both an act of solidarity with those who were suffering and a means of educating the readership. Both columns are concerned to widen the definition of motherhood, gainsay the "common sense" attitudes that could not see beyond the conventional, and remove the stigma attached to unmarried, separated and working mothers. There were differences of course: the fact that *Noi donne*'s target readership was female and *Epoca*'s mixed made for a different tone—and some combative answers to male readers on the part of de Céspedes—and of course the political allegiance of *Noi donne* meant that it had a particular focus on the issues of working-class women.

When it comes to the stereotype of *mammismo*, in *Grazia* it is assumed to exist, but treated superficially, as a clash in power relations between daughter-in-law and mother-in-law—essentially an annoying fact of life that is best avoided where possible. In *Famiglia cristiana* it does not really fit the very simple scheme of the family—with a paterfamilias and devoted wife and mother—that distinguishes the column. In *Noi donne*, too, it is given little space and this is hardly surprising as part of the purpose of the magazine was to counter negative stereotypes about women.

De Céspedes was also very concerned to counter prejudice and discrimination against women, and much of her column is devoted to arguing that they should be taken seriously as workers and artists as well as in their private lives (which she considered just as important). Her novels too, all of which are set in the period in which they are written, are striking for their commentary on the lives of women and often described as feminist. So it is perhaps all the more surprising that the stereotype of *mammismo* does appear in de Céspedes' advice column and, unlike the novels of other women writers of the time,[77] is given considerable space in her best-selling *Quaderno proibito*. It is an indication, therefore, that de Céspedes considered the stereotype both a reality and a particular problem for Italian society. However, while there is a suggestion that the recent war and the threat of war have had an emasculating effect on Italian men, she does not approach it as a failing inherent to the Italian nation and its mothers and sons, but focuses rather on the specific historical circumstances and domestic worlds that produce these female monsters.

If, for de Céspedes, the domineering and suffocating mother exists, then it is as a result of a society which denies women the physical and mental space to be individuals, which values motherly self-sacrifice but diminishes the importance of any other work, and which imprisons women in loveless marriages while their husbands can behave as if they are unattached. In her advice column there is considerable sympathy for women who find themselves in this situation, but her answers also act as a warning about the drastic effects of this kind of "selfish mothering" on (male) children and the focus remains on the women. In her novel, a medium that clearly offered more freedom, and perhaps also because she was addressing a mainly female readership, mothers are blamed for unconsciously perpetuating a cycle of dependency and discrimination, but it is the male characters who are contemptible and entirely feckless. Unthinkingly patriarchal in their attitudes, they collude willingly in their own infantilization. Despite the choices she makes at the end, the reader's sympathy remains with Valeria and the life in which she is trapped. Indeed, in 1950s Italy it is possible that the novel was so popular precisely because de Céspedes' female readers identified with a protagonist who is unable to leave her family and clings to her traditional role, for all the damage it does to herself and to those around her. It is the character of Mirella, on the other hand, who suggests, far more explicitly than the advice in de Céspedes' column, that the only true means of escape for women is to ignore rules and break conventions—in a vision of female fulfilment in which motherhood is tellingly absent.

NOTES

1. D'Amelia, *La mamma*, p. 15. Alvaro, "Il mammismo."
2. The Catholic Church and Christian Democrat government were vociferous in promoting an idealized image of self-sacrificing, devoted motherhood, at its most perfect in the impossible example of the Virgin Mary, but the Communist Party too, despite its apparent advocacy of equality, also put forward a largely traditional view of the role of women. See Willson, *Women*, pp. 112–48 and Morris, "Introduction," *Women in Italy*.
3. See Anna Lisa Carlotti, "Editori e giornali a Milano," p. 184, quoted in Forgacs and Gundle, *Mass Culture*, pp. 95–123.
4. See Forgacs and Gundle, *Mass Culture* and Bellassai, *La morale comunista*.
5. See Morris, "A Window" and Morris, "From Private to Public."
6. Claire Langhamer's *The English in Love* considers advice columns alongside other sources, while David Gudelunas looks at newspaper advice columns to analyse sexual education in America (*Confidential to America*) and Paul Ryan focuses on a single advice column in *Asking Angela Macnamara*.
7. In *Noi donne*, for example, readers' full names and addresses sometimes appear, and at other times readers are invited to correspond privately with the columnist on particularly awkward issues (this also happens in *Famiglia cristiana*). Giuliana dal Pozzo and Alba de Céspedes both argue strongly that they do not invent letters.
8. West, "'What' as Ideal."
9. For a more detailed discussion of advice columns as discursive space in 1950s Italy, see Morris, "A Window," pp. 309–14.
10. See Orton-Johnson, "Mummy Blogs." For a discussion of "Mamme blog" in Italy see Marina d'Amelia, "Cambia il mestiere."
11. Publishing was still a very patriarchal industry. Apart from the left-wing women's magazine *Noi donne*, all the magazines discussed had male editors, and, as will be discussed, not even all the "agony aunts" were actually female.
12. Donna Letizia, *Il saper vivere*, updated in 1990 as *Il nuovo saper vivere di Donna Letizia*. A collection of letters from the column was published in 1981 under her real name, Colette Rosselli (*Cara Donna Letizia...*).
13. Throughout the chapter Signora Quickly will be referred to as "she" as the discussion centres on the fictional persona.

PROBLEMS AND PRESCRIPTIONS: MOTHERHOOD AND *MAMMISMO...* 101

14. "Ditelo pure," *Grazia*, 14 October 1950.
15. "Ditelo pure," *Grazia*, 7 July 1951.
16. "Ditelo pure," *Grazia*, 7 July 1951.
17. "Ditelo pure," *Grazia*, 26 June 1950.
18. "Ditelo pure," *Grazia*, 11 July 1954.
19. "Ditelo pure," *Grazia*, 3 July 1955.
20. "Ditelo pure," *Grazia*, 30 September 1950.
21. "Ditelo pure," *Grazia*, 27 July 1955.
22. "Ditelo pure,"*Grazia*, 30 September 1950.
23. "Ditelo pure," *Grazia*, 6 Sept 1953.
24. "Saper vivere," *Grazia*, 8 July 1956.
25. "Ditelo pure," *Grazia*, 13 January 1951.
26. "Ditelo pure," *Grazia*, 17 January 1953.
27. "Ditelo pure," *Grazia*, 8 July 1956.
28. "Ditelo pure," *Grazia*, 30 May 1954.
29. "Ditelo pure," *Grazia*, 25 December 1955.
30. "Ditelo pure," *Grazia*, 17 June 1956.
31. See Reich, *Beyond the Latin Lover.*
32. In 1954 the magazine had a print run of 250,000, which grew to 1 million by 1960 (Forgacs and Gundle, *Mass Culture*, p. 258). For print runs of other magazines at the time see Ajello, *Lezioni di giornalismo*, p. 89.
33. Forgacs and Gundle, *Mass Culture*, p. 259.
34. "Just as parents are both responsible for generating children, God has established that both parents should co-operate with each other" ("Cerchiamo," *Famiglia cristiana*, 4 January 1953).
35. "Cerchiamo," *Famiglia cristiana*, 11 December 1955.
36. "Cerchiamo," *Famiglia cristiana*, 7 June 1953. The view is echoed in later years. In 1956, for example, he approved of a mother who continued to have children against medical advice (8 January 1956).
37. "Cerchiamo," *Famiglia cristiana*, 7 March 1954.
38. *Noi donne*, May–June 1957. Topics included teenage motherhood, abortion, maternity services, work and motherhood, the law and motherhood.
39. On UDI, see Willson, *Women*, pp. 139–44. See also, Harris, "*Noi donne* and *Famiglia cristiana*," and Rothenburg, "The Catholic and Communist Women's Press."
40. On Communism, consumerism and modernity in 1950s Italy, see Gundle, *Between Hollywood and Moscow.*
41. Estimated by *Noi donne* in 1957 to be around 28,000 per year ("Forbidden Maternity," 26 May 1957).
42. In the late 1940s and early 1950s, UDI was involved mainly in PCI campaigns, but from the mid-1950s distanced itself somewhat from the party. Once Giuliana dal Pozzo became editor, "*Noi donne* frequently diverged

from the official PCI line in matters connected to the private sphere" (Willson, *Women*, p. 141).

43. A typical example is when in 1951 she offers her reader a "motherly piece of advice" (17 June 1951).
44. "Fermo posta," *Noi donne*, 3 June 1951.
45. On the maternal and the Resistance more broadly, see Bravo and Bruzzone, *In guerra senza armi*.
46. Seymour, *Debating Divorce*, pp. 171–72.
47. "Parliamone insieme," *Noi donne*, 9 February 1958.
48. "Parliamone insieme," *Noi donne*, 16 June 1956.
49. "Parliamone insieme," *Noi donne*, 23 January 1959.
50. "Parliamone insieme," *Noi donne*, 17 February 1957.
51. "Parliamone insieme," *Noi donne*, 29 March 1959.
52. Forgacs and Gundle, *Mass Culture*, p. 110.
53. The column appeared from 1952 to 1958. Another significant letters column in *Epoca* was "Italia risponde," penned originally by Cesare Zavattini.
54. De Céspedes, *Dalla parte di lei*.
55. Prior to *Dalla parte di lei*, de Céspedes had published short stories, and, in 1938, the hugely successful *Nessuno torna indietro*. For a full annotated bibliography and a series of excellent in-depth essays, see Zancan, *Alba de Céspedes*. See also Carroli, *Esperienza e narrazione* and Nerenberg, *Writing beyond Fascism*.
56. See Morris, "From Private to Public."
57. "Dalla parte di lei," *Epoca*, issue 90, 1952.
58. "Dalla parte di lei," *Epoca*, 20 December 1952.
59. "Dalla parte di lei," *Epoca*, 20 December 1952.
60. Caldwell, *Italian Family Matters*, p. 151.
61. "Dalla parte di lei," *Epoca*, 4 January 1953.
62. "Dalla parte di lei," *Epoca*, 20 September 1952.
63. "Dalla parte di lei," *Epoca*, 20 September 1952.
64. "Dalla parte di lei," *Epoca*, 17 January 1953.
65. "Dalla parte di lei," *Epoca*, 21 November, 1953.
66. "Dalla parte di lei," *Epoca*, 28 March 1953.
67. "Dalla parte di lei," *Epoca*, 3 October 1954.
68. "Dalla parte di lei," *Epoca*, 31 January 1953.
69. "Dalla parte di lei," *Epoca*, 20 February 1955.
70. "Dalla parte di lei," *Epoca*, 20 February 1955.
71. "Dalla parte di lei," *Epoca*, 14 November 1954.
72. References to homosexuality are not entirely absent from advice columns in the 1950s, but usually it was a matter of euphemistic inferences (Morris, "A Window," pp. 323–24).
73. "Dalla parte di lei," *Epoca*, 14 November 1954.
74. "Dalla parte di lei," *Epoca*, 23 August 1952.

PROBLEMS AND PRESCRIPTIONS: MOTHERHOOD AND *MAMMISMO...* 103

75. See "Dalla parte di lei," *Epoca*, 8 May 1955.
76. *Quaderno proibito*, p. 217.
77. See Ursula Fanning's chapter in this volume.

BIBLIOGRAPHY

Ajello, Nello. *Lezioni di giornalismo*. Milan: Garzanti, 1985.

Alvaro, Corrado. "Il mammismo", in Corrado Alvaro, *Il nostro tempo e la speranza. Saggi di vita contemporanea*. Milan-Rome: Bompiani, 1952, pp. 183–190.

Bellassai, Sandro. *La morale communista: pubblico e privato nella rappresentazione del PCI (1947–1956)*. Rome: Carocci, 2000.

Bravo, Anna. *Il fotoromanzo*. Bologna: Il Mulino, 2003.

Bravo, Anna and Anna M. Bruzzone. *In guerra senza armi. Storie di donne 1940–1945*. Rome: Laterza, 1995.

Caldwell, Lesley. *Italian Family Matters: Women, politics and legal reform*. London: Macmillan, 1991.

Carlotti, Anna Lisa. "Editori e giornali a Milano: continuità e cambiamento," in *Libri giornali e riviste a Milano. Storia delle innovazioni nell'editoria milanese dall'ottocento ad oggi*, edited by Fausto Colombo. Milan: AIM-Abitare Segesta, 1998.

Carroli, Piera. *Esperienza e narrazione nella scrittura di Alba de Céspedes*. Ravenna: Longo, 1993.

d'Amelia, Marina. *La mamma*. Bologna: Il Mulino, 2005.

d'Amelia, Marina. "Cambia il mestiere di mamma? Dai manuali novecenteschi alle mamme blogger." Paper delivered at the "Storia in Piazza" Festival on Sexual Identity, Genoa, 20 April, 2013. http://www.palazzoducale.genova.it/storia/2013/files/audio/449.mp3

de Céspedes, Alba. *Dalla parte di lei*. Milan: Mondadori, 1949.

de Céspedes, Alba. *Nessuno torna indietro*. Milan: Mondadori, 1938.

de Céspedes, Alba. *Quaderno proibito*. Milan: Mondadori, 1952.

Forgacs, David and Stephen Gundle. *Mass Culture and Italian Society: From Fascism to the Cold War*. Bloomington and Indiannapolis: Indiana University Press, 2007.

Gudelunas, David. *Confidential to America: Newspaper advice columns and sexual education*. New Brunswick: Transaction Publishers, 2008.

Gundle, Stephen. *Between Hollywood and Moscow: The Italian Communists and the Challenge of Mass Culture, 1943–1991*. Durham, NC: Duke University Press, 2000.

Harris, Jessica L. "*Noi Donne* and *Famiglia Cristiana*: Communists, Catholics, and American Female Culture in Cold War Italy," *Carte Italiane*, 2, 11 (2017): pp. 93–114.

Langhamer, Claire. *The English in Love: The intimate story of an emotional revolution*. Oxford: Oxford University Press, 2013.

Morris, Penelope. "A Window on the Private Sphere: Advice columns, marriage, and the evolving family in 1950s Italy," *The Italianist* 27 (2007): pp. 304–332.

Morris, Penelope. "From Private to Public: Alba de Céspedes' Agony Column in 1950s Italy," in *Gender and the Private Sphere*, edited by Paola Filippucci and Perry Willson, Special Issue of *Modern Italy*, 9, 1 (2004): pp. 11–20.

Morris, Penelope, ed. *Women in Italy, 1945–1960: An Interdisciplinary Study*. New York: Palgrave, 2006.

Nerenberg, Ellen, ed. *Writing Beyond Fascism: Cultural Resistance in the Life and Works of Alba de Céspedes*. Cranbury: Associated University Presses, 2000.

Orton-Johnson, Kate. "Mummy Blogs and Representations of Motherhood: 'Bad mummies' and their readers," *Social Media + Society*, 3, 2 (2017): pp. 1–10.

Palazzi, S. and D. Bencetti. *Dizionario domestico (tutto per la casa)*. Milan: Ceschina, 1952.

Reich, Jacqueline. *Beyond the Latin Lover: Marcello Mastroianni, Masculinity, and Italian Cinema*. Bloomington: Indiana University Press, 2004.

Rosselli, Colette. *Cara Donna Letizia … venticinque anni di confidenza*. Milan: Rusconi, 1981.

Rosselli, Colette (pseud. Donna Letizia). *Il saper vivere*. Milan: Mondadori, 1960.

Rosselli, Colette. *Il nuovo saper vivere di Donna Letizia*. Milan: Mondadori, 1990.

Rothenburg, Nina. "The Catholic and Communist Women's Press in Post-War Italy—An Analysis of *Cronache* and *Noi Donne*," *Modern Italy* 11, 3 (2006): pp. 285–304.

Ryan, Paul. *Asking Angela Macnamara: An intimate history of Irish lives*. Dublin and Portland, Oregon: Irish Academic Press, 2012.

Seymour, Mark. *Debating Divorce in Italy: Marriage and the Making of Modern Italians 1860–1974*. New York: Palgrave, 2005.

Viganò, Renata. *L'Agnese va a morire*. Turin: Einaudi, 1949.

West, Rebecca. "Lost in the Interstices: A Postwar, Pre-Boom 'Enciclopedia della donna'." *Annali d'Italianistica*, 16 (1998): pp. 169–194.

West, Rebecca "'What' as Ideal and 'Who' as Real: Portraits of wives and mothers in Italian postwar domestic manuals, fiction and film," in *Women in Italy, 1945–60: An interdisciplinary study*, edited by Penelope Morris. New York: Palgrave, 2006.

Willson, Perry. *Women in Twentieth-Century Italy*. Basingstoke: Palgrave Macmillan, 2010.

Zancan, Marina, ed. *Alba de Céspedes*. Milan: Mondadori, 2005.

CHAPTER 5

Conceptualizing the Maternal: Representations, Reflections and Refractions in Women's Literary Writings

Ursula Fanning

INTRODUCTORY REFLECTIONS

Italian women writers, almost without exception, reject maternal stereotypes of differing kinds over the course of the twentieth century. The period of the Unification had its own particular conceptions of the maternal, rooted in the establishing of the new nation.[1] Fascism, with its demographic campaign, and its exaltation of a specific kind of sacrificial motherhood, provided another set of prescriptions, stereotypes and legal constraints around the maternal. Marina d'Amelia notes Corrado Alvaro's use of the term *"mammismo"* in his eponymous 1952 essay as something that signals what she defines as a postwar "invented tradition." This new tradition, as d'Amelia describes it, centres especially on a close and emasculating mother–son relationship (which offers a backhanded domestic power to the mother), and it radiates from there to become an oft-cited source of the so-called stereotypical "Italian vices" of amorality, relentless familism, lack of civic responsibility, and political immaturity.[2] The mother,

---

U. Fanning (✉)
University College Dublin, Dublin, Ireland
e-mail: ursula.fanning@ucd.ie

© The Author(s) 2018   105
P. Morris, P. Willson (eds.), *La Mamma*,
Italian and Italian American Studies,
https://doi.org/10.1057/978-1-137-54256-4_5

thus, becomes partly responsible for the social and political ills of Italy, much as in mainstream psychoanalysis she has been made responsible for the psychological maladies of her children. It is scarcely surprising that Italian women writers are keen to reject this tradition, as well as its predecessors, and to elaborate different maternal modes and models.

Equally unsurprisingly, the maternal is a problematic area of representation in Italian women's writings, particularly in the twentieth century. While the nineteenth century finds some room for what we might term a form of maternal discourse (about and around maternity, and often voiced through the figure of the mother, rather than from the perspective of the daughter),[3] the twentieth opens with the shock of Sibilla Aleramo's prescient articulation of issues of identity and conflict around the maternal in *Una donna* of 1906; this is followed initially by either silence or negativity in oblique approaches to the maternal and, eventually, in the second half of the century, there is a (by now well-recognized) proliferation of daughterly discourses around the maternal;[4] these last find their intriguing counterpoint in a collection of narratives that strive to relocate a maternal perspective, while explicitly engaging with many of the contradictions identified by Aleramo.

Difficulties in conceptualizing the maternal through the course of the twentieth century were not, of course, confined to the Italian context, nor to the domain of literature. Steph Lawler, reflecting on the field of sociology, has noted that: "the perspective of the mother has rarely been explored."[5] Discussing the lack of attention to the mother as subject in psychoanalysis for much of the twentieth century, Garner, Kahane and Sprengnether point out that:

> psychoanalysis [...] has yet to develop a story of the mother as other than the object of the infant's desire or the matrix from which he or she develops an infant subjectivity. The mother herself as speaking subject, as author, is missing from these dramas.[6]

History, too, was remarkably uninterested in maternal experiences. As Marina d'Amelia indicated in 1997, in her introduction to a collection of essays: "contrary to what one might assume, historians' attention to the phenomenon of maternity is [...] relatively recent."[7] The mother as subject was, then, under-visited in many respects throughout the twentieth century (and this is the case not only in the Italian context) and it should scarcely surprise us if that is reflected, to some degree, in Italian women's writing.

CONCEPTUALIZING THE MATERNAL: REPRESENTATIONS, REFLECTIONS... 107

What Annarita Buttafuoco terms "the cult of motherhood,"[8] which she locates between the 1890s and the advent of Fascism, is partly responsible for a recurring silence, or an outright negativity, around the maternal in Italian women's writing. It is a cult full of contradictions. On the one hand, it offered nineteenth-century first-wave feminists a context in which motherhood might be positively evaluated, and the maternal positively evoked, in its provision of a justification for women's right to education and full citizenship (albeit merely as a means to the end of effectively raising the next generation of Italians, as presented in conduct manuals and scientific discourse). On the other hand, it led to a one-dimensional and restrictive view of womanhood *as* motherhood. Fiorenza Taricone's study of the *cataloghi* (conduct literature, intended primarily for middle-class readers) of the early 1880s, for example, led her to conclude that women's primary function in the new nation was constructed as familial: "woman's mission was being transformed and extended, leaving intact the basic principle of the happiness of her husband, and the education of their children."[9] Fascism exacerbated this woman-mother connection. As Chiara Saraceno has stated: "both the apparent biological formulation of the maternal function, reducing women to producers of the race, and its linking with the interests of the nation are characteristic of fascism."[10] Thus, a link in existence from the foundation of the state was strengthened and made ever less palatable to women under Fascism. Evidence for this is to be found in the stubborn and continuous fall in the birth rate, in spite of the regime's best efforts.[11] It is also reflected in both the silences around—and the sometimes negative descriptions of—the maternal experience in women's writing. This is not terribly surprising, given the politically loaded potential of the maternal.

Later in the twentieth century, the cult of motherhood was effectively dismantled by Italian feminism. Despite a focus on the figure of the mother, and on sexual difference, Italian feminism was largely negative in its discussions of the maternal. Luisa Passerini notes "the critique of motherhood in the feminism of the early 1970s,"[12] and comments on its possible effects in modifying women's lifestyles, in terms of its encouraging them to either postpone or reject childbearing. Adalgisa Giorgio observes how "feminist analyses of women's cultural and social subordination published in the 1970s put the mother on trial for her complicity with patriarchal norms,"[13] while I suggest elsewhere that there is a real taboo around voicing the maternal in women's writing late in the twentieth century in the Italian context for precisely these reasons.[14] It is interesting to consider how those writers who write against the prevailing critique of, and silence around, the maternal go about this, and also to link their work right back to that of Aleramo in its probing of questions of identity and self-definition.

Writers who engage with the maternal, and in particular with finding a maternal voice, throughout the twentieth century seem to be cognizant that motherhood poses specific issues in the context of discussions on identity. It entails a particular kind of self-division, and the representation of that division may be especially challenging. As Cristina Mazzoni has it: "pregnancy and childbirth, with their challenges to bodily boundaries and to self-definition, physically illustrate the disruptions to the self that are entailed by the encounter with an Other, with difference."[15] The pregnant woman is always-already more than one and, as such, can be a truly disturbing figure in her embodiment of the split self. From Aleramo onwards, we see this kind of divided self explored in Italian women's literary output, albeit often with considerable tentativeness. This tentativeness is understandable, given that maternal discourse lacks an established cultural framework, well beyond the Italian context. As E. Ann Kaplan points out, in the American context there was a lack of cultural discourses setting forth women's subjective experiences of mothering (or, we could say, voicing the maternal) through the twentieth century.[16] For women writers in the Italian context, against the idealizing discourses of Unification, the pro-natalist discourses of Fascism, and the corrective discourses of 1970s feminism, this is an enterprise fraught with difficulty and open to misunderstanding. For critics, too, writing the maternal is tricky at best. Mazzoni wryly reflects that "whenever the maternal is invoked by a feminist [...] paradox and contradictions, leading to implacable (self) criticism, are just around the corner."[17] In spite of this, untangling maternal representations, noting their reflections of earlier works, and investigating their refractions of identity is a fascinating enterprise, not least in its recognition of the importance of the maternal in women's writing, despite the challenges involved in its representation. I will begin this analysis early in the century, with Aleramo, and move through the work of some of the better-known later writers for whom the maternal resurfaces (sometimes in the form of asides), noting in particular where they touch on common concerns. Much of my attention, later in this chapter, will be focused on those writers who grapple specifically with the maternal voice and the maternal perspective.

THE CHALLENGE OF SIBILLA ALERAMO

We take as read, at this stage, Aleramo's character's investigation of her relationship with her mother, against which she defines herself in the first instance.[18] We are also more than familiar with her rejection of her marriage and with that, in light of the legal position of women at the time, her inevitable rejection of motherhood. What is less recognized is Aleramo's challenging reconfiguration of the maternal, from the point of view of her protagonist. Although she delivers a daughterly discourse for much of the novel, Aleramo also accesses a maternal voice and, in many respects, this maternal voice is shocking in its context, quite apart from the controversial denouement of the novel in which the protagonist, in choosing to leave her marriage, must also decide to leave her son. In fact, Aleramo thoroughly engages with the maternal in this novel, from her depiction of its physical pleasures (probably no less striking than the protagonist's abandonment of her son, if overshadowed by that event), to her absolute rejection of the role of mother as it is understood in her society and her gritty problematization of what motherhood may mean for the self.[19]

In terms of an overt embodiment of the maternal, Aleramo's courageous and graphic (for her time) descriptions of pregnancy and childbirth are arresting. Childbirth is figured as a near-death experience, one that involves a sundering (and almost a surrender) of the self: "I thought I was dying at the moment in which my son entered the world, I cried out in revolt in the name of my torn flesh, my devoured entrails."[20] The body is literally rendered here. The labouring woman is both subject and object of a division in process. The physical threat to the integrity of the protagonist is unmistakeable. The intense, and lengthy, centralizing of the physicality of motherhood breaks new ground.[21] The negativity of some physical descriptions is, interestingly, offset by their counterparts in jouissance— there is, for the protagonist, a real physical pleasure in breast-feeding: "when I saw his little mouth sucking avidly, and I heard him swallow the liquid that gushed from my breast [...] I felt a new surge of inexpressible emotion."[22] The body is threatened, racked and pleasurably engulfed in its maternal experience within the space of a few paragraphs of text here.

This contradictory physical experience is mirrored in the conflicting emotions felt by the protagonist. The interdependence of mother and child gradually becomes overwhelming (as well as inescapable) for the narrator-protagonist. After the birth, she registers that her child: "was all of me [...] and demanded all of me [...] for ever: I gave him life [...]

through the offer of my life."[23] This intense interdependence appears to involve an abdication of subjecthood that is not only physical, predicated as it is on an ongoing interaction. The image of self-sacrifice persists until remarkably close to the end of the novel. A mere 60 pages before the denouement, the protagonist reflects (as her son recovers from a serious illness that has pushed her to think of suicide): "only one thing [...] really lived in me [...] the maternal bond."[24] The threat of the child's death brings the mother close to death—it is an existential as well as a physical threat, which mirrors the moment of childbirth described earlier in the novel. The abnegation of self is repeated at the very close of the novel, just as the protagonist leaves. She fantasizes about her own disappearance, in an inverse moment of oneness from that described earlier—here the child is not "all of [her]," rather she wants to: "grasp him, enclose him in me ... and disappear myself."[25] The pull between self and Other is constantly enacted in this text, and the threat to the self involved in that pull is repeatedly stated. In this respect, *Una donna* becomes a kind of cautionary tale. It hits a nerve, I argue, not only in its denouement, but also in its powerful representation of the pull of motherhood, which is clearly and repeatedly figured as threatening to the self. The threat of the maternal (not just of pregnancy and childbirth, absolutely understandable in its historical context) is inescapable. In this respect, it seems to me that *Una donna* is partly responsible (alongside the discourses of Fascism and feminism) for a silencing of the maternal, and for a predominantly negative discourse of the maternal, in women's narratives for some time. This threatening pull of motherhood exists, however, alongside what I have termed Aleramo's enactment of a murderous maternal fantasy (murderous not towards the child, but towards the rest of the cast of characters, most specifically the husband). The protagonist wishes everyone around her erased, apart from herself and her son.[26] This maternal fantasy (which could be read as dystopian, but which is firmly presented here in utopian terms) is the first in a series of fantasies which we will encounter in several of the writers who grapple with the maternal later in the century.

In the end, Aleramo rejects the already-established image of the mother who dotes on her son, setting her writing squarely at odds with the maternal discourses of Unification. She reconfigures and refracts the stereotype, but not without having made manifest its power and its potential seductiveness. Motherhood here is figured as transformative primarily in the sense that it is potentially threatening to the self and its integrity. I would contend that, in *Una donna*, we are confronted not so much with what Barbara Spackman calls "motherliness as masquerade" in her critique of the novel,[27] as with motherhood as self-sundering. Notions of integrity and wholeness are undone in this narrative, precisely through maternal discourses. The mother here is a truly disturbing figure, for she literally embodies the split self.

In Aleramo, the pleasures of the maternal are writ large, but so too are its dangers. Her representations of both reflect (and reject) stereotypical norms, but go far beyond them in exploring a maternal jouissance. Located precisely in this jouissance, however, is the threat to the self. And this threat is so great that it refracts, rather than reflects, the maternal image into a broken-mirrored jigsaw of motherhood that necessitates the sundering of the mother–child bond (since mass murder, however appealing to the protagonist, is not really an option). To save the self, the maternal must be abnegated. *Una donna*, on some levels, is a paradigmatic nightmare tale of maternity that casts a long literary shadow. It poses dilemmas that will not be fully confronted, engaged with and reworked until close to the end of the century.

BEFORE THE 1970S: VIVANTI, DELEDDA, BANTI, GINZBURG

Annie Vivanti's *The Devourers/I divoratori*, published in English in 1910 and in Italian in 1911, follows closely behind Aleramo's *Una donna* and, in its title, may well draw inspiration from Aleramo's "devoured entrails."[28] While there is no doubt that children are predominantly the devourers in Vivanti's text, and mothers are mainly the ones who are devoured, it is worth noting that Vivanti's definition of devourers also involves genius and that her representation of prey includes daughters and employees.[29] Nonetheless, the maternal role seems to lend itself particularly well to victimhood in this narrative. There are three significant mother characters in this novel: Valeria, Nancy and Anne-Marie. Valeria, first in the generational chain, is devoured by her daughter Nancy, from being prevented from forming romantic/sentimental attachments when she is still a young widow to (arguably) sacrificing her life for her daughter.[30] Nancy, in turn, falls victim to Anne-Marie, both in terms of rejecting possible romantic relationships and in turning her back on an artistic career (she is a failed writer). Nancy, indeed, could be read as an inverse image of Aleramo's protagonist—rather than being saved by her writing, she abandons it almost willingly to serve her daughter's needs. Nancy explains both her inability to write her book and her unwillingness to commit herself to a relationship in a letter to her suitor, towards the close of the narrative: "I am one of the 'devoured.' I no longer exist [...] I—like all mothers—enraptured and on my knees, give my life to the unaware creature who demands it."[31] Clearly, mothering (rather than genius) is primarily at issue at this point in the novel. And yet, this representation of the maternal is rather suspect. Vivanti excels, throughout her narrative work, in presenting her readers with a performative femininity.[32] It seems that, in *I divoratori*, she presents us with a performative maternity. She overtly draws our attention to conventional expectations of femininity, and particularly of maternity. Nancy, in the above citation, is not just herself; rather, she is "like all mothers." The generic type slips into parody towards the end of the novel, when Anne-Marie marries and leaves her mother: "Nancy cried and screamed—she screamed loudly, like a wounded animal, kneeling by the window, stretching her despairing arms out to the heavens."[33] The image of the animal is interesting here; we will encounter it in more detail in Banti; here, it is signalled rather than fully developed. Nonetheless, the description is clearly marked by excess. It offers what Judith Butler might term "hyperbolic exhibition[s]" of "the natural" that, in its very exaggeration, reveals "its fundamentally phantasmatic status."[34] Of the three maternal characters in this novel, Nancy is the most dramatically evoked, the most obviously excessive in her inhabiting of the maternal role. Vivanti returns to a more generic typology in the closing pages, as she casts Anne-Marie as a new mother, who dreams of returning to her music, as Nancy before her had dreamed of returning to "the book," only for both to have their dreams truncated by the cry of the newborn baby. The circular, repetitive, self-generating narrative underlines the inevitability of conventional maternal experience (even, Vivanti suggests, for geniuses).

It seems highly likely that Vivanti's images of the maternal function here, on the one hand, as representations of the acceptable feminine in order to deflect criticism, or to reassure conventional readers. On the other hand, the very excess of these representations calls them into question and raises the possibility of parody. If it is indeed the case that Vivanti presents us with the obverse conclusion of that reached in Aleramo (none of these mothers would dream of leaving their offspring to save themselves), she may be read as either highly conventional or as slyly subversive in her denouements.

Grazia Deledda approaches the maternal from the outside, looking in. She is silent in some important respects in relation to the maternal in her writing. Her posthumously published autobiographical work, *Cosima*,

CONCEPTUALIZING THE MATERNAL: REPRESENTATIONS, REFLECTIONS... 113

never gets as far as providing an account of her own maternal experience, though whether this is a function of intent or accident is impossible to say. In some of her other works, most notably *Cenere* and *La madre*, she clearly links the maternal and the sacrificial, and most recently critics have suggested that she does so in critical and combative fashion. In *Cenere*, the maternal figure of Olì (like Aleramo's protagonist in *Una donna*) abandons her son (at the time of his birth in her case), for his own good (given his married father's wealth and her own shameful status as unmarried mother). Maria Giovanna Piano defines the character of Olì as "mater absoluta" in Deledda's output,[35] as at the close of the novel the character demands recognition of her important role from her son, Anania, the novel's protagonist. Olì disappears at a relatively early stage in the novel, but she remains a haunting presence throughout its pages, and her return at the close of the text is dramatic. Her kind of mothering is juxtaposed with a more conventional maternal, encapsulated in the character of Anania's father's wife, who functions, in effect, as his caring surrogate mother. Olì chooses death, in the end, rather than an old age beholden to a resentful son and her death, in that light, may be read as "assertive," to borrow the term used by Margherita Heyer-Caput.[36] Within the economy of the narrative, however, it remains the case that Olì is sacrificed (perhaps for abandoning her son?). In this respect, *Cenere*, like *I divoratori*, provides a different, and differently pessimistic, take on the maternal from that of Aleramo. Maternal sacrifice of a sort also informs *La madre*, with another maternal death at its close. Here the mother invests so much of herself in her son, the priest, that she dies from the stress of his possible shaming before the congregation. The situation in this text is complex too; the mother over-identifies with her son, but also with his status in the community and with the status which she has accrued as a result, and thus her death is not to be read as wholly selfless, any more than is that of Olì. Maternal death, occasioned by the maternal experience, however, is something of a recurring theme for Deledda; the loss of the self is clearly associated with the maternal in her work.

Anna Banti is not particularly interested in representing the maternal, but where she does deal with it (again, most often looking from the outside in, rather than taking on the point of view of the mother characters with whom she presents us), her representation is overwhelmingly negative.[37] Banti's technique of indicating distance from her maternal characters is most often enacted through her use of animal imagery. This is crystal clear in the short story "Vocazioni indistinte" where the protagonist, Ofelia, a failed musician (and thus undeserving of the narrator's sympathy), loses herself (and her mind, in a manner befitting her name) in motherhood. She is, variously, a hen,[38] an ant,[39] a serpent[40] and a dog.[41] Motherhood is categorically blamed for her transformation; as she says herself: "what a state you find me in ... it was suckling the baby, you know; from that point on I haven't been well."[42] Ofelia is repeatedly linked with the physical, and specifically with the animalesque through the representation of her as a mother; in this respect, as well as in the negativity with which she is viewed, she is typical of Banti's maternal characters. D'Amelia, interestingly, notes Corrado Alvaro's repeated identifications of the maternal with the animalesque in his 1952 essay on *mammismo*. Banti, like Alvaro after her, is drawing on an old trope which, as d'Amelia notes, "winds its way through the social imaginary."[43] Less stereotypical in some respects is Banti's most interesting and complex maternal character, Artemisia, of the eponymous novel. We do not automatically think of Artemisia as a mother first and foremost—rather, we think of her as emblematic of Banti's preferred protagonists in her role as artist. It is the conflict experienced by Artemisia between maternity and art that makes of her Banti's most fascinating embodiment of the maternal. Embodiment, indeed, is what we are first presented with here. Banti figures mother-love as highly physical and intense: "Artemisia's embrace was violently strong [...] she experiences a wild maternal calling, a tenderness for the little one that rises in her throat tasting of blood."[44] Prior to this, Artemisia was figured as a cat, "purring as it gave birth."[45] The link between the animal and the maternal is just as clear here as in Banti's other writings. What crucially differentiates Artemisia from other Bantian mothers is her art, which she prioritizes over her love for her daughter while: "Maternal love [...] moans, struggles, raves. In silence, naturally."[46] Artemisia is like Aleramo's protagonist in her prioritization of the self and art over the maternal. Artemisia is also reminiscent of her predecessor in her construction of a utopian maternal fantasy, albeit Banti's representation of this fantasy is sacrificial rather than murderous: "These obsessive longings to be alone together, longings for a great warm embrace which would take them bound together to the grave, are eccentric."[47] Banti thus reflects some of Aleramo's images, albeit from a different angle, refracting them in a largely negative light. Jouissance is quickly jettisoned, and maternal sacrifice replaces self-assertion. Beyond the literary context, it is also worth noting that, in these texts from the 1940s in particular, Banti is writing squarely against the backdrop of

CONCEPTUALIZING THE MATERNAL: REPRESENTATIONS, REFLECTIONS... 115

Fascism. Her negative images of the maternal deviate sharply from the dominant discourses of Fascism around marriage and motherhood, and serve to undercut them.

Natalia Ginzburg begins writing fiction from a male perspective. Her first short story, "Un'assenza" of 1933, for instance, focuses on a male protagonist and his experiences and viewpoint. She admitted in her later essay "Il mio mestiere" that she really wanted to "write like a man, I was terrified that you would see I was a woman from the way I wrote. I almost always had male characters, so that they could be as far removed as possible from me."[48] She is very far removed, initially, from either daughterly or maternal perspectives. When she eventually begins to touch on the maternal, it is from the point of view of the daughter.[49] There are asides in *Lessico famigliare*, though, which access a maternal voice, and they do so in a very interesting fashion. The narrator-protagonist, Natalia, mentions how she has hired a nurse (she is facilitated in this by her own mother, who finances the enterprise) to help her with the children. In Natalia's reaction to the nurse, which is overtly intertextualized, we see both her financial concerns (always a consideration for Ginzburg when she discusses children, whether in her fiction or in her essays), and certain of her recurring images of the maternal. The intertext here is Vivanti's *I divoratori*— Natalia directly compares herself with Nancy in that novel: "it seemed to me that I was Nancy, in *I divoratori*, when she looks from her window at her little girl walking hand-in-hand along the avenue with the sumptuous nurse, and knows at the same time that they've lost all their money in the casino."[50] The "sumptuousness" of the nurse here marks her as maternal in Ginzburg's typology. Her maternal figures are usually larger than life images of fertility, while Natalia, like the mother in "La madre," as well as other characters who represent Ginzburg herself in her writings, is thin, tense and, by extension, goes against the maternal grain. Natalia's financial worries here echo those of Vivanti's Nancy (albeit on a less dramatic scale), and this is overtly why she is invoked. Nancy and Natalia share more than this, though—both struggle to find time to write, and this struggle is occasioned, for both, by the day-to-day work of mothering. This connection is implied, rather than stated clearly here, but the reader is pushed to think about the ways in which these (temperamentally very different) characters are analogous to each other, and about why it is that Ginzburg chooses to draw so clearly on Vivanti here. It is the mother-artist dilemma which constitutes their common ground, in fact; their financial concerns, after all, provide only superficial commonalities.

116   U. FANNING

Interestingly, it is in her essays that Ginzburg addresses the maternal most directly, rather than in her fiction. In "Il mio mestiere," for instance, she is more open about the writing/mothering balancing act. There is a definite conflict here: "The children seemed too important to me to waste time on stupid stories [...] But I felt a real yearning and sometimes at night I almost cried when I remembered how lovely my work was."[51] Ginzburg, then, reflects certain of Vivanti's representations of the maternal, seriously rather than parodically, sometimes obliquely and occasionally overtly.

THE 1970S TO THE 1990S: GINZBURG, FALLACI, RAVERA, MARAINI

It is in "Dell'aborto," ironically, that Ginzburg really faces the maternal head-on. In this essay, she describes abortion as a silent and dark choice and, in that sense only, she sees it as strangely similar to the choice made in becoming a mother. She explains the mother–child relationship, in this context, as follows:

> The relationship between the mother and that living, unknown and hidden form is in reality the most closed, the most enchained and dark relationship that exists in the world, it is the least free of relationships and it is nobody's business.[52]

It is notable here that the image of the chain used by Ginzburg originates with Aleramo in the Italian literary context. Ginzburg's vision of the intensity and the darkness of the mother–child relationship is also strongly reminiscent of its representation in Aleramo. Echoes of Aleramo's concerns around the maternal, indeed, seem to be more noticeable from the 1970s than in the decades in between.

Ginzburg's essay on abortion, written in 1975, is timely in the political context of debates on abortion, both within and without the feminist movement. So too, of course, is *Lettera a un bambino mai nato* by Oriana Fallaci. Often considered primarily as a novel about abortion (and it is as much a *roman à thèse* in its considerations of the legal system and its limitations in relation to women as is *Una donna*), *Lettera* is much more than that and would better be described as an embryonic fantasy. I would suggest, moreover, that this work is almost as influential for late twentieth-century approaches to the maternal as Aleramo's turn-of-the-century

CONCEPTUALIZING THE MATERNAL: REPRESENTATIONS, REFLECTIONS... 117

novel. Fallaci, while discussing abortion in remarkably few pages of this short work, sets out instead, it seems, to reconceptualize the maternal. Her protagonist (anonymous, like that of Aleramo) speaks in a maternal voice, and only rarely in a daughterly discourse. The protagonist's concern is both for herself, and for the "bambino," who is destined never to be born. The discovery that the "bambino" has died in utero at a relatively early stage in the pregnancy means that the event of childbirth and the day-to-day undertakings of mothering remain outside the narrative in an experiential sense, but the latter certainly form part of the textual fantasy. The narrative voice repeatedly flags this fantastical dimension of the work, through the dream-sequences and fairytale interpolations in the narrative, as well as through the protagonist's avowal that the "bambino" is "like my moon, my moon-dust,"[53] alerting the reader to the insubstantiality of both at a relatively early stage. There are, too, early recurring references to "fancies/phantoms of unborn babies,"[54] which perform an analogous function.

In this novel, Fallaci both "clarifies the designs of the institution [of motherhood] as social imperative [and] expands the meaning of motherhood in its personal and social dimensions," as Robin Pickering-Iazzi has noted.[55] *Lettera* certainly reveals the uses of motherhood and the maternal in the service of patriarchy (as Aleramo does in *Una donna* and, in many respects, little has changed here), but also presents it as both potentially revolutionary and transformative. The narrator tries, through the tales she tells the "bambino," to make him socially and politically aware, as well as to reject, for herself, maternal stereotypes. These transformative depictions of the maternal, though, are held in the realm of the protagonist's imaginary. They are never enacted in the novel; in this respect, they are reminiscent of the fantasized maternal universes briefly evoked by both Aleramo and Banti.

As in Aleramo and Banti, too, Fallaci's version of the maternal is represented with an extraordinary physicality. John Gatt-Rutter has rightly commented that *Lettera* presents us with "one possible version of an *écriture féminine*" in which "the female body is the protagonist and speaks with a 'bodily' voice."[56] The bodily dimension evoked here is closer (at least some of the time) to the kind of maternal *jouissance* we find in Aleramo than to the physicality portrayed by Banti (and, indeed, by Morante) through her retreat into animal imagery. The protagonist of *Lettera* discovers, to her surprise, that she suddenly believes that man's inability to carry a child is an impoverishment: "There is something glorious in enclosing another life within one's own body, in knowing that one is two, rather than one. Sometimes you feel a real sense of triumph and, in the serenity that accompanies that, nothing bothers you."[57] Clearly central to this bodily dimension, moreover, is Fallaci's dualistic and interdependent conception of the pregnant woman. Comments made by other characters about abortion strike the protagonist as "a conspiracy, a plot to divide us."[58] The sense of duality evoked by Aleramo is reflected and writ large in Fallaci. Laura Benedetti suggests that "perhaps no other Italian writer has investigated in such detail pregnancy as an event that challenges a woman's notion of self"[59]; it is true that Fallaci devotes more space in her novel to the pregnant body than do the other writers discussed thus far, but her focus on this aspect of the maternal was to be taken up and developed later by other writers who were to prove just as concerned with it. The two versions of the novel written by Fallaci offer us differing conclusions to the maternal loss of self in the Other. The 1975 version remains theoretically open, if implicitly pessimistic about the mother's survival, while later versions close off this possibility.

As significant as this strong physical bond and interdependence, however, is the meeting of minds conjured here. The novel is addressed to a fantastical entity, for the most part, to an extension of the self that is called into being mentally as much as physically. In the dream-trial sequence, the unborn "bambino" constantly refers back to what he has been taught by his mother. Some kind of understanding seems to have been reached between the narrator and her fantasized creature. The imagined addressee is crucial to the narrative, and the intellectual bond proves as significant as does the physical. It is in this respect, in particular, that I think Fallaci is important for later writers. Her focus on the intellectual, as well as the physical, aspects of the maternal will be reflected in later writers; her successors will also maintain that concept of the divided maternal self that has its origins in Aleramo.

An immediate sequitur to Fallaci's 1975 novel is Lidia Ravera's 1979 novel, *Bambino mio*. Like Fallaci, Ravera has her narrator directly address the unborn child (and later the baby, once it is born); the structure of her work mirrors that of Fallaci's. Just as the political sphere forms an important backdrop to Fallaci's work, so too for Ravera; like her predecessor, Ravera directly engages with traditional views of the maternal and sets out to reshape these in her own way. As an active feminist in the 1970s, Ravera was well aware of the denigration of motherhood that was part and parcel of the movement. In this novel, the very idea of becoming a mother is

CONCEPTUALIZING THE MATERNAL: REPRESENTATIONS, REFLECTIONS... 119

"the forbidden thought."[60] When the (again anonymous) narrator finds she is pregnant, she is unable to discuss her pregnancy with her female friends: "When I'm with women, I can't even mention you."[61] There is, Ravera makes clear, a real taboo around pregnancy and mothering within feminism. Indeed, once the narrator's friends eventually discover the pregnancy, she becomes the object of their concern: "for the most part, they encourage me to get rid of you."[62] The distaste for the maternal extends to Ravera's narrator's reaction to her own mother—the daughterly discourse developed here is wholly negative, and this marks one of the points of difference between this novel and its immediate predecessor: "I reject my mother, I hate sacrifice."[63] The narrator's life is organized in deliberate opposition to that of her own mother; the terms in which she discusses the maternal are reminiscent of Aleramo's discourse even more than that of Fallaci. A mother, she believes, "is not a person."[64] Ravera's narrator essentially outlines in fiction the path traced by Anna Scattigno, the:

> trajectory of emancipation from the family [...] from earlier history [...] the strong [...] opposition [...] to mothers and the image of the feminine represented by them [...] a violent aversion, a deep "rejection". The mother was everything one didn't want to become in life.[65]

Ravera's character's dislike of the traditional family structure is, if anything, stronger than that of Fallaci's narrator: "I've always hated families, mine, others."[66] The narrator also specifically takes issue with fascist discourses on the maternal, just as she has mirrored feminist suspicion of mothering: "the old lullaby of motherhood as a fundamental mission suited the regime's propaganda well."[67] Following the birth of the baby in this novel (after a miscarriage and a second pregnancy), the narrator furiously rejects the notion, expressed by some of her acquaintances, that becoming a mother makes her a woman: "and what was I before this, to what confused category did I belong, if you don't mind?"[68] Ravera has here interrogated both patriarchal constructions of motherhood, and feminism's troubled response to these, in rather more detailed fashion than did Fallaci.[69]

From inside the maternal experience, however, this author explores the disruption to identity, and the concept of the divided maternal self, even more fully than did Fallaci before her. Ravera highlights the sense of duality inherent in motherhood and even questions the possibility of returning to any form of singularity, equating the maternal experience to a fundamental, irremediable, splitting of the self. In a direct address to the foetus, her narrator asks: "How can one be two for nine months and then have to return to being, from one day to the next, one alone again, one once more? Explain to me what is natural about this madness."[70] The narrator's encounter with otherness is what Cristina Mazzoni might term a "risky disruption to subjectivity."[71] Ravera constantly stresses the disruption to subjectivity in her depiction of childbirth and early motherhood (areas that remained outside of Fallaci's remit). Immediately after her son is born, Ravera has her narrator reflect: "who knows [...] where my I ended up. Maybe it stayed in the labour ward."[72] There is, though, a suggestion here that more than one new self is created through childbirth, as the narrator reflects: "I am a newborn, as a mother."[73] The self/other identity-encounter, indeed, only intensifies towards the close of the novel. The narrator finds herself using the pronoun "I," when she actually means "he/the baby." The novel, thus, may be read as an example of what Brenda Daly and Maureen Reddy would define as a "maternal story [...] where selfhood is constructed, or reconstructed, in more complex patterns."[74]

In terms of embodiment, corporeality and emphasis on the physical experience of the maternal, there is a kind of jouissance experienced by the narrator after the baby's birth, where she spends hours simply staring at him, losing herself in him.[75] The negative flip side of this is explored in the narrative of the pregnancy itself, where the narrator feels, for instance, that "so much corporeality weighs on me like a hump on my back."[76]

It is not until her 1993 novel, *In quale nascondiglio del cuore* that Ravera takes on the more intellectual aspects of the maternal that Fallaci had begun to consider in *Lettera*. In this work (whose subtitle identifies it as a letter),[77] the narrator (once more anonymous) is keen to impart to her adolescent son the ways of thinking that have meaning for her. The kernel of her advice to him is to look outwards, to have an other-directed way of being in the world. For the narrator, "the exercise of looking" is crucial.[78] The son is advised: "Travel. Even without going far [...] what's important is your baggage: lighten your Self, open your eyes."[79] This is reminiscent of Sara Ruddick's formulation of maternal thinking, with the stress on thinking, as an extending of "maternal" attentiveness to the human race as a whole; it can be considered both deeply ethical and profoundly political. It mirrors the process described by the narrator of *Bambino mio* as a lightening of self, and an investment in the Other, consequent on motherhood.[80] Thus, mothering seems to be envisaged in Ravera as an important way in which to come to terms with Otherness, which can be used as a model for

CONCEPTUALIZING THE MATERNAL: REPRESENTATIONS, REFLECTIONS... 121

interacting with many Others. Kristeva speaks of motherhood in strikingly similar fashion as a "slow, difficult and delightful apprenticeship in attentiveness [...] forgetting oneself."[81] This recurring thread of the maternal as, on the one hand, that which splits the self but, on the other, in so doing, opens it up to others allowing for both emotional and intellectual permeability, is a fascinating one in both the literature and criticism of the latter part of the twentieth century. It is here that Aleramo's concerns around the split in the self are most clearly addressed and responded to. It is also here that *mammismo*, with its supposed individualism, its amorality, and lack of civic responsibility, is most roundly rejected.

Just a few years after Ravera's *Lettera*, Dacia Maraini tried out a maternal voice for the first time.[82] Like Natalia Ginzburg, she chose to do so through the medium of an extended essay, rather than through her fiction. *Un clandestino a bordo* is a reflection on women, on writing and on bodily experiences. The title essay was written in circumstances that directly mirror those of Fallaci's *Lettera*—it is a response to a request from an editor (and friend) to write an essay on debates around the abortion issue. Exactly like Fallaci, Maraini chooses not to do this. Instead, reflecting Fallaci's work, she chooses to write her experience of miscarriage (albeit in less overtly fictionalized fashion). Maraini explains her decision as follows:

> I can't speak about abortion but I keep circling around images of the maternal. It must be because for me miscarriage was above all an expropriation,[83] something unwanted and unexpected that ended my happy waiting, that never ended in [...] meeting that other, not-me.[84]

This sense of the maternal experience as an event-encounter with the other recurs throughout Maraini's text and links her work closely with that of Fallaci and Ravera. Like so many of her literary predecessors in the Italian context, too, Maraini uses an evocative tone in her descriptions of the maternal, often veering towards fantasy. Indeed, the fantastical elements of the text specifically link it with another of its intertexts, Conrad's *The Secret Sharer*, variously described as an essay or a short story and thus inhabiting the same literary terrain as Maraini's *Un clandestino* (stowaway). Maraini here is rethinking Conrad's work as one which parallels the experience of pregnancy in which the "bambino" (Maraini employs the same term as Fallaci) is a secret sharer of the mother's body, analogous to Conrad's ship, while the relationship between the pregnant woman and the "bambino" corresponds to that between Conrad's anonymous captain and Leggatt. This other within the self is, variously for Maraini, transformative (as we have seen most clearly in Ravera), possibly unwelcome and genuinely strange (and this is an aspect of pregnancy and the maternal that almost all of the writers discussed here have touched on), but most importantly, constitutive of a new kind of relationship. Conrad's captain, Maraini notes, "establishes [with the sharer] an intense bond of familiarity, understanding, indulgence and tenderness. Exactly as a mother does with her child."[85] Perhaps most interesting here is that notion of understanding, which implies a bond that contains an intellectual dimension. There is, of course, a strong corporeal root to the mother–child bond, acknowledged by Maraini: "It is a bond formed in a deep bodily knowledge, unspeakable, which precedes reason."[86] In a sense, though, this unspeakability is undone by Maraini as she sets out, as other writers have done before her, precisely to speak it, to narrate it, and to do so by analogy with a well-known and critically acclaimed literary text.

Il clandestino, like *Lettera* and *Bambino mio*, roundly rejects patriarchal representations of the maternal: "Mothering, in the culture of our fathers, was transformed into an event of extreme passivity for women."[87] To the contrary, Maraini holds that both pregnancy and mothering involve women in an intense and active relationship with their children and with their physical selves; borrowing Conrad's marine metaphor, she notes that, in childbirth, a woman "will do everything in her power to bring her child to land, even at the cost of battering her body against the rocks of haemorrhage and septicaemia."[88] The mention of septicaemia here specifically recalls Fallaci's *Lettera*, while also returning the reader to the corporeal dimension.

In this essay crammed with intertexts, Maraini privileges the maternal perspective and specifically associates it with the literary, hence with both the intellectual and the imaginative. She had already made an association between the maternal and the literary in another essay from 1986.[89] There she provocatively described writing as "profoundly feminine and maternal."[90] In this respect, Maraini knowingly takes issue with what Margaret Homans has described as "a framework of dominant cultural myths in which writing contradicts mothering."[91] She is, as Susan Stanford Friedman would have it, risking the maternal metaphor's dangerous biologism "to challenge fundamental binary oppositions between word and flesh, creativity and procreativity, mind and body."[92] In this respect, she is part of a body of women writers who take on the maternal in its corporeal dimension, certainly, through their writing but who also push it beyond this into the literary and philosophical domain.

Concluding Considerations

There are, of course, other writers whose work might profitably have been discussed in this chapter. I have omitted discussion of a number of writers who produce daughterly discourses, who look at the maternal from a critical distance, largely because this aspect of their work has been the subject of a good deal of critical analysis already.[93] Still more produce maternal subjects who are very like their counterparts in Fallaci, Ravera and Maraini and discussion of these has been omitted for reasons of space.[94] Perhaps the most obvious omission, though, is Elsa Morante and, most specifically, her maternal protagonist in *La storia*. I have made only passing reference to Ida Ramundo here because, although she is undoubtedly one of the most memorable literary mothers of the twentieth century, she is also, in many respects, uncharacteristically reflective of *mammismo*. As Laura Benedetti puts it, Ida is "inseparable [...] from her maternal function, to the point that her life loses all meaning when Useppe dies."[95]

It is obvious from the above that, throughout the twentieth century, there have been particular concerns around the maternal in women's writing. These range from considerations of patriarchal discourses on (and stereotypes of) the maternal, and their long-felt effects, through daughterly objectifications of the mother, to the taking on of maternal perspectives and, most importantly, the creation of maternal subjectivities; these representations of maternal subjectivities deal with the disruptions to identity occasioned by the maternal experience, the corporeal aspects of maternity (both negative and positive) and, alongside this corporeality, constant returns to the intellectual dimension of mothering and the possibilities it might offer for an other-directedness which arises precisely from the potentially threatening undoing/doubling of the self. The writers considered here challenge, in their reconceptualizations of the maternal, all notions of sameness and integrity. That challenge is initially represented as disturbing, but gradually shifts its meaning to a much more positively construed possibility. This brings much of their work close to the elaboration of subjectivity posited by Adriana Cavarero in "Il pensiero femminista." Cristina Mazzoni accurately summarizes Cavarero's position as proposing "a feminist metaphysics that, through the ethical bond to the other exemplified by birth, aims to avoid the destructive alternative of either the full subject of metaphysics or the fragmented self of postmodernism."[96]

In the end, while never avoiding the ambivalence of the maternal, these writers are awake to its possibilities. They provide us with challenging mosaics of identity, in which the intensely personal becomes highly political. Their conceptualizations of the maternal reflect each other and, in most cases, refract prescribed norms.

NOTES

1. See Fanning, "Maternal Prescriptions and Descriptions," for an analysis of nineteenth-century prescriptions around mothering in the advice literature of the early 1880s, and in scientific discourse close to the end of the century. Woman's maternal mission is central to both, and mothers are seen as indispensable to the formation of the new state.
2. See d'Amelia, *La mamma*, p. 7 for an elaboration of this tradition in the aftermath of the Second World War, which she locates as part of the national search for unifying myths.
3. See, for an example of maternal discourse in the fiction of the late nineteenth and early twentieth centuries, Fanning, "Maternal Prescriptions and Descriptions." This recurring theme with its concomitant articulation of a maternal perspective sharply differentiates Italian women's writings of the post-Unification period from their English and French equivalents.
4. These daughterly discourses are investigated in Giorgio, "The Passion for the Mother," as well as in Fanning "Some Segments of Daughterly Discourse."
5. Lawler, *Mothering the Self*, p. 5.
6. Garner et al., *The (M)Other Tongue*, p. 25.
7. D'Amelia, *Storia della maternità*, p. v.
8. Buttafuoco, "Motherhood as a Political Strategy," p. 179.
9. Taricone, "I cataloghi femminili," pp. 13–14.
10. Saraceno, "Redefining Maternity and Paternity," p. 199.
11. De Grazia, *How Fascism Ruled Women*, p. 46.
12. Passerini, "The Women's Movement in Italy," p. 177.
13. Giorgio, *Writing Mothers and Daughters*, p. 5.
14. Fanning, "Touching on Taboos," p. 46.
15. Mazzoni, *Maternal Impressions*, p. 100.
16. Kaplan, *Motherhood and Representation*, p. 4. Kaplan actually uses the term "subjective pleasures"; the observation also applies more generally to subjective experiences.
17. Mazzoni, *Maternal Impressions*, pp. 99–100.
18. See, for instance, Caesar, "Italian Feminism and the Novel," Bassanese "*Una donna*" and Fanning, "Sibilla Aleramo's *Una donna*."

CONCEPTUALIZING THE MATERNAL: REPRESENTATIONS, REFLECTIONS... 125

19. See Fanning, "Maternal Prescriptions" for a detailed analysis of these aspects of the novel.
20. Aleramo, *Una donna*, p. 71.
21. If Aleramo's nineteenth-century predecessors (e.g. Carolina Invernizio) sometimes depicted childbirth quite graphically, their accounts of it tended to be brief.
22. Aleramo, *Una donna*, p. 71.
23. Ibid., p. 70.
24. Ibid., p. 143.
25. Ibid., p. 203.
26. See ibid., p. 193 and Fanning "Maternal Descriptions," p. 34.
27. Spackman, "Puntini," S210.
28. Aleramo, *Una donna*, p. 71.
29. One of the notable portraits of a devourer in the novel is that of an elderly male poet who cannibalizes his daughters, as well as the maid, in the service of his genius. See Vivanti, *I divoratori*, p. 237.
30. Valeria is run over when going to borrow money for her spendthrift daughter, and is distracted while crossing the road precisely by her concerns for Nancy—she is mentally elsewhere. Her death is represented in gruesome detail.
31. Vivanti, *I divoratori*, p. 294.
32. See, for instance, *Marion*, her earliest novel, where performance is, in part, her subject-matter and where performative femininity is central to the text.
33. Vivanti, *I divoratori*, p. 297.
34. Butler, *Gender Trouble*, p. 147.
35. Piano, *Onora la madre*, p. 59.
36. Heyer-Caput, "*Cenere* by Grazia Deledda and Eleonora Duse," p. 199.
37. See Fanning, "'Feminist' Fictions?" for a detailed consideration of the mother as inalienably other in Banti's narratives.
38. Banti, "Vocazioni indistinte," p. 68.
39. Ibid., p. 79.
40. Ibid., p. 74.
41. Ibid., p. 75.
42. Ibid., p. 100.
43. D'Amelia, *La mamma*, p. 18.
44. Banti, *Artemisia*, p. 88.
45. Ibid., p. 86.
46. Ibid., p. 94.
47. Ibid., pp. 88–89.
48. Ginzburg, "Il mio mestiere," pp. 847–48.
49. *Le voci della sera*, for instance, is a wholly daughterly discourse. *Lessico famigliare* is almost entirely so. The short story, "La madre" is an exception in

its focus on the character of the mother, although here too the perspective of the children is the initial (if somewhat ironized) focus. The output of Elsa Morante may also be categorized in this way for the most part (*Menzogna e sortilegio* is an obvious example); it is invariably centred on the perspective of the child, with the exception of Ida in *La storia* (in fact, Ida is the apotheosis of the mother-animal and provides the title for Laura Benedetti's study of the mother in twentieth-century Italian literature, in her guise as tigress). Later in the century, these discourses predominate and a good deal of critical work has been done on them. Francesca Sanvitale's *Madre e figlia* and Fabrizia Ramondino's *Althénopis* are but two of the narratives that may be characterized as focalized on daughterly discourses.

50. Ginzburg, *Lessico famigliare*, p. 145.
51. Ginzburg, "Il mio mestiere," p. 849.
52. Ginzburg, "Dell'aborto," p. 1302.
53. Fallaci, *Lettera a un bambino mai nato*, p. 74.
54. Ibid., p. 32 (on three occasions).
55. Pickering-Iazzi, "Designing Mothers," p. 337.
56. Gatt-Rutter, *Oriana Fallaci*, p. 79.
57. Fallaci, *Lettera a un bambino mai nato*, p. 12.
58. Ibid., p. 22.
59. Benedetti, *The Tigress in the Snow*, pp. 90–91.
60. Ravera, *Bambino mio*, p. 10.
61. Ibid., p. 14.
62. Ibid., p. 40.
63. Ibid., p. 11.
64. Ibid., p. 17.
65. Scattigno, "La figura materna," p. 283.
66. Ravera, *Bambino mio*, 24.
67. Ibid., p. 35.
68. Ibid., p. 106.
69. It is notable that, despite the multiple echoes of Fallaci in Ravera's work (not all of which are revisionary), she explicitly rejects her predecessor in this novel. See Ravera, *Bambino mio*, p. 54.
70. Ibid., pp. 43–44.
71. Mazzoni, *Maternal Impressions*, p. 64.
72. Ravera, *Bambino mio*, p. 100.
73. Ibid., p. 100.
74. Daly and Reddy, *Narrating Mothers*, p. 12.
75. Ibid., p. 32.
76. Ravera, *Bambino mio*, pp. 98–99.
77. This does not seem quite coincidental; Ravera may not have quite finished with Fallaci, hence her subtitle *Lettera a un figlio adolescente*.

CONCEPTUALIZING THE MATERNAL: REPRESENTATIONS, REFLECTIONS... 127

78. Ravera, *In quale nascondiglio del cuore*, p. 127.
79. Ibid., p. 144.
80. See Ruddick, "Maternal Thinking." Obviously, this lightening of self and engagement with others is viewed by neither Ravera nor Ruddick as exclusive to a biological maternity. Ravera's narrator suggests it is attainable for a young man, while Ruddick derives her theory from the other-centredness of the biological maternal experience, but sees it as ultimately non-gender specific.
81. Kristeva, "Women's Time," p. 206.
82. Maraini's work is almost entirely made up of daughterly discourses. Even *La nave per Kobe*, which is flagged as "Topazia Maraini's [...] copybooks" in the blurb on the back cover, is a narrative controlled by the voice of the daughter, in which the mother's writing occupies only a small proportion of the volume.
83. The "aborto" of the original, of course, could mean both abortion and miscarriage, but the latter is clearly what is intended here.
84. Maraini, *Un clandestino*, p. 20.
85. Ibid., p. 15.
86. Ibid., p. 16.
87. Ibid., p. 18.
88. Ibid., pp. 16–17.
89. Maraini, "Reflections on the Logical and Illogical Bodies of my Sexual Compatriots."
90. Ibid., p. 29.
91. Homans, *Bearing the Word*, p. 22.
92. Stanford Friedman, "Creativity and the Childbirth Metaphor," p. 51.
93. Among those writers not already mentioned here are Rosetta Loy, Francesca Duranti and Carla Cerati.
94. Particularly important in this regard are the works of Gina Lagorio, Clara Sereni and Lalla Romano. I have discussed Romano's take on the maternal in my "Touching on Taboos."
95. Benedetti, *The Tigress in the Snow*, p. 80.
96. Mazzoni, *Maternal Impressions*, p. 190.

BIBLIOGRAPHY

Aleramo, Sibilla. *Una donna*. [1906] Milan: Feltrinelli, 1982.
Banti, Anna. *Artemisia*. [1947] Milan: Rizzoli, 1989.
———. "Vocazioni indistinte." In *Il coraggio delle donne*, pp. 61–100. [1940] Milan: La tartaruga, 1983.
Bassanese, Flora A. "*Una donna*: Autobiography as Exemplary Text." In *Donna: Women in Italian Culture*, edited by Ada Testaferri, pp. 131–152. Toronto: University of Toronto Press, 1989.

128 U. FANNING

Benedetti, Laura. *The Tigress in the Snow: Motherhood and Literature in Twentieth-Century Italy.* Toronto: University of Toronto Press, 2007.

Butler, Judith. *Gender Trouble: Feminism and the Subversion of Identity.* New York: Routledge, 1990.

Buttafuoco, Annarita. "Motherhood as a Political Strategy: the Role of the Italian Women's Movement in the Creation of the Cassa Nazionale di Maternità." In *Maternity and Gender Policies: Women and the Rise of the European Welfare States 1880s–1950s*, edited by Gisela Bock and Pat Thane, pp. 178–195. London: Routledge, 1991.

Caesar, Ann. "Italian Feminism and the Novel: Sibilla Aleramo's *A Woman.*" In *Feminist Review*, 5 (1980): pp. 79–87.

Cavarero, Adriana. "Il pensiero femminista. Un approccio teorico." In *Le filosofie femministe*, edited by Franco Restaino and Adriana Cavarero, pp. 111–163. Turin: Paravia, 1999.

Conrad, Joseph. *The Secret Sharer.* [1909] Charlottesville: University of Virginia Press, 1996.

d'Amelia, Marina. *La mamma.* Bologna: Il Mulino, 2005.

———. edited by. *Storia della maternità.* Rome: Laterza, 1997.

Daly, Brenda O. and Reddy, Maureen T., *Narrating Mothers: Theorizing Maternal Subjectivities.* Knoxville: University of Tennessee Press, 1991.

Deledda, Grazia. *Cenere.* [1907] Milan: Oscar Mondadori, 1973.

———. *Cosima.* [1937] In *Romanzi e novelle*, edited by Natalino Sapegno, 691–820. Milan: Mondadori, 1971.

———. "La madre." [1919] Milan: Mondadori, 2003.

de Grazia, Victoria. *How Fascism Ruled Women: Italy, 1922–1945.* Berkeley, Los Angeles and Oxford: University of California Press, 1992.

Fallaci, Oriana. *Lettera a un bambino mai nato.* Milan: Rizzoli, 1975.

Fanning, Ursula. "'Feminist' Fictions? Representations of Self and (M)Other in the Works of Anna Banti." In *Women in Italy, 1945–1960: An Interdisciplinary Study*, edited by Penelope Morris, pp. 159–76. New York: Palgrave, 2006.

———. "Maternal Prescriptions and Descriptions in Post-Unification Italy." In *Women and Gender in Post-Unification Italy: Between Private and Public Spheres*, edited by Katharine Mitchell and Helena Sanson, pp. 13–37. Oxford: Peter Lang, 2013.

———. "Sibilla Aleramo's *Una donna*: A case study in women's autobiographical fiction." In *The Italianist*, 19 (1999): pp. 164–177.

———. "Some Segments of Daughterly Discourse: Dacia Maraini's Return to the Mother." In *La lunga vita di Mariana Ucrìa, Bagheria* and *La nave per Kobe.*" In *Recent Italian Fiction*, edited by Roberto Bertoni, pp. 121–135. Dublin and Turin: Trauben, 2005.

———. "Touching on Taboos: Imagining and Reconceptualizing Motherhood in Some Post-'68 Autobiographical Narratives by Women." In *La modernità letteraria*, 4 (2001): pp. 49–58.

CONCEPTUALIZING THE MATERNAL: REPRESENTATIONS, REFLECTIONS... 129

Garner, Shirley N., Kahane, Claire and Sprengnether, Madelon. "Introduction." In *The (M)Other Tongue: Essays in Feminist Psychoanalytic Interpretation*, edited by Shirley N. Garner, Claire Kahane and Madelon Sprengnether, pp. 15–32. Ithaca and London: Cornell University Press, 1985.

Gatt-Rutter, John. *Oriana Fallaci: The Rhetoric of Freedom*. Oxford: Berg, 1996.

Ginzburg, Natalia. "Dell'aborto." [1975] In *Opere*, II, edited by Cesare Garboli, pp. 1299–1303. Milan: Mondadori, 1987.

———. "Il mio mestiere." [1962] In *Opere*, I, edited by Cesare Garboli, pp. 839–854. Milan: Mondadori, 1986.

———. "La madre." [1957] In *Opere*, I, pp. 203–215.

———. *Lessico famigliare*. [1963] Turin: Einaudi, 1996.

———. *Le voci della sera*. [1961] Turin: Einaudi, 1999.

———. "Un'assenza." [1933] In *Opere*, I, pp. 171–177.

Giorgio, Adalgisa. "The Passion for the Mother: Conflicts and Idealisations in Contemporary Italian Literature by Women." In *Writing Mothers and Daughters: Renegotiating the Mother in Western European Narratives by Women*, edited by Adalgisa Giorgio, pp. 119–54. Oxford: Berghahn, 2002.

———. edited by. *Writing Mothers and Daughters: Renegotiating the Mother in Western European Narratives by Women*, pp. 119–54. Oxford: Berghahn, 2002.

Heyer-Caput, Margherita. "*Cenere* by Grazia Deledda and Eleonora Duse." In *The Challenge of Modernity: Essays on Grazia Deledda*, edited by Sharon Wood, pp. 189–213. Leicester: Troubador, 2007.

Homans, Margaret. *Bearing the Word: Language and Female Experience in Nineteenth-Century Women's Writing*. Chicago and London: University of Chicago Press, 1986.

Kaplan, E. Ann. *Motherhood and Representation: The Mother in Popular Culture and Melodrama*. London: Routledge, 1992.

Kristeva, Julia. "Women's Time." In *The Kristeva Reader*, edited by Toril Moi, pp. 187–213. Blackwell: Oxford, 1986.

Lawler, Steph. *Mothering the Self: mothers, daughters, subjects*. London: Routledge, 2000.

Maraini, Dacia. *La nave per Kobe*. Milan: Rizzoli, 2001.

———. "Reflections on the Logical and Illogical Bodies of my Sexual Compatriots." In *The Pleasure of Writing: Critical Essays on Dacia Maraini*, edited by Rodica Diaconescu-Blumenfeld and Ada Testaferri, pp. 21–38. Lafayette, IN: Purdue University Press, 2000.

———. *Un clandestino a bordo*. Milan: Rizzoli, 1996.

Mazzoni, Cristina. *Maternal Impressions: Pregnancy and Childbirth in Literature and Theory*. Ithaca and London: Cornell University Press, 2002.

Morante, Elsa. *Menzogna e sortilegio*. [1948] Turin: Einaudi, 1994.

———. *La storia*. [1974] Turin: Einaudi, 1995.

130   U. FANNING

Passerini, Luisa. "The Women's Movement in Italy and the Events of 1968." In *Visions and Revisions: Women in Italian Culture*, edited by Mirna Cicioni and Nicole Prunster, pp. 167–182. Oxford: Berg, 1993.

Piano, Maria Giovanna. *Onora la madre: autorità femminile nella narrativa di Grazia Deledda*. Turin: Rosenberg & Sellier, 1998.

Pickering-Iazzi, Robin. "Designing Mothers." In *Annali d'Italianistica: Women's Vision in Italian Literature*, 7, edited by Rebecca West and Dino Cervigni, pp. 325–340. Chapel Hill: University of North Carolina, 1989.

Ramondino, Fabrizia. *Althénopis*. Turin: Einaudi, 1981.

Ravera, Lidia. *Bambino mio*. Milan: Bompiani, 1979.

———. *In quale nascondiglio del cuore: lettera a un figlio adolescente*. Milan: Mondadori, 1993.

Ruddick, Sara. "Maternal Thinking." In *Mothering: Essays in Feminist Theory*, edited by Joyce Trebilcott, pp. 213–230. Lanham, MD: Rowman & Littlefield, 1983.

Sanvitale, Francesca. *Madre e figlia*. Turin: Einaudi, 1980.

Saraceno, Chiara. "Redefining Maternity and Paternity: gender, pronatalism and social policies in fascist Italy." In *Maternity and Gender Policies*, edited by Gisela Bock and Pat Thane, pp. 196–212. London: Routledge, 2012.

Scattigno, Anna. "La figura materna tra emancipazione e femminismo." In *Storia della maternità*, edited by Marina d'Amelia, pp. 273–299. Rome: Laterza, 1997.

Spackman, Barbara. "Puntini, Puntini, Puntini: Motherliness as Masquerade in Sibilla Aleramo's *Una donna*." In *MLN*, 124.5, (2009): S210–S223.

Stanford Friedman, Susan. "Creativity and the Childbirth Metaphor: Gender Difference in Literary Discourse." In *Feminist Studies*, 13.1 (1987): pp. 49–82.

Taricone, Fiorenza. "I cataloghi femminili dell'ottocento." In *Operaie, borghesi, contadine nel XIXe secolo*, edited by Fiorenza Taricone and Beatrice Pisa, pp. 11–24. Rome: Carucci, 1978.

Vivanti, Annie. *I divoratori*. [1911] Milan: Mondadori, 1949.

———. *Marion, artista di caffè concerto*. [1891] Palermo: Sellerio, 2006.

CHAPTER 6

Neapolitan Mothers: Three Generations of Women, from Representation to Reality

Gabriella Gribaudi

Literary representations, stereotypes that have embedded over time, have cut across an extremely complex and irregular reality to create monolithic and enduring images of southern Italian women and mothers, divided between two antithetical extremes. On the one hand we have women oppressed by violent and chauvinistic men, confined to the domestic space, victims of an archaic and patriarchal society: women in mourning black, mothers and wives destined for sacrifice. This image fitted neatly, and still fits, with the paradigm that links the Italian South with chronic and deeply rooted social and cultural backwardness.

On the other hand, we have strong and protective Mediterranean mothers who watch over their husbands and children, impose their own rules, and snare everyone in their web of cloying emotionality. While this image contrasts starkly with the first, it too has been used to confirm and transmit stereotypes that are at the same time both anti-southern and anti-feminist. This is the idea that southern society is ruled by the law of the protective and retrogressive mother: individualist, defiant towards society's rules, and in conflict with the laws of the state and civil society, which represent the law of the father. At the end of the nineteenth century, in

G. Gribaudi (✉)
Università di Napoli Federico II, Naples, Italy
e-mail: gribaudi@unina.it

© The Author(s) 2018
P. Morris, P. Willson (eds.), *La Mamma*,
Italian and Italian American Studies,
https://doi.org/10.1057/978-1-137-54256-4_6

131

132 G. GRIBAUDI

this vein, Niceforo wrote that "the peoples of the North have a collective conscience and therefore have social organization, institutions, and discipline. The dissolute and weak-willed Neapolitans are a 'feminine-people,' while the others are a 'masculine-people'."[1]

In the case of Naples, this second image has been the principal one to emerge from literary texts, and it has become the dominant representation. Much nineteenth- and twentieth-century writing on Naples describes a world dominated by women: mothers and wives who make or break the fortunes of their husbands and sons; neighbours who protect, or lead into damnation; insatiable and ruthless moneylenders. The vanquished and subservient female victims who appear in some works are young, often on their own, sometimes foreign, and vanquished precisely because they are isolated within the city's female society. Men, by contrast, are described as fragile beings unable to cope with real life and make their mark on the female world. Where do these images come from, and how do they relate to social reality? If women are viewed through other lenses and other sources, what images emerge?

Stereotypes and representations stem from choices: from a complex reality, elements are selected which either confirm previously deep-rooted ideas or have dramatic literary potential. This process is continually repeated in interactions and social communications; it is very vividly illustrated in representations of the Naples area, which has many features encouraging the creation of strong images: a huge population, a large working class with a long history, and strong cultural traditions.

Some of the best-known literary and theatrical representations are discussed in the first section of this chapter. This is followed by stories drawn from lived reality: in the second and third sections, we examine the lives of two women which to some extent echo the literary images. Rosa is an example of quite a traditional mother but her story also introduces the theme of the life-cycle and social transformation across the generations. The final section offers a more panoramic view of three different generations of rural and urban women, which allows us to explore trajectories of cultural and social change.

The sources include life stories and family histories collected by myself and by female students on my courses at the University of Naples, from 1994 onwards.[2] There are hundreds of these life stories, referring to a very broad and disordered world; I have had to select lives that seem in some way emblematic, and simultaneously try to convey the complexity of real life. I have chosen stories that start within social strata that can be described

NEAPOLITAN MOTHERS: THREE GENERATIONS OF WOMEN... 133

as "working class,"[3] from both urban and rural origins, and that include three age cohorts: women born in the 1910s and 1920s who often experienced unsettled family and material conditions, growing up before the modernization processes that developed in Italy from about the 1960s onwards; women born in the 1950s and 1960s, years of extraordinary material and cultural change that either involved them personally or helped to determine the framework they offered their daughters; the daughters themselves, young women born after the 1970s who are pursuing new ideas about being a woman, sometimes with great difficulty. This might seem a straightforward path from tradition to modernity, but in reality change sometimes occurs haphazardly, and tradition and modernity do not always correspond to the values and features that a stereotyping approach might attribute to them.

LITERARY REPRESENTATIONS

Two women face each other: the mother and lover of a man on trial for murder, competing for his affection. "You're taking my son from under my nose," the mother protests to the woman who has stolen him from her, thus leading, she claims, to his arrest and ruin. This occurs in *Assunta Spina*, a play of 1909 by Salvatore Di Giacomo, which on three occasions has been made into a film (1915, 1930 and 1948) and twice into a television mini-series (1992 and 2006). The scene, set in the court waiting room, is completely dominated by female characters; while the man is being tried in the court itself, we see the women waiting, quarrelling, and talking. In another of Di Giacomo's comedies, *'O voto* (*The Vow*) of 1889, the male lead Vito, "affected by nervousness" (we would now say "neurotic"), is a weak character and prey to both his *mamma* and his lover, who this time are allies. Vito has vowed to marry and rescue a young woman who has fallen into prostitution. He chooses Cristina, with whom he falls in love, but his mother and previous lover weave a plot of deception and obstruction around him which derails his intentions, to the point where he gives in. The loser here is another woman, Cristina, who has neither family nor support network in the neighbourhood: she has no idea what is happening around her, no-one explains the deceptions to her, and no-one puts her on her guard. Cristina is a symbol of the innocence of youth, against the shrewdness and toughness of mature women.

These two mothers portrayed by Di Giacomo are "Mediterranean": enmeshed, enveloping, and determined to shape their sons' destinies. The

134 G. GRIBAUDI

archetypal southern Italian mother, however, is Filumena Marturano, the protagonist of the well-known comedy by Eduardo De Filippo.[4] The unfortunate Filumena has been seen as a symbol of Italian familism and, especially, Neapolitan familism.[5] Formerly a prostitute out of financial necessity, she has had three children by different men. She lives for many years with one of them—Domenico Soriano—and looks after his house and his financial affairs without any emotional or material recognition. At a certain point, by pretending to be at death's door, she tricks him into marrying her; she then summons the three sons that she has secretly supported all this time and presents them to her new husband, but refuses to tell him which son is actually his. There follows a bitter quarrel in which Filumena stands her ground: if her husband fails to accept all three children, she will leave. "Children are children," she repeats.[6] In the end, faced with her obstinacy, he gives in and accepts them all. The law of the mother thus triumphs over the laws of blood and the father. Filumena Marturano, as grounded and resolute as Domenico Soriano is vain and ineffective, thus manages to confound her fate as an oppressed woman, reducing the man to total submission.

Another portrayal of a woman which played an important role in Neapolitan constructions of femininity was that of Amalia Jovine, in De Filippo's play *Napoli milionaria* of 1945:

> Amalia is a woman aged thirty-eight, and still attractive. Her way of speaking, her tone and her gestures, immediately give the impression of a decisive character: someone accustomed to being in charge. Her restless eyes see and note everything. She is always conscious of her own actions, including when these are not entirely proper. Grasping in business and hard-hearted, she sometimes conceals her resentment for a setback with honeyed words, leaving people to guess at her real thoughts from the irony of her look. She is animated and impetuous.[7]

The story relies on Amalia's character traits. She lives in a ground-floor apartment with her husband Gennaro, a tram driver, whose fragile temperament is further weakened by his inability to meet his family's material needs. We are in 1942, with Naples under punishing bombardment, and the tram network is destroyed. Gennaro loses his job, and with that what little recognition his family had given him; as their youngest daughter's bitter refrain goes, "Dad is an idiot." He is then arrested by the Germans during the Naples uprising, and sent as a prisoner to Germany. On his

NEAPOLITAN MOTHERS: THREE GENERATIONS OF WOMEN... 135

return, he finds Amalia fully involved in the trafficking that characterized Naples during the Allied occupation. She has supported the family by her black market activities, pursued with a relentless cunning. Conflict is inevitable.

The clash between Amalia and Gennaro is one between psychological frailty and toughness, honesty and cunning, legality and illegality, idealism and pragmatic opportunism. This is an extreme example of a way of thinking that is to some extent apparent in all De Filippo's plays, and that expresses a widespread male perspective.

Almost all the women portrayed by De Filippo are stronger and more powerful than the men, who in his comedies are solitary and obsessive: they concentrate on one particular activity, while around them, and beyond their comprehension or control, are their wives, daughters and sons, in-laws, brothers and sisters, all in frenzied motion. In his *Natale in casa Cupiello* of 1931, Luca Cupiello, a perpetual child engaged in peripheral tasks like assembling the nativity scene, is excluded and willingly excludes himself from family life, whose language he does not even understand: it is a "wireless telegraph," whose messages he stops trying to decipher. Ferdinando Quagliolo, in *Non ti pago* of 1941, is up on the roof watching the clouds with an assistant in search of potential messages for playing the lottery, while in the apartment below his wife and daughter manage all the busy comings and goings. Alberto Stigliano, in *Mia famiglia* of 1955, having realized his impotence and inability to deal with his relationships with his wife and children, withdraws into total silence, pretending to be mute. The men are fragile and temperamental creatures, embodying reason and honesty against trickery and deception. Their guilt lies in their absence, which is often the cause of the family's ruin and their ultimate return to save everyone.

De Filippo celebrates Neapolitan men: poets and dreamers facing female pragmatism, the defeated and the just, they are men overpowered by the sticky webs that women weave around them. His female characters emerge from the Neapolitan context, but above all relate to the writer's imagination, perhaps to the imaginary world of Neapolitan men, in which women are powerful and dangerous spectres. They tell us more about how women are seen by men than about women themselves. However, they also throw light on the difficulties families face, and the uncertain position of fathers who, according to social norms, should be supporting their families, but fail in this.

136 G. GRIBAUDI

There is another aspect that literature highlights, through female characters engaged in trading and trafficking, both legal and illegal. In her novel *Il paese di Cuccagna* of 1891, Matilde Serao paints an intense portrait of one of these, the money-lender Concetta Esposito, who is described among the crowd of tortured and emaciated lottery players waiting for the numbers to be drawn:

[A]mong the few gray women's faces and torn calico dresses, discoloured from too frequent washings, quite a different woman's face showed. She was a tall, strong lower-class woman, with a high-coloured dark face; her chestnut hair was drawn back, elaborately dressed—the fringe on her narrow forehead even had a touch of powder; and heavy earrings of uneven, round, greeny-white pearls pulled down her ears, so that she had had to secure them by a black silk string, fearing they would break the lobes; a gold necklace and a thick gold medallion hung over the white muslin vest, all embroidered and tucked with lace. She pulled up a transparent black silk crape shawl every now and then, to show her hands, which were covered with thick gold rings up to the second joint. (vol. 1, p. 7)[8]

There are angry mutterings from the crowd, who know her and know that her task at that point is to warn her sister, an organizer of "*small games*" (a kind of illegal lottery), should the results favour the players, so that she can flee with their stakes. In response, Donna Concetta scornfully shrugs her shoulders and crosses her bejewelled hands on her stomach: "[s]he looked at the crowd severely twice or thrice—rather proudly. The voices ceased; the woman's eyelids fluttered, as if from gratified pride" (1, 7).

This is the portrait of a woman who is beautiful, rich, and proud of her wealth, and who tirelessly protects her own interests and her money. Serao later depicts her in a period of crisis, when repayments are not being made and she relentlessly and angrily hunts down her debtors through alleys, up staircases and into hovels:

She wandered about all day from one street to another, from cellar to attic, from shop to factory, running after her own money, till she was out of breath; for she always went on foot. Consumed with rage from the constant refusals, she began by asking for her interest at least, coldly insistent, and ended up by making a scene, yelling, demanding her "blood," as she passionately called her money. (vol. 2, p. 51)

NEAPOLITAN MOTHERS: THREE GENERATIONS OF WOMEN... 137

Serao describes her at home with a throng of people who flatter, beg, and cajole her, but her response is sarcastic and unbending; she allows no-one to move her to pity, in the name of her "blood," which she regards as legitimately accumulated wealth.

Usury was, and still is, the preserve of women. Contemporary judicial inquiries provide us with similar images: it is women who manage the money-lending networks of the Camorra. We find them collecting debts, making threats, and using and commissioning violence,[9] and thus it can hardly be said that the representations do not reflect people who really exist; the problem is that they have been projected onto the entire Neapolitan world.

What now follows relates to one of those characters who actually seem to confirm the literary model. Geppina's story, which she herself told a few years ago, could have come straight from a theatre script.

THIS COULD BE A LITERARY PORTRAIT...

Geppina, born in 1936, grew up with her grandmother and grandfather from her own choice and this greatly influenced the development of both her character and her history. Her grandmother Concetta, she said, was no less than the daughter of Tore 'e Crescienzo, the renowned *camorrista*, and was one of those then known as a "*zi' maesta.*"

My grandmother was ... at the time they used to say "a zia maesta," meaning she was a woman of honour. And so I inherited from my grandmother the character that I have. For example a girl would get in trouble and then they would go to this woman. She says: look, that man has behaved badly, but not if he wants to marry her, she's expecting a baby. And rather than having him hurt, my grandma would call someone, who'd call someone else ... she was a peacemaker ... that was my grandmother, the lady of the area. She brought me up, my grandmother, and so I turned out different to my sisters. [...] My grandmother, I remember, used to carry a knife.

Her grandfather, an "*acquafrescaio*" (drinkseller), coffee shop manager, and then bar manager on via Foria, rose to the role of *guappo*,[10] she said, due to his father-in-law's renown. Power, generosity and wealth are the mythical qualities linked to portrayals of grandparents:

They used to weigh the coins on scales, we didn't have time to count them, we weighed them. [...] My grandmother had eighteen children, and with every child my grandfather would give her a string of pearls.

At the beginning of her story, she signalled her rejection of identification with her mother and her choice of her grandmother:

> They brought me up, because I was too difficult, mamma couldn't bear me. My mother was the daughter of a site foreman, for an iron factory in the port, so, they were self-controlled people who preferred not to argue with anyone, while I was a real character! [...] One had to stay inside, and not go out ... not ... instead, with my grandma, I was used ... to talking to people.

Her life story began with a firm foundation, and everything that followed stemmed from this: her roots were in the part of the family that becomes felt in the "blood." Her identification with her grandmother provided the elements for her subsequent self-representation, explaining her life choices and success.

Due to gossip and unfounded rumours, common features of that time, she found herself married very young, almost before she could think. According to her, her husband was useless:

> When I realized the mistake I'd made, that I'd married this big mistake, my character cut in. They had bought me a bit of furniture, while I was dying of hunger, and had no money. I went down ... at the time I was seventeen. I called on someone who bought old furniture and I sold everything, even the bed from under me. That way I had capital, and I started to sell ties. I was a good-looking girl, all the men stopped to buy ties, and I earned money.
>
> My husband was a weak man, and I played the parts of both father and mother.

After selling ties, Geppina launched further commercial enterprises, which later became a starting point for her children. She also worked as a cleaner in the local government offices. She portrayed herself as someone with a strong sense of self-worth and a boundless faith in her own abilities. She also saw herself as a strong woman: her strength was shown on many fronts, social and psychological for example, and so she was a courageous woman. Whoever lacked courage did not become strong:

> The important thing is to fight, fight, keep on fighting, because if you stop for five minutes and think that you're beaten, you won't be able to fight on. When something happens? You have to toss your hair back, wipe your brow, and tomorrow is another day!

NEAPOLITAN MOTHERS: THREE GENERATIONS OF WOMEN... 139

She believed that you have to earn, you have to struggle to make money, but you should not get too fond of it. Money should be spent with largesse:

I've always earned. But I spend the money, I spend it all. We shouldn't hold onto money, you shouldn't be a slave to cash! You should keep what little you would need if you fell ill, or something. [...] It doesn't matter to me, what I don't need I spend. [...] For example I have something I like to do. To go around the stores. Recently, for example, I bought myself three dresses. That's how I let off steam, it's my safety valve. Now, for example, I don't feel well, but I'll go and have my hands, hair, and feet done. I'm always at the hairdresser's.

I like going to Capri, for ten days. On my own, and I like going alone. They think I'm a billionaire, when I go there. Because I dress like a billionaire! In fact I go further up, to Anacapri [*You go to a hotel? Alone?*] Yes. But I'm never alone, my child! It's my bad luck, I don't know. When I stop, a whole crowd of people stop to talk to me. It's they who make friends with me. I don't look for them ... they even write to me. [*Later in the interview: Don't you go on holiday with your husband?*] What would I do with him! He goes with our daughters! As for me, in August, I really like to be on my own. Yes, because it gives me time to think, about my life, I feel as if I'm in a film, all alone...

Geppina said that she had betrayed her husband, claiming that he was fully aware of this and knew that her last child was not his. However, she defended the institution of the family:

A family must stand together against everyone and everything! That's what a real mother does! I do what I want with my life, outside the house, but at home I'm the mother

Geppina's words have no real need of comment. They convey, better than any analysis, her personal strength, her very strong identity and her world view. She seems to walk out of the pages of Matilde Serao: her resemblance to a literary portrait, the representation of the archetypal strong Neapolitan woman, is striking. If the lengthy interview had not been recorded, we might think she had been invented. Geppina struggled to finish her second year of primary school, and certainly had not read Serao. She might have gone to the theatre, certainly might have seen De Filippo, and would perhaps have identified with his dramas.

140 G. GRIBAUDI

In Geppina strength, assertiveness, autonomy and tradition all coexisted. Her story emphasized her autonomy in relation to her husband and the surrounding world, while at the same time it extolled her role as mother. Geppina's idea of family is certainly not the intimate marriage that the sociologists now tell us about, and that, in Naples as elsewhere, is the reference point for many other individuals and groups; rather, above all, it is a necessary institution with lineage at its core. The mother is a mother, and not necessarily a wife: a good mother can be a bad wife. There is a conflictual relationship with the male world, which we will discuss again later. To be a strong mother means, as in nature, to both protect and control one's children, from the emotional sphere to business activities (with her children, Geppina established a business in the clothing trade). In the figure of Geppina, documentary sources are almost perfectly consistent with literature.

A recurring theme of theatrical representations is women's role as mediators of emotional and family relationships, a role that our protagonist exercised forcefully. The importance attributed to this role strengthens women's authority in the family. This is particularly evident, as we have seen, in the plays of De Filippo. Serao, who pays more attention to social and gender differences, gives us a range of contrasting female characters: we have a money-lender and a "small game" organizer, both genuinely proud women, but also a girl who suffers the arrogance and abuse of a violent man, and an aristocrat's daughter who sacrifices herself to her father's despotic whims: a spectrum of both class social differences, and differences among women. Women are oppressors, but also victims, and can exchange these roles during the life-cycle, as the next section about Rosa demonstrates.

LIFE-CYCLES: ALTERNATIONS OF POWER AND VULNERABILITY

Rosa was born in 1925 to two caretakers in the "Monte di Dio" quarter, in central Naples:[11]

> We were very poor, my mother worked as a caretaker and the building was sold ... because the water supply pipe burst and three buildings collapsed, one after the other, and mamma was the caretaker and had to leave, I was a little girl ... we were out in the street, then my mamma took on another house and we lived in the entrance hall ... we lived there for years without water or electricity, and then the war came.

Rosa was an only child. Her father died during the war. She and her mother suffered countless hardships. She took in ironing, and then worked as a housemaid. She had three children during the 1950s, by three different men, then married a professional thief who gave his name to the children; he was in and out of prison, and Rosa supported him. She was the real mainstay of the family, and continued to work as a maid. Despite her husband's activity, well known locally, her own reputation for honesty remained intact.

In this first part of Rosa's life, she seems a victim. Her first three men each left her on her own with a child. The thief married her—only a complete madman, she said, would have married her with three children to support—but as a result she experienced numerous problems, including physical violence, until he left her for a younger woman. At this point her image was anything but powerful, but this changed in the next phase of her life.

This was Rosa's golden period. She no longer had to suffer the anxieties linked to her husband's "trade," nor his harassment. An invalidity pension had built up from her hourly pay as a maid, and her sons started to earn. In this phase her relationships with her children and in the neighbourhood indicated her social position. She lived amid an intricate neighbourhood network, in which relationships between young people would also develop, and Rosa could thus steer her sons towards particular girls. While this was not an entirely conscious calculation, and the girls were not necessarily good matches, her desire to manage her sons' lives led her to put in motion a complicated set of interactions which eventually got out of control. Following a maelstrom of pressure, gossip and slander two of the young men, before they could stop and think, ended up married. One wife came from a family linked to criminal gangs, the other from an almost destitute family. Their vulnerable situation made Rosa's presence alongside her sons essential, and thus a burdensome period of involvement in the lives of the new couples started. One daughter-in-law accepted her intrusions, but quarrels started with the other. Rosa sought allies in the neighbourhood. Rumours gradually spread that the daughter-in-law had a relationship with her own father, and that Rosa's son was not the father of the couple's second child. In the end, in a crescendo of outlandish stories, the couple separated. The young man went to work in Germany, and then came back, more mature, to re-marry; once again the bride was a local girl, but they then moved a long way from his mother. Rosa remained near to the other son, whose oldest daughter she brought up, and her youngest

142   G. GRIBAUDI

son still lived with her. In this period of her life Rosa was clearly dominant. There then came a third phase, in which her fate changed again.

Displaced by the earthquake, Rosa was given a council apartment in the city's eastern area, where new public housing was being built. This was big enough for her to take in her third son, who had just married. He had always been quite reserved, protecting himself from the neighbourhood, and had often argued with his mother due to their different personalities. While Rosa was expansive, lively, extrovert and chaotic, her son was reserved and obsessively neat, and had profoundly different social and cultural norms from his mother. His wife naturally sided with him; she was educated and worked as a nursery school teacher and child-minder. Their wedding was very expensive and, as custom dictated, took place in a restaurant outside Naples, concluding with a honeymoon in the Canaries. All this was faithfully recorded by a cine camera. On their return, the newlyweds went to live with Rosa, who had every intention of ruling the household. At this point, however, a fierce war developed, with protests, cries and swearing on one side, and on the other silences and the gradual conquest of spaces. And Rosa lost. Gradually, her son and daughter-in-law took over the house, without officially evicting her. Rosa, an excellent cook, initially did the cooking, but then she was forced away from the stove. The reason given was diet, which was at odds with her kind of cooking: rich dishes, fried food, hot sauces, and every kind of high-calorie creation. Her old furniture was gradually jettisoned, and modern furniture introduced instead: polished, lacquered, and covered in knick-knacks and ornaments that were not to be touched. At this point Rosa was confined to her room. To distract herself she often went to visit her oldest son, who now had many children and numerous problems, and had remained much closer to his mother (not least because his wife had been the only one to accept her mother-in-law). Rosa, however, fell ill. She had always been an incredible talker and great story-teller, but started to go quiet and fell into a depression. Eventually her son and daughter-in-law sold or threw away (this was unclear) the furniture in her room, which she had inherited from an old friend and which she was really fond of, replacing it with children's furniture, including bunk beds, where Rosa slept. This couple now had two small children but the apartment was not large enough for a children's bedroom, an essential status symbol, and so the mother's room was camouflaged for the purpose. The children naturally continued to sleep with their parents. Perhaps innocent guests might have thought that this was actually the children's room, and perhaps the son and his wife hoped thus to drive Rosa into her grave. The defeated Rosa no longer spoke her mind. The final years of her life were spent in the home of her oldest son, who had remained emotionally and culturally closer to his mother.

Rosa's story echoes in certain ways some of the literary characters, but it tells us something more. It shows how the relationship between the genders can alter across different phases in life and in relation to the configurations of relationships that develop, and that subjects themselves have taken part in creating. Strength and weakness alternate. Rosa seemed a victim in her youth, then ruled over the destinies of others, becoming in some sense an oppressor, and then in the final phase was again a victim. We see how female power is at risk in relationships with men, but also in conflicts between women, and often between women of different generations. In Rosa's story some interesting factors play a part, relating to her ascent from the "*basso*" (ground-floor apartment)[12] to the small apartment in a "traditional" neighbourhood, to the apartment in the city outskirts. In this trajectory different cultures came together and collided: the conflict with her son and daughter-in-law was exemplary in this respect.

In this case, the individual's very identity changes along the arc of her life. Rosa's identity seems inextricably linked to the power play and the relationships in which the maternal role is crucial. By leaving the city centre, Rosa lost the neighbourhood relationships which had been so important to her. She then encountered another mother, who at that precise moment was stronger than her for various reasons: she had her husband on her side, he shared her ideals regarding the family, and so on. As in other situations, female strength is almost always linked to adulthood, and to the moment of full motherhood. If a woman does not have the wherewithal to defend herself (financial means, or relationships, as with Geppina), she may have to yield.

Rosa's tale relates to the life-cycle and inter-generational conflict, but also to historical change: the progression between different models, values and cultural codes. Her son and daughter-in-law aspired to the ideal of an intimate conjugal family, and to the myths of a modernity experienced as a form of social progress: an inwardly focused family life no longer open to the neighbourhood, the children's bedroom, and the joint parenting of fathers and mothers. Rosa, by contrast, had been the real head of a fatherless family.

This brings us to the wider story of the generations across the twentieth century.

THE GENERATIONS: HISTORICAL PERIODS, INDIVIDUAL LIVES

The life stories of Geppina and Rosa fit within an urban and working-class social space. They have some elements in common: a maternal role emphasized and consciously managed for their own self-determination, and financial management of the family, although with varying success. Many other elements mark their stories as different. Geppina's family enjoyed higher social status than Rosa's: her grandparents had a place in the quarter's hierarchy of honour and her parents had a business, while Rosa, an only child in an era when the number of children and siblings was synonymous with strength, was born into a vulnerable family that quickly lost the financial basis for its survival, and soon after that also lost its head. The precariousness of Rosa's beginnings, the events of the era (the war, and then the earthquake with the loss of home and the move to the outskirts), and the phases of her life, together triumph over the strength of character that she showed as an adult in her escape from marginalization, and reduce her in old age to a position of weakness. In Rosa's story, however, we also see the imprint of events common to her age cohort, and traces of the transformations of the era which involve other generations: the lifestyle, aspirations, and behaviour of her and of her son and his wife are profoundly different, and in conflict. These are changes that, in different ways, involve the generations spread across the twentieth century.

This section examines the stories of three cohorts of women born between 1915 and the 1980s, and widens the picture to include areas outside the city itself. These generations have lived through huge changes: the demographic revolution, the revolution in material conditions (from scarcity and sacrifice to the consumer society), and the revolution in sexual morality and gender roles. These stories offer us a much more complex reality than the literary images, and allow us to analyse the dynamics of these changes.

Our first generation, women born in the 1910s and 1920s, was marked by the war and by extremely difficult material conditions. Emigration, captivity and early deaths often deprived families of their men, and broadened the maternal role. Caterina, born in 1921, is a good example. Having lost her father when she was aged 10, she married just before the war and had a daughter in 1940. At this point her husband left for the front, was taken prisoner, and returned six years later. He then left again, for Argentina, then France and then England. Moreover, Caterina had a second child:

"I'd always been on my own, working, with the child, and then another one arrived." This was her terse comment at the end of her tale.

The frequent absence of fathers and husbands is striking. This absence was both material and psychological, as many of the stories underline. Lia M., for example, was born in 1922. Her parents separated, having had four children, two boys and two girls, and she was sent to boarding school, emerging aged 18. She never saw her father again after the split. Both her brothers died in the war, one from illness and the other as a soldier in Greece, leaving Lia and her mother and sister. Lia married an American soldier in 1944 and had a son. Her husband left for the United States, but she never wanted to join him:

> I'd have liked him to come here, but since he couldn't come, he wanted me to go over there. [...] He would say, 'Have you decided to come now? Have you decided? The child is two years old, I love him' ... No! From then on he didn't write any more, but every month an American Express money order from New York, this continued for twenty years, me sending photographs and him sending money, me sending Christmas greetings. However I always bless him as he gave me the chance to bring up my son how I wanted, with all means possible and imaginable. My son has been the apple of my eye [...] I stood in for his father, I was both father and mother.

In Lia M.'s story, in the first phase the men either disappeared or died. The women remained, and our protagonist consciously gave up the man and father who emerged from the war.[13]

N.N., born in a village in the province of Caserta in 1915, instead told of an arranged marriage and a life "alongside a man who always remained a stranger" to her.

> In a house that never really felt like mine, my life went by with no excitement, in the most complete indifference. I felt as if I was in a life and a world that weren't my own. [...] My husband Alfredo passed on about five years ago leaving absolutely no trace, he passed away quietly, just as he had spent his life.

This was a very intense account, an extreme case which nevertheless helps us to consider the problem of male–female and mother–father relationships. The woman's story referred back to the man's story. In this, as in other cases, we need to listen to the man as well, as he too was a victim: he passed away quietly, without leaving any trace ... What would he have told us if we had interviewed him? One man, interviewed by another female student, claimed that he had had to communicate with his sons by letter because, he said, they were dominated emotionally by his wife. This, too, could have come straight out of a De Filippo play. Then there are the many instances of men who for long periods lived their lives far from their families, which was hard for them: emigrants, sailors, deep-sea fishermen and so on. We cannot spend time on their stories here, but we should not forget their presence in the background. The history of gender is a history of relationships, as has been said many times. In this first generation, the relationship between the sexes seems to have been a difficult one, dominated by the uncertainties of material conditions, by premature deaths, and often by the irresponsibility of fathers and husbands. Many working-class wives and mothers either worked alongside their husbands, or also went to work to support their families, if they were present, whereas the emotional sphere and the roles of father and mother seem to have been divided and symmetrical. This would change in the next generation, born in the 1950s and 1960s. Furthermore, the maternal role appears to have been distributed socially: many children, especially girls, were fostered by aunts, grandmothers, female neighbours and well-to-do childless female friends.

Rosa D., from a fishing family in the Neapolitan suburb of Santa Lucia, was born in 1915. A year later her mother died in childbirth and Rosa was passed to a childless aunt:

> I've always been unlucky, I lost my mother when I was a year old. She died giving birth to my sister, whom I never saw because she was given to the Annunziata,[14] a Roman lady took her. I only know that she's called Maria Addolorata. My father had to give my sister to the Annunziata because he was left without a wife, he worked all day so he couldn't look after us smaller ones, so he gave me away too, having me fostered by my mother's sister, who hadn't had children for eleven years.

In the background there is the figure of the fisherman father: a sad man, scarred by life's difficulties, who chose to commit suicide on the day of the Piedigrotta festival, the day the entire fishing quarter celebrates.

Concetta (1919–2000), mother of eight children, lost her husband when her youngest daughters were aged 4 and 2. Two of her daughters were taken in by a boarding school, while other children were fostered by their paternal uncle's family. There had in fact already been a similar story in her family of origin: her mother (1885–1965) had had two illegitimate

NEAPOLITAN MOTHERS: THREE GENERATIONS OF WOMEN... 147

daughters and was very poor, so to survive sold fruit and vegetables without a proper licence and placed her second daughter with her immediate neighbours, who subsequently officially adopted her.

We see fragmented families and children without parents: an uncertain world, where the web of relationships with neighbours and the wider family can produce solidarity. The mother is the only important person of reference, and if she disappears the family crumbles. Even she, however, can be replaced by another mother, although not without difficulty: a childless sister, or a better-off neighbour. In their daughters' memories, these mothers are tragic figures, often hardened by life events, hard workers, and rarely emotional. A rejection of this model and attempts to create different relationships with their children, characterize the subsequent generation of women: those born in the 1950s and 1960s.

From the vast neighbourhood networks, trajectories branch out that also often represent paths of social advancement. These have their origins in choices that vary in relation to territory, employment, education, and paternal and maternal roles. This is a radical transformation of the family model, as it moves towards what has been described as the "intimate conjugal family."[15] These trends naturally coexist with those examined earlier, contributing to the creation of a composite reality that is full of contrasts, from ideal aspirations to real possibilities.

The women had often had tough childhoods, growing up in large families with many siblings, and not experiencing the tenderness of maternal care. Many had grown up constrained by rigid sexual morality, and suffered from gender discrimination at school. This is particularly evident in rural areas, as illustrated by the story of Maria Cristina, born in 1963, who lived in a small village in the province of Caserta.

Maria Cristina's parents worked all day selling agricultural produce and entrusted her to her grandmother, a strict woman who saw a woman's role and her future as domestic. "The man can do anything, the woman must stay in her proper place": these were the grandmother's words, and her views were perfectly reflected in those of her daughter and son-in-law. By way of example, Maria Cristina told a story of the gender discrimination she experienced in the period when at the national level, and in nearby Naples, feminism was developing:

The darling of the family was my brother, being the youngest, and the only boy ... He grew up wrapped in cotton wool. Consequently if, say, he made

148 G. GRIBAUDI

a mess, if he turned the house upside down, I and only I would be told off, and I'd have to make up for what he'd done. I was often slapped by my mother when he was at fault ... [...] he'd be quite happy about all this. I'll never forget what happened on the sixth of January in 1969 or 1970.[16] The worst and most disappointing day of my life. Two enormous parcels arrived at our house, one for me and one for my brother. I was glowing with joy and happiness, I was so happy, as for the first time ever I'd received a present. My brother opened his first, and he had a great big tractor to play with and enjoy himself. His first toy, his first *befana*. It was my first *befana* too, my first parcel to unwrap. My present? A bowl and a table, for washing clothes. I'll be honest, my first thought was to throw them away, I don't know where or who at, but, because I was well behaved, and out of the respect that I had and still have for my mother, I bowed my head and kept quiet while my brother had fun.

As she grew up, Maria Cristina encountered other forms of discrimination. She was unable to carry on studying:

Simply for being a girl, I wasn't given the chance to study. I dreamt of becoming a lawyer, going to university, but it wasn't possible. My father was possessive: I couldn't take the train, I couldn't leave the village, I couldn't wear make-up or short skirts, I was restricted in every way. My only outings were to Sunday mass. I had friends, but all girls. Men couldn't get anywhere near ... I went on hunger strike, I rebelled! I even started to rage against my mother, as she'd never done anything for me. To realize this dream, my dream!

The world of her relationships was held within a sort of female or family enclosure, as shown by the description of her engagement. It began with silent glimpses:

He courted me, and knew what to do. How? By shadowing me, following my every step, when I went to mass, or shopping, or the market. In every place, on every corner, he was there.

Then the fiancé was accepted, and entered the house:

My husband, then my fiancé, came to the house, introduced himself to my family, we had coffee and at the end of the evening my father said: in this house you're very welcome, we'll treat you like a son, but there are two rules: no going out alone, and you must always toe the line! [...] I had my

NEAPOLITAN MOTHERS: THREE GENERATIONS OF WOMEN... 149

first kiss from my husband and straight after a rain of blows from my father. I shouldn't have done it, and what's more outside, not in the courtyard, but out in the open air. [...] I couldn't be alone with my fiancé, we never went for a sandwich, a pizza, a coffee, or for a walk, and even at home I was watched by him, my mother, my grandma, and my brother.

Eventually Maria Cristina got married and her parents gave her a big wedding, which she was proud of and grateful for. Her husband came from a coastal town and had much more modern ideas:

I'd grown up in a small village, he in a town, Torre del Greco, and he wasn't used to women like me. In his town, the women were different. They had more freedom, they could kiss someone without trouble, and they could even travel with a man.[17]

This marriage produced two children. The new family nucleus was built on new models: friendship and love were now the dominant words in descriptions of relationships between parents and children, as in many other life stories. The mother became a friend. While grandmother and mother had described their childhood as hard, one of Maria Cristina's daughters, Stefania, said she had had a wonderful childhood. Both she and her sister studied to degree level, and her account shows how this choice had been a conscious projection of their mother so that her daughters should in some way make good for what she had suffered:

Thanks to my parents, I had the chance to study. My mother, due to my grandpa's absurd way of thinking, hadn't been able to fulfil her dream of becoming a lawyer, but she gave her daughters the chance to realize their dreams.

Most of the women of the generation born in the 1950s and 1960s talk of tough mothers, limited freedoms, and incomprehension; they portray themselves, instead, as mothers who are open to discussion, responsive and "friends of our daughters." This contrast is seen in the account of a woman born in 1950:

I've had three fantastic sons, I've also had the daughter that I wanted so much, and I've been lucky that my children have all been good. For me they are the most important thing in my life, and my love, my life I dedicate to them. My mother behaved differently with us children, and even now she

150   G. GRIBAUDI

tells me off if I give them too much time; right from when I was little, she gave me only chores. She would pile up tasks for us, and we would have to obey. It's true that in this way she made us responsible, but it meant that our childhood was all chores. I, on the other hand, tried to behave differently with my children, trying to do everything myself, even little things like putting out the rubbish or paying their taxes, even now that they're married.[18]

The investment of both parents in their children changed. In this regard the transformation of the man's role was important: he became responsible, looking for a steady job and ensuring the family's sustenance, but his role had to narrow. While the model of the woman as "angel of the hearth," a perfect wife and mother had dominated fascist propaganda, it was not until the postwar period that this became a reality for these social groups.

From this perspective women's space in this generation was in some respects restricted compared to their mothers, which had been open to the neighbourhood. Both in town and in the country, much of life had unfolded outside the walls of the house, as in the Calabria described by Siebert:

The old social exchange between women was linked to the poverty of their material life: almost nothing came in or had to be done within the house, from the water, to the vegetable garden, to things they made for their own use. [...] The material configuration of the house, without precise boundaries with the alley or the courtyard, offered opportunities for meeting and moving about that the new well-being made redundant. Now, everything is inside [...] and the house, or really the apartment, contains a comfortable space, but an extremely closed one. The figure who reigns supreme and alone within these walls is a new and modern one: the housewife.[19]

Obviously, there were women who worked, but many chose to stay at home to look after their children. There were also the difficulties of the labour market, especially pronounced in the South. These were the years, especially in Naples, when all those skilled activities that had provided work for a great number of women (dressmaking, stitching together gloves, bags, and shoes, for example) experienced a crisis and were greatly scaled down, and in the country there was a permanent contraction of agriculture. Much of the work traditionally done by women was thus cut back, while only a few managed to enter the burgeoning tertiary sector. Moreover, those who wanted to leave behind the conditions of their childhood rejected manual jobs, nor did they want to get involved in informal trade networks like many women of the previous generation.[20] In some ways the women of this generation seem weaker in social terms, but they retained considerable status in the family as mothers, strengthened by the intense emotional investment that had previously been absent.

We thus have the husband at work and the wife looking after the home and children. This was the model energetically promoted in Italy by the Catholic Church and by the legislation of the new Italian republic, which until 1975 gave the man and husband a central role: head of the family, and undisputed leader and ruler. The principle that sanctioned this situation was "*patria potestà*" ("paternal authority"), only abolished in 1975, when the rights and responsibilities for ensuring children's development were extended to women.[21]

It should be said that these stories follow paths of limited or moderate social mobility: from conditions of relative neediness and vulnerability, people reached satisfactory standards of living. The shrinking of the nuclear family, with the reduction in numbers of children, was a central element of this transformation.[22] Mothers who were housewives wanted something different for their daughters: fulfilment of their true identity as women through motherhood remained a fixed element, but was no longer exclusive, coexisting with study and work. Education, which they regretted missing, was the central focus of their hopes for their sons and daughters.[23]

In the stories of the third generation, women born after the 1970s, we see momentous changes. All of them have studied, many at university. All aspire to fulfilment in their work, and for some this is a priority. Very many of them stated explicitly that their ideal was to combine the roles of wife, mother and worker. In practice this meant that the women of the previous generation would have to help look after their grandchildren. Italian public welfare policy, much focused on the waged head of family, reinforces this model.[24] Cultural models, legislation and institutions combine to maintain the model of motherhood and female care, strengthening the relationship between the generations of mothers. This includes negotiation, exchange and conflict, as seen in the extracts from interviews that follow. Parents speak first, then their daughters:

Husband: We were hoping that Raffaella wouldn't pass the admission exams for Medicine, because we thought it was very hard work and not the best choice of work for a woman.

152   G. GRIBAUDI

Wife:

Especially me. I asked her: do you want to be ful-filled as a woman as well? And she said yes, she liked children. And I said to her: well look, I'm advising you against it because it's a really hard job. My greatest hope ... it was ... if you are a woman, you have to take a path that brings you to teaching, in the subject you want, but in teaching ... because a woman who does teaching has the summer free and can be with her children, two weeks at Christmas, a week at Easter, it's different, you have a break so you can be at home and be there for your children. I tried to go that way but they didn't listen to me, any type of teaching, because I saw it as the only way possible for a woman, that could fit in with the role of mother...

Daughter (age 37):

She says she doesn't want to influence us but actu-ally it was clear to us all ... for me and for Carmen the paths were clear: I was supposed to choose Classics after high school, and so I'd have been a Latin teacher and would have been all right. Carmen was supposed to take Languages and be a language teacher. For her [the mother], being a teacher was the ideal job for a woman, as you can also look after your family. And so ... in fact, she never approved of me choosing Medicine. Even when I sat the entrance exam, she never prayed for me, so that I would pass ... and she's always prayed for everything: for the state exam, for Carmen ... in my case she didn't say a single prayer ... nothing ... she didn't want to...
[*But is she happy now?*] Look, I think she is happy, that is a mother is always pleased that her own daughter has become a doctor, a professional, but in her heart, I think, she wanted something else. She finds it very hard that I work long hours, I'm often not at home and I can't watch over my children...

The mother described with great clarity the model that still prevails in Italian society. The daughter, however, distanced herself from this mater-nal model. In this case there was an explicit discontinuity between the

NEAPOLITAN MOTHERS: THREE GENERATIONS OF WOMEN... 153

generations over the models to conform to. The daughter had chosen fulfilment through study and work in conflict with her mother, who, however, while still critical, gave in and looked after her grandchildren.

I would like to conclude by quoting part of a presentation by one of my female students:

> The work is based on three interviews, with three women in the same family. The grandmother, Elvira, aged 71, was the third of five children. She and her family were abandoned by the father, and she and her mother and siblings were forced to support themselves by working. Married at seventeen to a man who had lost both parents through the war, she had seven children. Her daughter Angela, aged 47, fifth of the seven, suffered during childhood from the family's financial situation; she is married with two children, and her husband is a mechanic. The granddaughter Michela, 21, Angela's first child, has one younger brother. She had a lovely childhood and a carefree youth, and hopes for a good job and the attainment of her ambitions.

This extract neatly summarizes the transformation experienced by the three generations of women I have presented in this section. The grandmother embodied the generation who lived through dramatic absences and difficult material conditions, working from a young age onwards; they were mothers with numerous offspring, to whom they could not give especial attention. The mother nicely represented the generation that Ginatempo has called "women on the border": having grown up in a traditional family with six brothers and sisters and great financial difficulties, she instead chose to have just two children to whom she could guarantee care and attention. She was a housewife, and her husband's earnings supported the family financially. Her student daughter represented the first generation able to have a cared-for and carefree childhood, and expressed the new ideals of emancipation through a job appropriate to her studies.

Told like this, their story seems a perfectly unilinear path: from multifarious starting points (the grandmothers), via the housewife mothers, we arrive at a homogeneous model that conforms to the ideal typologies of "modernity" (the grand-daughters). As we have seen, however, historical periods can involve territories and individual stories in different ways, and generate fresh hybrids. In the lives of the young women, different worlds often coexist: they are immersed in and identify with the relationships and values constructed in the spheres of work and social friendship, but are also helped and advised by their mothers, mothers-in-law, and other female relatives, who provide an essential material and psychological reference point. In the lives of this generation, models, customs and values come together in new ways, which are often not acknowledged in their accounts; these young women are consciously trying to cultivate a female ideal that differs from the traditional one. In Naples, the need to emphasize difference is more pressing than elsewhere: difference from a generation or from models that are known and rejected, but also from the negative stereotypes that the rest of the nation has about the South, which are so much stronger when discussing the position of women. An educated young Neapolitan woman primarily wants to show that she is not what others would have her believe; from the information acquired through, for example, education, books, mass media and travel, she has developed an image of herself as modern and European that she wants to conform to both in reality and in representation.

Reality, however, is more problematic as regards the dreams and aspirations of youth. Female unemployment, especially in the South but right across Italy, is currently rising, and consequently young women are often compelled to make painful adjustments to their ambitions and ideal models.[25] This is a terrible defeat for mothers who dreamed of a different future for their daughters, and for daughters unable to achieve the dual role they had aspired to.

From this perspective, the path taken by these three generations is more complex than it might initially seem. Working grandmothers, housewife mothers, graduate daughters: this has been a classic sequence of the family memories of women in twentieth-century Europe, within which the housewife mothers delegated their own emancipation to their daughters; in some countries these daughters, in honouring their mothers' aspirations, were often the main protagonists of the European feminist movement of the 1970s, and achieved real progress in their social and political lives. In this case, however, the new generation faces an economic crisis rather than a boom, interrupting a path of emancipation and social mobility. In the background the traditional strength of Geppina demonstrates how the trajectory of gender transformations is much more tortuous and contradictory than that seen in a stereotyped and unilinear representation of the passage from traditional society to modernity.

Translated by Stuart Oglethorpe

NOTES

1. Niceforo, *L'Italia barbara*, p. 293. References to a North that follows the rules of the father and a South that follows the rules of the mother are common, including within the most learned debates. This concept, with reference to Italy as a whole, was revisited by Antonio Gambino in *Inventario italiano* (1998), which has a very telling sub-title: *Costumi e mentalità di un Paese materno* ("The customs and mentality of a maternal country"). On the cover it says about Italy's chronic ills: "they can be identified in the predominance of a maternal family model which has very deep roots. For Italians, the *mamma* and the family come first, and against civil society. Protective, enveloping and always ready to forgive, tradition's Great Mother has for centuries exercised a possessive protection that embodies the negation of society and history." Some writers and essayists should be reminded that in the twentieth century it has been totalitarian states that have embodied the law of the father with greater force and conviction, committing the most shameful acts in its name. On stereotypes and representations arising in Italy during its unification process, see a body of criticism and analysis in Gribaudi, "Images of the South" and Patriarca, *Italian Vices.*
2. The stories and recordings are conserved in the Archivio multimediale di Storia Orale, Dipartimento di Scienze Sociali, Università di Napoli Federico II.
3. "Working class" in this case means that the first generation belonged to a world with low levels of education and engaged in manual employment, as workers and peasants in the urban and rural contexts respectively.
4. Quotations from the comedies of Eduardo De Filippo (1900–84), the greatest writer of plays in Neapolitan and known and loved throughout Italy, are taken here from the 1979 edition of *I capolavori di Eduardo.* The comedy *Filumena Marturano* is from 1946.
5. See the analysis by Gambino: "The public (in this strong exaltation of maternal and familial values, to which there implicitly corresponds an equally strong denial of any significant 'paternal' need) is also all on the side of Filumena, and of the phrase ('children are children') with which she explains and justifies her behaviour. Beyond its apparently circular reasoning this phrase is the motto for maternal and familial mentality, inasmuch as it indicates that for the sake of one's children anything is permissible, and that it would be neither possible nor right to make any distinction between them on the basis of some criterion of merit" (*Inventario italiano*, p. 48).
6. De Filippo, *I capolavori*, vol. 1, pp. 322 and 346.

7. De Filippo, *I capolavori*, vol. 1, pp. 175–76.
8. This and the quotations that follow are taken from the English translation, *The Land of Cockayne*, published in 1901.
9. Gribaudi, "Donne di camorra."
10. The term "*guappo*" indicates a respected figure, or man of honour, who puts himself forward to resolve conflicts in the quarter. A *guappo* is a complex figure who moves between the mythical role of protector of the vulnerable and the violent imposition of his own authority.
11. I first recorded the life story of Rosa (not her real name) in 1991, and then periodically followed this up thereafter.
12. The "*bassi*" are single-room or two-room ground-floor apartments, opening directly onto the street, linked both materially and symbolically to the population's poorest social strata.
13. In this case it should be emphasized how the mother's experience influenced her daughter's choices. On this issue see Mercer et al., *Transitions in a Woman's Life*, especially ch. 5, "The Awesome Mother: Her Influence on Her Daughter," pp. 91–110.
14. The Annunziata foundling hospital in Naples took in newborn abandoned children from the fourteenth century until 1980.
15. Marzio Barbagli, in *Sotto lo stesso tetto*, introduced the concept of the "intimate conjugal family" as the new family model, established during the twentieth century at different speeds depending on context and social group. In this the roles of husband and wife became more flexible, authority relationships were modified, more attention was paid to the children, and relationships were based on love and intimacy. This concept has been revisited by Chiara Saraceno, who defines it as "the family in which the couple's relationship is central, and the two partners expect from each other more than the division of labor within a common enterprise and the availability for sexual relations either for reproductive purposes or in order to contain their drives, especially those of the male. They also expect love and, especially, intimacy" (*Coppie e famiglie*, p. 33).
16. On 6 January (Epiphany) it is traditional, especially in southern Italy, to give children presents. The "Befana" is an old woman who supposedly secretly brings these presents.
17. Until the 1970s and 1980s, long after the legendary 1968, there was still strict control in the countryside over young women in public spaces. In this regard there was a significant difference between Naples and the coastal towns. As a woman born in 1961, who grew up in a village on the slopes of Vesuvius, explained: "My dad was from Naples and so he gave us a more open mentality than that of the village. In fact I always found the narrower mentality of the place very difficult ... […] We were always more free, I, my sister, and my brother." She went about freely and went on trips

NEAPOLITAN MOTHERS: THREE GENERATIONS OF WOMEN... 157

and holidays with her boyfriend, while her female friends only went out accompanied by older sisters or their brothers.

18. Similar feelings emerge from the stories of Calabrian women collected by Renate Siebert: "Those mothers (the grandmothers) were distant, unapproachable for their daughters, and were not seeking a relationship of intimacy. Modern ideas about childhood, the sensitivities of the adult towards the specific needs of their young son or daughter, had not yet penetrated the grandmothers' culture: for many of the mothers, as well as being a painful memory, this served to help establish a different relationship with their daughters. [...] *With my mother, there's more distance. I feel closer to my children, I feel I'm entirely for my children. I try to make them happy in every way possible, and my mother didn't do this. She never did this*." ("*È femmina, però è bella*", pp. 76–77).

19. Siebert, "*È femmina, però è bella*," pp. 98–99.

20. Nella Ginatempo calls women from Messina, of the same generation, "women on the border": "[w]omen in Messina live on the border of two different worlds with friction between them. Two worlds as universes of symbols that give meaning to their identity and actions: one is the world of tradition presented by the mothers [...] and the other is the world of modernity with its objects, symbols, and myths, especially that of emancipation, longed for by many but reached only by a few" (*Donne al confine*, p. 10).

21. Willson, *Women in Twentieth-Century Italy*, p. 159.

22. However, the models of the first generation persist in some social groups, including camorra gangs and marginal strata linked to the illegal economy. In these cases, the model of the very large family still exists, with women taking on a role similar to that outlined for Geppina, the Neapolitan woman of the first generation. See Gribaudi, "Clan camorristi a Napoli," and "Donne di camorra."

23. See, again, Siebert's analysis regarding Calabrian women of the same generation: "[e]ducation symbolizes the opening to the world, the chances of a better future, in terms of social welfare and greater personal dignity. Even mothers wary of the dangers of today's freedoms are sure of this: education breaches the otherwise impassable wall of tradition, which wants women kept within the domestic space" ("*È femmina, però è bella*," p. 88).

24. Saraceno, *Mutamenti della famiglia*; Naldini and Saraceno, *Conciliare famiglia e lavoro*.

25. According to the Istituto Nazionale di Statistica (ISTAT), in the fourth quarter of 2014, female unemployment was 14.7 per cent nationally and 24.2 per cent in the South, while the rate of female economic inactivity (women of working age not currently employed or actively seeking work) was 59.5 per cent in the South as against 36.3 per cent in the North

158 G. GRIBAUDI

(ISTAT, "Occupati e disoccupati," pp. 5, 12). Furthermore, there was a growth in the proportion of women who were in employment when pregnant but were no longer working two years after childbirth: from 18.4 per cent nationally in 2005 to 22.3 per cent in 2012, and as high as 29.8 per cent in the South (ISTAT, *Rapporto Annuale 2014*, pp. 127–28).

BIBLIOGRAPHY

Barbagli, Marzio. *Sotto lo stesso tetto. Mutamenti della famiglia in Italia dal XV al XX secolo*. Bologna: Il Mulino, 1984.

De Filippo, Eduardo. *I capolavori di Eduardo*. 2 vols. Turin: Einaudi, 1979.

Di Giacomo, Salvatore. *Opere*. 2 vols. Edited by Francesco Flora and Mario Vinciguerra. Milan: Mondadori, 1952.

Gambino, Antonio. *Inventario italiano: costumi e mentalità di un Paese materno*. Turin: Einaudi, 1998.

Ginatempo, Nella. *Donne al confine. Identità e corsi di vita femminili nella città del Sud*. Milan: Franco Angeli, 1994.

Gribaudi, Gabriella. "Images of the South," in *Italian Cultural Studies: An Introduction*, edited by David Forgacs and Robert Lumley, pp. 72–87. Oxford: Oxford University Press, 1996.

Gribaudi, Gabriella. "Clan camorristi a Napoli: radicamento locale e traffici internazionali." In *Traffici criminali. Camorra, mafie e reti internazionali dell'illegalità*, edited by Gabriella Gribaudi, pp. 187–240. Turin: Bollati Boringhieri, 2009.

Gribaudi, Gabriella. "Donne di camorra e identità di genere." *Meridiana* n. 67 (2010): pp. 145–154.

ISTAT, "Occupati e disoccupati." *Flash Statistiche*, 2 March 2015.

ISTAT, *Rapporto Annuale 2014*. Rome: ISTAT, 2014.

Mercer, Ramona T., Elizabeth G. Nichols, and Glen Caspers Doyle. *Transitions in a Woman's Life: Major Life Events in Developmental Context*. New York: Springer, 1989.

Naldini, Manuela, and Chiara Saraceno. *Conciliare famiglia e lavoro. Vecchi e nuovi patti tra sessi e generazioni*. Bologna: Il Mulino, 2011.

Niceforo, Alfredo. *L'Italia barbara contemporanea. Studi ed appunti*. Milan–Palermo: Sandron, 1898.

Patriarca, Silvana. *Italian Vices: Nation and character from the Risorgimento to the Republic*. Cambridge: Cambridge University Press, 2010.

Saraceno, Chiara. *Mutamenti della famiglia e politiche sociali in Italia*. Bologna: Il Mulino, 2003.

Saraceno, Chiara. *Coppie e famiglie. Non è questione di natura*. Milan: Feltrinelli, 2012.

Serao, Matilde. *The Land of Cockayne*. 2 vols. New York: Harper, 1901. [First published in Italian as *Il paese di cuccagna*. Milan: Treves, 1891.]

Siebert, Renate. *"È femmina, però è bella"*. *Tre generazioni di donne al sud*. Turin: Rosenberg e Sellier, 1991.

Willson, Perry. *Women in Twentieth-Century Italy*. Basingstoke: Palgrave Macmillan, 2010.

CHAPTER 7

Mammas in Italian Migrant Families: The Anglophone Countries

Maddalena Tirabassi

INTRODUCTION: ARCHETYPES AND STEREOTYPES

Stereotypes of the Italian *mamma* in Italy and abroad have developed following separate trajectories, only coinciding at certain points. The models of the Risorgimento mother and the Catholic mother, shaped in the years before and after Italian unification, have been reconstructed by Marina d'Amelia: the first had as its essential feature the educative function of the maternal figure while the second focused on motherhood as a vocation, and neither was relevant to the overwhelming majority of those who wished to emigrate.[1] These models never reached the women of the lower classes, especially in the Italian South, who were subject to entirely different religious and behavioural codes. In other words, the archetype of the new mother figure that the Italian bourgeoisie developed—a mother close to her children, being neither rich enough to afford a nanny nor poor enough to have to leave her children for work—was conceived for the growing middle classes.[2] This new model of the maternal figure had nothing to do with southern peasant women, who started to develop their own, different model, linked in particular to migration.

M. Tirabassi (✉)
Centro Altreitalie sulle Migrazioni Italiane, Turin, Italy
e-mail: redazione@altreitalie.it

© The Author(s) 2018
P. Morris, P. Willson (Eds.), *La Mamma*,
Italian and Italian American Studies,
https://doi.org/10.1057/978-1-137-54256-4_7

161

162   M. TIRABASSI

We will be looking in this chapter at the transition of the Italian *mamma* from archetype to stereotype, analysing a range of successful novels, films and television series. We will be focusing mainly on the United States since, to paraphrase the Canadian historian Francesca L'Orfano, the Anglophone cinematic world is dominated by that country's film industry, which "disseminate[s] one-dimensional stereotypical renditions of Italian culture."[3] It was here, in fact, that the contemporary stereotype of the Italian *mamma* in emigrant communities was created and popularized, first through literature and then through the mass media. North American research on Italian immigrant women has, over the last thirty years, underlined their conservatism and location in the domestic sphere, developing a discourse on domesticity and sexuality that reflected the parameters of the middle classes in the Anglophone world and led to the establishment of a paradigm for the entire Italian diaspora.[4]

The "American" image of the Italian family at the start of the twentieth century was still that of an extended patriarchal family held together by very strong family ties,[5] but, as the analysis of Italian sources of the period show us, the extremely close relationships attributed to the Italian American family were a novelty compared to the realities of family life prior to migration: they resulted, in fact, from the combination of improvements in living conditions in America and ideals held regarding the family in their homeland, rather than being simply the survival of Italian culture. We will see how the family models that were established by Italian American literary and cinematographic production sometimes faithfully reflected reality but came to influence behaviour, becoming models for generations of descendants of immigrants in search of an identity.

With the aim of deconstructing the stereotype, the analytical approach will be historical, transnational and comparative: there will be an examination of the evolution over time of the archetype (quickly descending into a stereotype) of the maternal figure, from the era of mass migration onwards; there will be a comparison of the histories of women in Italy and emigrant women; and there will be comparison with other ethnic groups.[6] An inter-disciplinary approach will be used, drawing on sociology, demography, statistics, and the analysis of literary and autobiographical texts in relation to a range of cinematographic, ethnographic and anthropological sources.

The Old World

In late nineteenth-century Italy most families in the South were nuclear, but among the lower classes the modern family, based on romantic choices rather than economic interests, was yet to arrive.[7] Italian sources, such as the investigations conducted, firstly by Stefano Jacini, who oversaw the agrarian survey carried out between 1877 and 1884, and secondly by Eugenio Faina in the first decade of the twentieth century, offer some insight into family life at the time.[8] However, it must be remembered that the investigators were men who belonged for the most part to the Italian bourgeoisie; their interpretations of behaviour relating to morality were influenced by the bourgeois principles that had taken shape in the post-unification period.

As regards the poorer strata of the population of southern Italy across the nineteenth century, family unity was more an aspiration, which would materialize through emigration or, in Italy, with the improvement in economic conditions some decades later, than a reality. Any sort of domesticity or closeness was hindered by the long absences of the men, working far from home, sometimes for days; by the women's obligation to work in every type of domestic industry (such as vegetable gardening, weaving or spinning) as well as working in the fields if they were close enough to home, preventing them from attending to their children; and by the living conditions themselves.

Some comments in the agrarian surveys make it clear how financial concerns rather than sentiment ruled the peasant family. In Campania, the investigator Fedele de Siervo observed that "here the family is a necessity not created by sentimentalism, but by mutual interest,"[9] and later expanded on this:

> Emotional ties [...] are neither the principal motive nor the foundation for their conjugal association [...]. In general, our peasants express the view that their wives make excellent working partners, and their children are a resource; it is thus the case that domestic society very often rests more on interests of convenience, imposed by the needs and the nature of our agricultural practices, than on ties of attraction and emotion.[10]

The official tasked with researching Sicily wrote that "in marriage, the man looks for a wife who is healthy and wealthy. [...] In general, the bridegroom wants a wife with savings, nothing else. [...] The countryman grieves for his donkey more than for his wife."[11]

164 M. TIRABASSI

These surveys shed light on aspects of the figure and responsibilities of the mother, and of her relationship with her children:

> While the husband rules the household for the brief time that he is resident, the wife oversees the marriage of her male children, chooses the bride, fixes the wedding, and imposes this on her husband and her sons. The woman marries having only just attained her majority, bringing her linen chest and her bed as her dowry. A good *mamma* cannot rest if she is not putting aside, a little at a time, linen and a trousseau for her daughters. [...] In Noto the peasant's wife always stays in the house, busy making socks and patching up linen and clothes, waiting for Saturday evening when her husband returns home. In Avola, when she is not looking after her husband, she works on the small bits of land that the family own. The wife has to address her peasant husband formally, serve him at table before she can sit down to eat, and ask him to say grace on every occasion. [On Sundays], in certain squalid locations lit by oil lamps, people smoke and drink, and the tarantella is danced to the sound of the violin by two men with some unscrupulous women (two dances for a penny). The peasant's wife, however, never takes part in these outlandish amusements and suffers in seeing him return home late, exhausted by his debauchery. [...] Leaving for work on Monday, he packs up all the bread he can find, leaving the family to feed itself on crusts and crumbs. On holiday evenings, after the rosary, the family converse.[12]

Among the poorer classes of agricultural society in southern Italy, the ties between parents and children were not especially strong. The relationships between mothers and their offspring were dictated by the rules of basic survival; in those areas where women were working at some distance from home, at the point of childbirth they only stopped work for a few days:

> then they take their children and nurslings into the fields [...]. When they can walk they are entrusted to old women that make this their profession, who put ten or twelve children together in a single room. Sometimes they are left to themselves. [One hears of] culpable homicides due to burns, scalding with boiling water, falls, bites from pigs and other animals, and every day stories in the newspapers report some of these cases.[13]

The minimal respect of children towards their parents was noted, with "children who deny support to their old and infirm fathers."[14] It was also observed that "paternal authority progressively declines as the children become self-sufficient and leave home to set up families."[15] Family dynamics were discussed again later in the report:

> Thus the family is a necessity created not by sentiment, but by mutual interest [...] they marry straight after military service [...]. These two existences are necessary to each other, since both work with equal zeal; the children they produce are only inactive within the family for a few years, and then contribute, at least in part, to supporting themselves by guarding the animals and undertaking other tasks. It is improper to remain without a companion: widows and widowers remarry.[16]

It was noted that in Basilicata and Calabria "the family is led by the parents, who become recipients of their children's wages," but in the Abruzzi children left home soon after becoming adults to establish a new family, and "the tie of paternal authority is of brief duration."[17] In the province of Catanzaro, it was observed that "family ties are very loose; sons leave at the age of 22 or 23, abandoning their elderly parents to abject poverty."[18] In the inquiry led by Jacini, figures were also compiled, for many Italian provinces, on the crimes of adultery, prostitution, incest and rape, and on illegitimate births.

THE UNITED STATES

In the United States a few studies, based on specific sources like reports by social workers and court records offering evidence as to the living conditions of the poorest immigrants, have demonstrated that the Italian family was nothing like as cohesive as the "fingers of the one hand" metaphor; it was not only minimally governed by sentimental/emotional attachments, but was afflicted by violence, rape and incest, just as in Italy.[19] Most of the research on immigrants, however, interprets family cohesion as representing continuity with the past, rather than a change.[20]

Italian peasant women were not used to articulating and verbalizing their feelings and this problem was destined to persist for a long time after they had settled in America. First- and second-generation immigrant women born between 1900 and 1920 were interviewed by the psychologist Elisabeth Messina, and from this series of interviews the continuities with Italy emerge: first, the meagreness of "emotional interactions" between parents and children, and above all the lack of "emotional intimacy and sexual fulfillment" between husband and wife.[21] As one inter-

166 M. TIRABASSI

viewee said, "[o]ur parents' marriages worked because there were no other options open to them."

Regarding these women and their emotions, Messina found that:

> [N]one of them had been educated in their families of origin to put their feelings into words. [...] [P]arents' and children's fulfillment was derived from their role in meeting family responsibilities rather than through fulfillment of one's personal desires or needs. [...] The women seemed to identify with their mothers as the centers of the household. [...] [M]arriage was often a source of inescapable suffering that provided little opportunity for the development of love and affection.[22]

However, Messina's interviews also suggest a break with the past in the emergence of a family cohesiveness that extended across the generations: "parental affection, combined with strong parental control as well as the presence of an extended network of kin and friends, contributed to the development and maintenance of family stability and cohesiveness."[23] In the United States there evolved a sort of familism, not necessarily amoral, that had its origins in the marked suspicion of state institutions that had developed in Italy; relocated to America, this could be seen in the reluctance of the first generations to register their children for school, or to turn to state bodies for help.[24] In general, it can be argued that, by emigrating, men and women were able to develop ideals of the family that in Italy had been prevented by poverty and ignorance.

GOOD *MAMMAS*, MADONNAS, MAFIA *MAMMAS* AND THE INVENTION OF A STEREOTYPE

Literary works depicting the first wave of emigration to the United States offer images of strong women, and tend not to show those who could not cope or who could not control inter-generational conflict. The latter remained deep within the tenements. Their images, immortalized in the photographic work of Jacob Riis and Lewis Hine, played an important part in the early twentieth-century American debate on social conditions.[25]

"When you turn to Italian American writers you begin to find strong portrayals of mothers, and most of them come from Mary's mould," according to the Italian American writer Fred Gardaphé. He argues that in

American literature the figure of the mother often reflects the Catholic image of the suffering Madonna, and expands on this:

> [F]or Catholics, the ideal of motherhood has always been the Virgin Mary, a mother who is pretty much defined in terms of a family's needs [...] the "mater dolorosa," or suffering mother. [...] It is the seriousness or *la serietà* that defines the woman who is the heart of the family that her husband heads.[26]

With time and improvements in economic conditions, the mother's role also came to include responsibility for preserving the honour and good standing of the entire family nucleus.[27]

In many novels and films, from the 1940s onwards, the figure of the father is replaced by that of the sons, not only in emotional terms but also as providers and decision-makers. Daughters, on the other hand, are expected to conform to the maternal model. Some features of the culture of origin, arranged or proxy marriages, in other words marriages without love, may explain the very close relationships that developed between mothers and their children, especially sons.[28]

For widowed mothers this was especially the case, as we see in Pietro di Donato's *Christ in Concrete*, a novel published in the United States in 1937 and set in the 1920s.[29] In its first few pages the close relationship between the mother and her first-born child is clearly portrayed: 12-year-old Paul is ready to take the place of his father Geremio, a skilled worker who has died on a building site the day before Good Friday. "Am I not he? [...] Am I not my father's son?" (46)[30] he cries silently at the funeral. Not long after, he reassures his mother, Annunziata: "Mama, do not cry—I—I—shall be the father" (49). He does in fact take his father's place on the site, and becomes "the father of his father's family" (160), looking after his seven siblings and even playing the role formally at mealtimes:

> At evenfall when from the street came distantly his step, at window, her head would bow in thanksgiving. [...]. Paul ... mine. Everything for him. Paul, Paul. [...] Head-chair of table and richest dish for my Paul. [...] Salt and pepper and clean serviette. (299–300)

Early Italian American literature included other detailed descriptions of family life and roles, by men who were seeking to reconcile their own identity as Italian males with American models of masculinity, and doing

168 M. TIRABASSI

this through their writing.[31] Paradoxically, it was they, through the very successful novels and films which we will be considering, who created the strongest image of the Italian male, that of the gangster, which replaced the images of the poor organ-grinder, the exploited worker and the exotic Latin lover personified by Rudolf Valentino.[32] If we accept Gardaphé's thesis, the identity of the Italian American male has been constructed, starting with the figure of the *mafioso*, by a continuous play of mirrors that saw facts become fiction, which in turn influenced reality: "[t]he gangsters created by Hollywood eventually come to represent all Italian and Italian-American men past, present, and future."[33] A long string of films and novels, often of mediocre quality, then contributed to the spread of the image of the macho *mafioso* and mother's boy that would endure for decades to come.

Returning to the portrayal of the Italian American mother, this was further developed in *The Fortunate Pilgrim*, a novel by Mario Puzo published in 1964, through the figure of Lucia Santa, which then provided the model for many other stories and screenplays.[34] The story is set in late 1920s New York, and tells of the endeavours of another strong mother, with five children, who arrives in America after a proxy marriage, is widowed, and remarries. In this novel the behavioural norms governing the Italian American family are spelt out. While arguing with her oldest son, Larry, she warns him that "[m]y children sleep under my roof until they are married. My children do not become drunkards or fight with drunkards, or go to jail, or go to the electric chairs" (66). However, when Larry defends his younger brother in a fight she is reassured: "[h]e still knew what a brother meant; that there was no obligation more sacred than blood, that it came before country, church, wife, woman, and money" (72). The children will live in the same building as their mother even when they get married, and will maintain their presence at her table because for Sunday lunch "everyone in the family, married or not, must attend" (246). Moreover, the children give their pay packets to their mother, as her daughter Octavia observes: "Larry gives you money every week. Vinnie hands over his pay envelope without even opening it" (209). Her sons are forgiven for their misdemeanours, as the youngest brother Vinnie recalls: "he remembered the pride hidden in his mother's voice when she reproached Larry for taking advantage of young girls" (215). The final requirement of the Italian mother is the choice of the appropriate wife, to take care of her sons as she would have done herself:

MAMMAS IN ITALIAN MIGRANT FAMILIES: THE ANGLOPHONE... 169

Lucia Santa wanted each of her sons to marry a good Italian girl who knew from the cradle, that man ruled, must be waited on like a duke, fed good food that took hours to prepare; who cared for the children and the house without whining for help. (191)

The Italian American writer Thomas Ferraro interprets this novel as a true story: a piece of autobiographical writing by Puzo on immigration and settlement in which he revisited his own history. Ferraro concludes that "the received stereotype of the peasant Italian mother *is* true, making it an archetype."[35]

Considerable time was in fact needed for writers to be able to recount their own experiences as descendants of immigrants. It took years for an Italian American literature to emerge that gave its protagonists a voice freed from clichés.[36] Gay Talese has admitted that he started writing his novel *Unto the Sons,* dedicated to his father, in 1955, but then had to break off half way through:

I was concerned that a book focusing on my father's past would bring him unwanted attention and perhaps even ridicule from his American friends and neighbors in the conservative Anglo-Saxon community along the New Jersey shoreline, where, after 30 years of residence, he was accepted as an assimilated citizen of the United States. The instinct to protect my father should come as no surprise to the American-Italian writers of my generation. Not to protect the privacy of one's family from the potential exploitation of one's prose was considered unpardonable within our ethnic group, which was overwhelmingly of southern Italian origin and was still influenced, even a generation or two after our parents' or grandparents' arrival in America, by that Mediterranean region's ancient exhortations regarding prudence, family honor and the safeguarding of secrets.[37]

For the women, all this seems even truer. As Mary Jo Bona says in her introduction to *The Voices We Carry:*

The writers collected in this anthology all acknowledge implicitly the dual and conflicting role involved in being a daughter of Italian or Sicilian ancestors and the writer who breaks away from the traditions imposed by the code of *omertà* (silence) in order to write the family's secrets [...] we leave the closely-knit Italian American culture which [quoting Tina De Rosa] "regardless of our education, expects us still to be more or less like them, which still expects us to get married and have babies." What this culture did not expect was for Italian American women to be married with children *and* write. Writing the family's secrets may very well border on treason.[38]

170   M. TIRABASSI

Another important element that helps to explain the delayed development of an ethnic literature is introduced by Talese's statement that he had not wanted to compromise his father's entry into the "WASP" world. As argued by Anthony Tamburri, taking up the analysis by Daniel Aaron, non-Anglo-Saxon writers went through three phases: in the first, they sought to ingratiate themselves with the American public by using their writing to eliminate the negative stereotypes regarding their own ethnic group; in the second, they humanized the stereotyped images in order to dispel the prejudice attached to them; only in the third phase, by which time they had become part of the dominant culture, did they no longer have to deny their ethnicity. Then they felt free from previous constraints and were able to start producing literature.[39]

This applies to another contemporary author, Fred Gardaphé, whose personal history provides an example of how stereotypes and reality sometimes coincide. Gardaphé told his story in an interview for the Turin newspaper *La Stampa*: born in Chicago into a Calabrian family, he saw his father, uncle and godfather all killed by the mafia, probably due to a settling of accounts within the organization.[40] His mother, left on her own with small children, entrusted him to another boss who had in fact been responsible for his father's death. As a young man, Gardaphé worked for the organization. At some point the boss, on the eve of a crisis within the gang, gave him money to start a career outside the mafia, and he took this opportunity to enrol at university, where in due course he became a lecturer. In a recent essay, published in the anthology *Italian Women in Chicago*, he continued his personal tale.[41] Not long after his divorce he entered analysis, and was encouraged by the analyst to get his mother to tell her own story. Initially, he felt confused:

> My mother, orphaned at the age of 7 and widowed at the age of 35 was a saint and none of my problems could possibly have been caused by a Saint Anna. And what could be wrong, I was the oldest son to an Italian American mother!

Having listened to her story, he wrote:

> She did raise four tough kids pretty much on her own. And that, for me, was enough to turn her into a saint. But the more I found out about her by listening to her story, the more human I realized she was, and how her failings might have contributed to the making of me. I went through some periods of anger, and then, having understood that anger, began to feel sorry for her, and then, came upon a new understanding of our relationship.

A less dramatic insight into contemporary relationships between mother and son can be found in a story by John Calabro, a second-generation Canadian of Sicilian origin. In "A Glass of Wine" he articulates the feelings of a son tiring of the excessive attentions of his mother, who continues to treat him like a child due to his inability to meet her expectations of seeing him established with a nice family, like his sisters:

He comes in and takes off his shoes.
She offers a pair of slippers and says, "The floor is cold, they *are* ceramic tiles after all".
He would have liked to refuse since he doesn't like slippers [...] but he doesn't and puts them on to make her happy.
As he walks into the family room, he looks at the old photographs huddled against each other in various sized frames, sitting on top of the TV cabinet.
There are no pictures of him as an adult, only of him as a child. His two sisters, their husbands and numerous children are there, displayed in full familial bliss.
He sits at the kitchen table, the same seat he takes every time, the one against the wall.
His mother removes the doily and the centerpiece from the table, and replaces it with a nicer one, the one reserved for guests. Solemn, with an exaggerated sense of gravity, she brings out a plate filled with homemade cookies that she keeps in the fridge and another smaller plate with roasted almonds. He watches her as she moves around the kitchen and he listens to the sound of the cupboards opening and closing. Mesmerized by the precision of her routine, he follows the serving dishes as they, in the quiet of the house, smack the surface of the table. The fridge door creaks open again and she comes up with a fruit platter that includes peeled and diced prickly pears, a dish she has prepared well in advance, and just for him. She sets each plate on the table without a word. It is a ritual of silent activities that he knows too well.[42]

In the tale of *Umbertina*, Helen Barolini portrays the change in the role of mothers over time in a transnational perspective, comparing the experience of Italian women in America with that of women in Italy.[43] This novel, written in the turbulent years of American feminism, takes a path that intertwines the searches for ethnic and gender identity. The four generations of women illustrate the changing role of the mother across more than a century. This starts with the female patriarch Umbertina, "the man of her family" as her fellow villagers described her, a shepherdess who marries the much older Serafino, forfeiting the love of Giosuè the charcoal burner. Love has little to do with this; when Serafino meets her:

> he saw she wore no ring. In another moment he knew he would ask for her hand. He had come back from America to marry a woman of his village and to start a family. Now that he saw this strong girl glowing with health and womanliness he thought, Why not the daughter of my friend? (36)

Umbertina marries him on the basis of considerations that exclude sentiment. Serafino is chosen because he is a returning emigrant from the United States, and in Castagna, their small village of shepherds in the Calabrian mountains, she judges him to be the only one capable of taking her to America where she thinks her children will have a better future: "[w]hat was important to her was that Serafino represented something new in her life. He had been to America, he knew the way" (42). She does in fact persuade him to return to America with the family, fifteen years later, by which time they have two children. After very tough times in New York tenements she subsequently persuades him to move the family to Cato, in Connecticut, where others from their village live. Here, Umbertina starts a successful family business and truly becomes the man of the family, having had six more children: "[h]er future was in her sons. They were becoming as American as anyone else" (96). All the children join the business except for Paul, whom his father throws out despite Umbertina's protest: "[l]eave him alone, [...] he's not a strong as the others. *È piu delicato*. He needs a different kind of work" (119). After Serafino dies, she asks her son Jack to look for a new house for himself and her two daughters who are still unmarried: "I can't stay alone in a flat with these unmarried girls [...]. It's not right without a man as head of the family. Your family is growing and you'll have to find a larger place anyway, so what you have to do is get a house large enough for all of us" (124). She orders her sons to go to college, but tries to prevent her daughter Carla: "[n]o daughter of mine is going off to sleep out of town under strange roofs. Girls should be married" (129). Carla in fact gives up her studies to work in the family business, and then to marry for love: "[f]or Carla, love was a Gloria Swanson movie" (132). Umbertina, on the other hand, "reacted as if to an indecent question when Carla, teasing, asked her if she had been in love with her husband. [...] 'What has that to do with anything? He was a good man—a little sentimental, but good; and I did my duty. That's what marriage is, not all this love and romance'" (132). Carla entirely fulfils her mother's expectations by becoming a "real American woman" with three children, including the protagonist of the second part of the novel, Marguerite. The latter rebels right from childhood and rejects the part her mother wants her to play, identical to her own and well integrated in America, as this exchange makes clear: "[w]ho cares about [...] being popular ... I'm not some damn Homecoming Queen. All you want me to do is smile, play golf, and have dates as if that's what life is all about" (146). She rejects a life in which money and appearances are more important than values. The novel thus moves from one mother totally dedicated to social acceptance to another entirely concerned with the search for herself, which takes her to a rushed marriage in order to leave home, quickly annulled with the family's support. While travelling in Italy she meets her second husband, a well-known Italian writer, older than her, whom she marries after an unfortunate romance with another Italian she met in London. She then has two children, Tina—on whom she projects her expectations just as her mother had done with her—and another daughter Weezy, and a son who dies as a child. However, her children take a marginal position in her life, as she herself would admit on reflection:

> Fifteen years after she had decided on marriage over love, if you asked Marguerite Morosini what it had brought her she would have answered bitterly: being a hausfrau, an au pair, mother hen, sister goose. (176)

The search for roots told in *Umbertina* bears witness to mobility, rather than the survival of an ancient past. Umbertina belongs to the cliché of the strong woman who abandons love and chooses a husband, a returned emigrant, because she wants her children to grow up in America. Once they have arrived in the United States, it is she who improves the chances for her family by getting it away from the New York tenements. Her rebellious grand-daughter Marguerite rejects the role her mother favours that would gain her entrance to the "WASP" world, studies Dante in postwar Italy, embraces Italian "high culture", and does not surrender to nostalgia for the ethnicity of her family. The moment of full understanding of the family's ethnic identity comes with the fourth generation, through her daughter Tina's trip to Castagna, in the Calabria of Magna Graecia, when she gains awareness of her multiple identities during an emancipatory journey. Barolini's novel, with its transnational perspective, traces an evolving portrait of Italian American women across four generations; although at times this seems influenced by clichés determined by the feminism of

174 M. TIRABASSI

the 1970s, such as the stereotyping of the different generations, it manages to transcend the temporally fixed characterization of women in most Italian American literature.

FILM: MAFIA, FOOD AND PSYCHOANALYSIS

The greatest contribution to the establishment of the stereotypical Italian family, within which the figure of the mother reigns supreme, has been made by cinema with the success of gangster films. As Ilaria Serra argues in an essay of 2007, "the family has always been a presence in representations of the Italian American, and constitutes one of the most enduring stereotypes in literary representations [...]. From the age of sound onwards, mothers have been present in all their shapely insistence."[44] The Italian American family *par excellence* is the Corleone family where, to use Serra's apt expression, "the family of blood and the bloodthirsty family" coincide.[45] In *The Godfather*, themes that recur in literature interweave. There is behaviour linked to tradition, such as the episode in which Carmela, "Mama" Corleone, sends her son Michael to Italy to find a wife (who will die in Sicily in an attack on Michael), or when she convinces his second wife to convert to Catholicism so that she can pray for her husband, as Carmela had done for Vito; this alternates with bloody deeds that follow mafia principles: Michael has his renegade brother Fredo killed only after their mother's death, thereby demonstrating his complete filial devotion.

This alternation of ordinary and criminal occurrences is found again in *The Sopranos*, in a more sophisticated representation of the gangster: no longer a romantic figure, but one seized by a full-blown existential crisis.[46] In the early episodes of this series we see Tony Soprano revealing to his psychoanalyst his feelings of guilt over choosing to put his mother into residential care. The issue of the relationships between children and their elderly parents proves especially thorny when they adjust to American behaviour, contradicting all the principles of the emigrant Italian family. This theme is not new: in the American cinema of the 1950s, which was influenced by Italian neo-realism, Delbert Mann's *Marty* (1955) won four Oscars for its neo-realist portrayal of the Italian immigrant community, using a family melodrama in which the Italian American mother is dominant.[47] The protagonist is an unmarried butcher, 34 years old, who lives with his elderly mother in the Bronx. When, in the presence of an aunt, he tells his mother that he is in love and about to set up house, the latter does not hesitate to signal the rupture of family codes: "[i]t is a very cruel thing when your son has no place for you in his home."

Sociological understandings of the Italian American family indicate that in this case cinema captures one of the most enduring features of this family culture. Research in the United States in the 1980s showed that Italian Americans used residential care for the elderly less than the other large white ethnic groups. Similarly, compared to these other groups they had the lowest percentage of their college-age population living in college dormitories.[48] In the 1970s the sociologist Colleen Johnson, while examining the maternal role in a comparative perspective, had noted that, in Italian families, the priority of the family over individual interests had been maintained, and emphasized that faithfulness to the family outranked all other allegiances and all personal preferences.[49]

William Egelman argues that in present-day America, too, the stereotype of the Italian American *mamma* "may come to have symbolic significance in the sense of romantic nostalgia, but will likely have little to do with the real lives of contemporary Italian-American women."[50] For a different perspective, we need to look to more recent independent films, which have seen the arrival of young second-generation Italian American directors. While Italian American gangsters continue to populate Hollywood cinema and television, these films have started to present a different reality in which the maternal figure, as in *The Sopranos*, is not a reassuring domestic presence. As Giuliana Muscio says, "as they get away from Hollywood, some of these films make significant modifications to the stereotype, correcting some of its features."[51] Here, Italian roots are those of a mid-twentieth-century Italy that has not been turned into a myth, as it was in the memories passed down from the period of mass emigration. In the feature film *Buffalo '66* (1998), which Muscio describes as a "melancholic autobiography,"[52] the Sicilian American director Vincent Gallo narrates the malaise of his protagonist, the neurotic Billy Brown, which can be traced back to his emasculating family background. In the film's opening scene Billy, just released after spending five years in prison for a crime he did not commit, telephones his mother and then goes to visit his parents, who are represented as bizarre characters. Presumably emigrants to the United States after the Second World War, they have quickly become Americanized: the father is a former singer in the mould of Frank Sinatra, and the mother an obsessive watcher of American football. Billy arrives with a pretend wife, kidnapped for the purpose, and relives the most frustrating experiences of his childhood, marked by his

176 M. TIRABASSI

mother's lack of interest. This is a *bildungsroman* film in which, in the course of a dramatic series of events, the protagonist rediscovers his own masculinity. Gallo has said that he used his own parents as models, and chose his childhood home as the film's location.[53]

Nancy Savoca's comedy *True Love* (1989) also uses a documentary style to present a snapshot of life in the Bronx, where she was born, as her two protagonists celebrate their marriage. In Edvige Giunta's words, she depicts "the domestic space as both nurturing and stifling."[54] Savoca manages to go beyond the romantic image of the Italian community as seen in the much better-known *Moonstruck* (1987), directed by the versatile Norman Jewison; perhaps because the description comes from an outsider, this reproduces, in a benevolent form, all the usual stereotypes, starting with the love of music. Here, too, it is the figure of the elderly mother, still in Italy, that influences the life of her son.

Independent film production has unfortunately remained a niche phenomenon, and has not yet managed to counter the imagery broadcast by Hollywood's large-scale production. In the English-speaking world, the influence of American cinema has to be acknowledged. Canadian film production has traditional content alternating with emergent themes. The comedy *Mambo Italiano*, directed by Émile Gaudreault (2003), tells the story of second-generation immigrant Angelo Barberini. Angelo's father, who arrived in Canada by mistake on his way to the United States, makes an assertion that shows how Italian-style familism has found its way into the new millennium: "[a] son leaves the household only when he marries or dies." However, the director also addresses a new feature for the iconography of the Italian family to accommodate: the son coming out as gay. Not long after shocking his parents by leaving home, Angelo reveals his sexuality. When he is subsequently abandoned by his partner, also of Italian origin and not ready to deal with the issue of his gayness, he too turns to psychotherapy.

The theme of homosexuality can also be found in Italian Australian cinema. In Thomas Scire's *Desolato* (2003) the protagonists are reproached by their respective mothers, who, as well as stressing all the sacrifices they have made for them, insist that they find respectable Italian girls.[55] The sons rebel against family traditions each in their own way; Daniele's mother is bewildered, to say the least, when he chooses a male Italian partner.[56] Another well-known Australian film, *Looking for Alibrandi* (2000), directed by Kate Woods and set in Sydney in the 1990s, depicts an adolescent's growing awareness of her ethnic identity.[57] Here the matriarchate emerges once more, through the history of three generations of Italian women. We see the control exercised by the Italian Australian community, and the persistence of traditions in the importance given to the preparation of Italian dishes: the film opens with the communal cooking of tomato sauce. As Gaetano Rando observes, "it is interesting to note that some third-generation writers [...] recognize themselves in situations described in *Looking for Alibrandi*, such as the themes relating to family ties."[58] Thus in some cases, in Australia as in North America, literature and cinema reach behind the stereotypes and help to express the concerns of the descendants of immigrants.

A sounding-board for Italian American family behaviour has been the situation comedy. Silvia Giagnoni has observed that the small screen uses "stereotypes of a superficial kind, although never in an abusive manner, inasmuch as produced by a generalist television that for obvious reasons of a financial nature [...] cannot allow itself to offend any particular group."[59] Even more than commercial cinema, situation comedies have exaggerated the more trivial aspects of Italian American culture, bringing them into the present day. The soap opera *Everybody Loves Raymond*, directed by Phil Rosenthal and broadcast in the United States between 1996 and 2005, has Raymond's parents living in the house opposite along with his brother, who still lives with them. Food provides the pretext for the daily exchange of visits between mother and son, and is the cause of endless arguments between husband and wife. The latter is repeatedly accused of not knowing how to make the mother's dishes.[60] On the screen, as in the literature, food and all its related rituals—Sunday lunches, wedding banquets, funeral receptions—seem to provide the strongest link with the past, although it remains to be seen whether this is not actually true for all ethnic groups. As Daniel Golden says, "[w]hether it is pizza or matzoh ball soup, czarina or black eyed peas, the ethnic mother in the kitchen insisting that we eat, *mangia*, is a standing joke of situation comedy and Alka Seltzer commercials."[61]

The Italian *mamma* is thus not the only mother subject to stereotyping. In American situation comedies the family and mothers, whether or not they are from ethnic minorities, are often victims of satire: the "WASP" mother in the series *The Gilmore Girls*, for example, embodies the stereotype of the Ivy League family who, alongside the stereotyped Korean mother, is the most intrusive of all screen mothers. In screen comedy, however, the image of the Jewish mother, as represented, for example, by Woody Allen in *New York Stories* (1989), outshines those of all other ethnic minorities.[62]

It has, however, been the success of gangster movies, which, as we have seen, have even contributed to the creation of gender roles for Italian Americans, that has perpetuated the stereotype by reflecting an Italian American culture from the past, and has thus played a part in spreading the stereotypical image of the Italian American *mamma*. Somewhat ironically, this image has played a part in disseminating the stereotype not just in America and other foreign countries but also in Italy itself.

CONCLUSIONS

Research has shown that male children represent the weak link in the transition between Italian peasant society and advanced industrial society. They saw their male roles in the old world, including that of breadwinner, eroded; in contrast, women, whether or not successful, through emigration started to achieve recognition for their activities, even if they were often confined to the domestic sphere. In the dominant literature and cinema, men seem fated to join youth gangs that will then channel them towards the world of organized crime, or to remain clinging on to a nostalgic and unrealistic image of the old world: these men have to turn to psychoanalysis to resolve their conflicts. From one perspective, the overseas experience has started to address the issue of the crisis of masculinity in the post-feminist age, although this is not bounded by ethnic divisions and is somewhat outside our remit. It is important to emphasize here that the success of portrayals of Italian Americans, which arguably started with cinema and then became more widespread through publishing and television from the 1970s onwards, has created very strong stereotypes of Italian Americans, and this has included disseminating the image of an Italian *mamma* of southern origins still tied to archaic practices and traditions. This has, in turn, contributed to the reinforcement of the stereotype in Italy.

A focus on emigrant women provides a further element to the analysis of the construction of the maternal figure in Italian society. It demonstrates that different models existed in Italy from the nineteenth century, and it encourages discussion of the development of a model of the mother that started in southern Italian culture, a culture that has still not had sufficient attention from Italian historiography.

Translated by Stuart Oglethorpe

NOTES

1. On the construction of the image of the *mamma* and *mammismo*, see d'Amelia, *La mamma*.
2. D'Amelia, *La mamma*, p. 159.
3. L'Orfano, "The Overwhelming Albatross," p. 138.
4. Tirabassi, "Bourgeois Men, Peasant Women"; Tirabassi, "Making Space for Domesticity."
5. Campisi, "Ethnic Family Patterns"; Tomasi, *The Italian American Family*; Yans-McLaughlin, *Family and Community*, pp. 18–19; Yans-McLaughlin, "Patterns of Work and Family Organization."
6. Gabaccia, "Italian-American Woman"; Tirabassi, "Italiane ed emigrate."
7. Barbagli, *Provando e riprovando*; Barbagli, *Sotto lo stesso tetto*; Saraceno, *Anatomia della famiglia*.
8. Tirabassi, "Bourgeois Men, Peasant Women"; Reeder, *Widows in White*.
9. *Inchiesta Jacini*, VII, p. 181.
10. *Inchiesta Jacini*, VII, p. 332.
11. *Inchiesta Jacini*, VII, p. 35.
12. *Inchiesta Jacini*, VII, p. 672.
13. *Inchiesta Faina*, IV, p. 264.
14. *Inchiesta Jacini*, VIII, p. 385.
15. *Inchiesta Jacini*, VII, p. 331.
16. *Inchiesta Jacini*, XII, p. 181.
17. *Inchiesta Jacini*, IX, fasc. I, p. 120; VII, p. 181.
18. *Inchiesta Jacini*, IX, fasc. I, p. 214.
19. Tirabassi, *Il Faro di Beacon Street*, pp. 199–203; Gordon, "Single Mothers and Child Neglect"; Gordon, *Heroes of Their Own Lives*.
20. Tomasi, *The Italian American Family*.
21. Messina, "Nine Italian-American Women," pp. 15–16.
22. Messina, "Nine Italian-American Women," pp. 15–28.
23. Messina, "Nine Italian-American Women," p. 19.
24. Banfield, *Moral Basis of a Backward Society*.
25. Tirabassi, *Il Faro di Beacon Street*.
26. Gardaphé, "Good Mammas," p. 172.
27. Nardini, *Che Bella Figura!*; Ferraro, *Feeling Italian*.
28. On the tradition of arranged marriages, which continued into the period after the Second World War, see Revelli, *Il mondo dei vinti*; Revelli, *L'anello forte*; Scarparo, "Italian Proxy Brides in Australia."
29. The film *Give Us This Day*, directed by Edward Dmytryk (GB, 1949), was based on the book.
30. Page numbers for quotations from this and other novels refer to the editions listed in the bibliography.

180 M. TIRABASSI

31. Bona, *The Voices We Carry*, p. 12. For an analysis of the autobiographies of Italian American men, see Boelhower, *Immigrant Autobiography in the United States*; Gardaphé, *From Wiseguys to Wise Men*.
32. Gardaphé, *From Wiseguys to Wise Men*, p. xiv.
33. Gardaphé, *From Wiseguys to Wise Men*, p. xii.
34. The book was adapted for the television mini-series *The Fortunate Pilgrim* (*Mamma Lucia* in Italy), directed by Stuart Cooper and broadcast in 1988, with Sophia Loren and John Turturro.
35. Ferraro, *Feeling Italian*, p. 74.
36. For one of many discussions on this topic see Merullo, "Working against Cliché," pp. 41–43.
37. Talese, "Where Are the Italian American Novelists?", p. 1.
38. Bona, *The Voices We Carry*, pp. 11, 13.
39. Tamburri, "Towards a (Re)definition of Italian/American Literature."
40. Anello, "Fred, il picciotto che insegna la mafia all'università."
41. Gardaphé, "Good Mammas: The Story of One," pp. 171–74.
42. Calabro, "The Children of Immigrants," p. 320.
43. Barolini, *Umbertina*. See also Barolini, *The Dream Book*.
44. Serra, "Forme e deformità della famiglia," p. 164.
45. Ibid., p. 165.
46. *The Sopranos*, created and principally produced by David Chase (USA: 1999–2007). There is a vast literature on *The Sopranos*. See, for example, Barreca, *A Sitdown with the Sopranos*; Gorlier, "The Sopranos."
47. Muscio, "Tony, Rosa, Vito e Guido," p. 87.
48. Femminella, "Italian American Family Life," pp. 56–57.
49. Johnson, "The Maternal Role," pp. 235, 238.
50. Egelman, "Traditional Roles and Modern Work Patterns," p. 84.
51. Muscio, "Tony, Rosa, Vito e Guido," p. 91.
52. Ibid., p. 91.
53. Serra, "Forme e deformità della famiglia," p. 169; Muscio, "Tony, Rosa, Vito e Guido."
54. Giunta, "The Quest for True Love."
55. See Rando, "Mezzo secolo di cinema italoaustraliano," p. 165.
56. The issue of homosexuality has also been addressed in two American films, Maria Maggenti's *Puccini for Beginners* (2005) and Tom De Cerchio's very successful short film *Nunzio's Second Cousin* (1994). See Rando, "Mezzo secolo di cinema italoaustraliano" and "Migrant images."
57. The film is based on the 1992 novel of the same name by Melina Marchetta.
58. Rando, "La narrativa italoaustraliana."
59. Giagnoni, "Tony, Ray e gli altri," p. 224.
60. See, for example, the episodes "Debra made something good," "Maria's meatballs," and "Call me mother."

61. Golden, "Pasta or Paradigm," p. 353. See also De Angelis, "Foodways in Italian-American Narrative," p. 207.
62. See the "floating mother" in *New York Stories*, where the mother, although dead, continues to follow her son from the sky, enveloped by cloud. As far as I am aware, no comparative analysis of the cinematic or televisual representation of ethnic minority mothers has yet been undertaken.

BIBLIOGRAPHY

PARLIAMENTARY INQUIRIES

Atti della giunta per l'inchiesta agraria e sulle condizioni della classe agricola in Italia ('Inchiesta Jacini', 1877–1885). 15 vols. Rome: Forzani, 1881–1886.

Inchiesta parlamentare sulle condizioni dei contadini nelle province meridionali e nella Sicilia ('Inchiesta Faina', 1906–1911). 9 vols. Rome: Bertero, 1909–1911.

Anello, Laura. "Fred, il picciotto che insegna la mafia all'università." *La Stampa*, 21 August 2013: p. 64.

Banfield, Edward C. *The Moral Basis of a Backward Society*. New York: The Free Press, 1958.

Barbagli, Marzio. *Provando e riprovando. Matrimonio, famiglia e divorzio in Italia e in altri paesi occidentali*. Bologna: il Mulino, 1990.

Barbagli, Marzio. *Sotto lo stesso tetto*. 4th edn. Bologna: il Mulino, 2013.

Barolini, Helen. *Umbertina*. New York: Seaview Books, 1979.

Barolini, Helen. *The Dream Book: An Anthology of Writings by Italian American Women*. New York: Schocken, 1985.

Barreca, Regina, ed. *A Sitdown with the Sopranos: Watching Italian American Culture on T.V.'s Most Talked-About Series*. New York: Palgrave Macmillan, 2002.

Boelhower, William. *Immigrant Autobiography in the United States: Four Versions of the Italian American Self*. Verona: Essedue, 1982.

Bona, Mary Jo. *The Voices We Carry: Recent Italian American Women's Fiction*. Montreal: Guernica, 1994.

Calabro, John. "The Children of Immigrants: Who Speaks for Them?" *Altreitalie* n. 38–39 (2009): pp. 315–23.

Campisi, Paul J. "Ethnic Family Patterns: The Italian Family in the United States." *American Journal of Sociology* 53, n. 6 (1948): pp. 443–9.

d'Amelia, Marina. *La mamma*. Bologna: Il Mulino, 2005.

De Angelis, Rose. "Foodways in Italian-American Narrative." In *American Woman, Italian Style: Italian Americana's Best Writings on Women*, edited by Carol Bonomo Albright and Christine Palamidessi Moore, pp. 206–14. New York: Fordham University Press, 2011.

182 M. TIRABASSI

di Donato, Pietro. *Christ in Concrete*. Indianapolis–New York: Bobbs-Merrill, 1937. Translated and published in Italian as *Cristo fra i muratori*. Milan: Bompiani, 1941.

Egelman, William. "Traditional Roles and Modern Work Patterns: Italian-American Women in New York City." In *American Woman, Italian Style: Italian Americana's Best Writings on Women*, edited by Carol Bonomo Albright and Christine Palamidessi Moore, pp. 78–86. New York: Fordham University Press, 2011.

Femminella, Francis X. "Italian American Family Life." *Center for Migration Studies Special Issues* 7, n. 2 (March 1989): pp. 49–61. https://doi.org/10.1111/j.2050-411X.1989.tb00593.x

Ferraro, Thomas J. *Feeling Italian: The Art of Ethnicity in America*. New York: New York University Press, 2005.

Gabaccia, Donna. "Italian-American Women: A Review Essay." In *American Woman, Italian Style: Italian Americana's Best Writings on Women*, edited by Carol Bonomo Albright and Christine Palamidessi Moore, pp. 307–32. New York: Fordham University Press, 2011.

Gardaphé, Fred. "Good Mammas: The Story of One." In *Italian Women in Chicago: Madonna mia! QUI debbo vivere? (You mean I have to live HERE?)*, edited by Dominic Candeloro, Kathy Catrambone, and Gloria Nardini, pp. 171–4. Chicago: Casa Italia, 2013.

Gardaphé, Fred. *From Wiseguys to Wise Men: The Gangster and Italian American Masculinities*. New York: Routledge, 2006.

Giagnoni, Silvia. "Tony, Ray e gli altri: gli italoamericani in televisione." In *Quei bravi ragazzi. Il cinema italoamericano contemporaneo*, edited by Giuliana Muscio and Giovanni Spagnoletti, pp. 218–28. Venice: Marsilio, 2007.

Giunta, Edvige. "The Quest for True Love: Ethnicity in Nancy Savoca's Domestic Film Comedy." *Melus* 22, n. 2 (1997): pp. 75–89. https://doi.org/10.2307/468136.

Golden, Daniel. "Pasta or Paradigm: The Place of Italian-American Women in Popular Film." In *The Italian Immigrant Woman in North America*, edited by Betty Boyd Caroli, Robert F. Harney, and Lydio F. Tomasi, pp. 350–7. Toronto: MHSO, 1978.

Gordon, Linda. "Single Mothers and Child Neglect, 1880–1920." *American Quarterly* 37, n. 2 (1985): pp. 173–92.

Gordon, Linda. *Heroes of Their Own Lives: The Politics and History of Family Violence, Boston 1880–1960*. New York: Viking, 1988.

Gorlier, Claudio. "The Sopranos." *Altreitalie* n. 29 (2004): pp. 120–6.

Johnson, Colleen L. "The Maternal Role in the Contemporary Italian-American Family." In *The Italian Immigrant Woman in North America*, edited by Betty Boyd Caroli, Robert F. Harney, and Lydio F. Tomasi, pp. 234–44. Toronto: MHSO, 1978.

MAMMAS IN ITALIAN MIGRANT FAMILIES: THE ANGLOPHONE... 183

L'Orfano, Francesca. "The Overwhelming Albatross: Stereotypical Representations and Italian-Canadian Political and Cultural Life." *Altreitalie* n. 38–39 (2009): pp. 137–57.

Marchetta, Melina. *Looking for Alibrandi*. Ringwood: Penguin Australia, 1992.

Merullo, Roland. "Working against Cliché." *Italian Americana* XVIII, n. 1 (Winter 2000): pp. 41–3.

Messina, Elisabeth G. "Narratives of Nine Italian-American Women: Childhood, Work, and Marriage." In *American Woman, Italian Style: Italian Americana's Best Writings on Women*, edited by Carol Bonomo Albright and Christine Palamidessi Moore: 15–31. New York: Fordham University Press, 2011.

Muscio, Giuliana. "Tony, Rosa, Vito e Guido: Hollywood tra padrini e commari." *Archivio storico dell'emigrazione italiana* 5 (2009): pp. 65–93.

Nardini, Gloria. *Che Bella Figura! The Power of Performance in an Italian Ladies' Club in Chicago*. Albany: State University of New York Press, 1999.

Puzo, Mario. *The Fortunate Pilgrim*. Greenwich, CT: Fawcett, 1964.

Rando, Gaetano. "Mezzo secolo di cinema italoaustraliano: una prima retrospettiva." *Altreitalie* n. 30 (2005): pp. 160–6.

Rando, Gaetano. "Migrant Images in Italian Australian Movies and Documentaries." *Altreitalie* n. 16 (1997): pp. 16–22.

Rando, Gaetano. "La narrativa italoaustraliana della seconda generazione." *Altreitalie* n. 50 (2015): pp. 133–42.

Reeder, Linda. *Widows in White: Migration and the Transformation of Rural Italian Women, Sicily, 1880–1920*. Toronto: University of Toronto Press, 2003.

Revelli, Nuto. *Il mondo dei vinti. Testimonianze di vita contadina*. Turin: Einaudi, 1977.

Revelli, Nuto. *L'anello forte. La donna: storie di vita contadina*. Turin: Einaudi, 1985.

Saraceno, Chiara. *Anatomia della famiglia. Strutture sociali e forme familiari*. Bari: De Donato, 1976.

Scarparo, Susanna. "Italian Proxy Brides in Australia." *Altreitalie* n. 38–39 (2009): pp. 85–108.

Serra, Ilaria. "Forme e deformità della famiglia nel cinema italoamericano." In *Quei bravi ragazzi. Il cinema italoamericano contemporaneo*, edited by Giuliana Muscio and Giovanni Spagnoletti, pp. 164–72. Venice: Marsilio, 2007.

Talese, Gay. "Where Are the Italian-American Novelists?" *New York Times Book Review*, 14 March 1993: pp. 1, 23, 25, 29. Also translated and published as "Dove sono i romanzieri italoamericani?" *Altreitalie* n. 10 (1993): pp. 33–43.

Tamburri, Anthony J. "Towards a (Re)definition of Italian/American Literature." In *Social Pluralism and Literary History: The Literature of the Italian Emigration*, edited by Francesco Loriggio, pp. 188–205. Toronto: Guernica, 1996.

Tirabassi, Maddalena. "Bourgeois Men, Peasant Women: Rethinking Domestic Work and Morality in Italy." In *Women, Gender, and Transnational Lives*, edited by Donna Gabaccia and Franca Iacovetta, pp. 106–29. Toronto: University of Toronto Press, 2002.

Tirabassi, Maddalena. "Making Space for Domesticity: Household Goods in Working-Class Italian American Homes, 1900–1940." In *Making Italian America: Consumer Culture and the Production of Ethnic Identities*, edited by Simone Cinotto, pp. 57–70. New York: Fordham University Press, 2014.

Tirabassi, Maddalena. "Italiane ed emigrate." *Altreitalie* n. 9 (1993): pp. 139–53.

Tirabassi, Maddalena. *Il Faro di Beacon Street. Social workers e immigrate negli Stati Uniti (1910–1939)*. Milan: Franco Angeli, 1989.

Tomasi, Lydio F. *The Italian American Family: The Southern Italian Family's Process of Adjustment to an Urban America*. Staten Island: Center for Migration Studies, 1972.

Yans-McLaughlin, Virginia. *Family and Community: Italian Immigrants in Buffalo, 1880–1930*. Ithaca, NY: Cornell University Press, 1977.

Yans-McLaughlin, Virginia. "Patterns of Work and Family Organization: Buffalo's Italians." *Journal of Interdisciplinary History* 2, n. 2 (1971): pp. 299–314.

CHAPTER 8

Queer Daughters and Their Mothers: Carole Maso, Mary Cappello and Alison Bechdel Write Their Way Home

Mary Jo Bona

Mother/Daughters and Experimental Narratives

Experimental daughters seek their mothers in frequently circuitous ways. Their narratives are often multi-perspectival, innovating on genre and style while interrogating the notion of representation itself. Such is the case for Carole Maso, Mary Cappello and Alison Bechdel, all of whom construct narratives of motherlove from the perspective of daughters who identify as lesbian.[1] Influenced by practices of postmodernism and feminist thought, Maso, Cappello and Bechdel implement an intersectional approach in their narratives in order to represent complicated relations between mothers and daughters. As a result, "new writing modes," are created, as Adalgisa Giorgio explains, as writers employ a "wide variety of strategies, ranging from free-flowing experimental styles … to the subversion … of established genres, and the inversion or rewriting of traditional plots to counter Freud's (male) Family Romance."[2]

M. J. Bona (✉)
Stony Brook University, Stony Brook, NY, USA
e-mail: mary.bona@stonybrook.edu

© The Author(s) 2018
P. Morris, P. Willson (eds.), *La Mamma*,
Italian and Italian American Studies,
https://doi.org/10.1057/978-1-137-54256-4_8

185

While each of the writers shifts away from traditional representations of ethnicity vis-à-vis the family institution, I also argue here that heritage culture continues to inflect these narratives in illuminating ways, informing a reading of the mother–daughter plot.[3] Of the three works examined in these pages, Mary Cappello's memoir, *Night Bloom*, focuses overtly on the ethnic culture of her Italian ancestors as she engages in eulogizing relatives who migrated from Italy to the United States during the period of migration in the late nineteenth and early twentieth centuries. In contrast to Cappello's narrative, Carole Maso's novel, *Ghost Dance*, signals *italianità*[4] through a story strand that focuses on the narrator's paternal Italian grandparents, whose cultural repression compels her to probe the silences informing their lives, affording her licence to construct tales that might account for her father's sorrow and her mother's mental suffering. While Alison Bechdel does not explicitly signify heritage culture in her graphic memoir, *Are You My Mother?*, her many references to Catholicism inform her childhood and the way her Italian American mother raised her. Bechdel's notable references to her mother's sewing expertise recall Italian foremothers whose needlework skills after migration to America ensured financial stability and increased the family's own sense of the artistic value inherent in cloth-work. In *Embroidered Stories: Interpreting Domestic Needlework from the Italian Diaspora*, editors Edvige Giunta and Joseph Sciorra demonstrate how immigrant women utilize "old skills" in new ways, inclusive of becoming their "families' most reliable breadwinners ... [and continuing] their domestic needlework for their family's use."[5] A generation later, Helen Bechdel extends the wealth of her own hands not to prepare a trousseau for her daughter, but to design costumes for the theatre. I argue in these pages that Bechdel's representation of Helen (née) Fontana's sustained silences about Alison's sexuality might also be read profitably through the lens of an implicit Italian American ethnicity.

Published between the years 1986 and 2012, the narratives of Carole Maso, Mary Cappello and Alison Bechdel perhaps reinforce a "twilight of ethnicity," but in doing so they simultaneously move beyond reductive media representations developed in early twentieth-century America, caricaturing the figure of "la Mamma."[6] I cannot provide a summary definition of *the* Italian American mother, since no such monolithic identity ever existed.[7] Nonetheless, media representations have insidiously trivialized this figure, reducing her to an "Italian mamma," dressed in black, lugubriously sorrowful, stirring the sauce.[8] Literary Italian America may portray mothers dressed in black, but offer cultural context that serves to deepen their characters, refusing to reduce this immigrant group to comedic or immutable types. Despite the hostile reception Italian immigrants received during their greatest period of migration, mothers have been represented as maintaining maternal authority through cultural retentions, inclusive of linguistic, culinary and religious customs. The literature of Italian America often represents immigrants adjusting to America, and, while Maso, Cappello and Bechdel do not situate their narratives in traditional immigrant plots, their work echoes earlier writing as it too is modified by culturally specific traditions and complementary forms of mothering.

Besides resisting forms of male domination in their lives and establishing primary relations with women, the writers examined here also wage an ongoing critique of normative heterosexuality and its attendant patriarchal practices. In doing so, they execute a paradigmatic shift away from portraying traditional matriarchal roles within patriarchy designated by wifehood and motherhood and toward examining the female figure of the lover and the artist, which each daughter recognizes in her own mother. Through experimental narrative techniques, each writer attempts to forge new narrative space where mother and daughter remain together, creating a textual landscape that unfixes sexual identity but also creates what Roseanne Quinn calls "places of rupture ... but it is precisely in those intervals where poetry and song, Italy and women connect."[9]

All three writers bridge second- and third-wave feminism. While they recognize the generation of their mothers as achieving important strides in freedom from traditional definitions of family, the daughters seek to transform such achievements not only through challenging existing structures but also through performing subversive acts of reading and writing. Because of their awareness of historical contexts that influenced how their mothers acted, the authors offer interpretative strategies of reading in order to investigate the mother–daughter bond. Each writer intellectually recognizes that she futilely longs for a mother she cannot have. To deepen an understanding of the generational rift between mother and daughter, the writers deploy elements of third-wave feminism, engaging differences of class, sex and ability, to examine that rupture. For example, by focusing on maternal mental illness, Carole Maso's narrator illuminates the limitations posed by heteronormative behaviour on all women from her mother's generation, those who came of age in the 1940s. That the mother figure is a famous poet who suffers from paranoid delusions permits Maso not only to place her in a genealogical line alongside Anne Sexton and

Sylvia Plath, but also to impress upon the reader the price paid for desiring motherhood and creativity concomitantly in the mother's era.

While she situates her queerness within the Italian American family, Mary Cappello interprets kin relations through the lens of migration and class, examining ongoing familial patterns of joblessness, minimum wage and ill health. Cappello pays heed to her second-generation mother, who inherited the pain resulting from the material deprivations of her immigrant parents. For Alison Bechdel, a willingness to explore intersections between lesbian sexuality alongside an ardent form of motherlove opens up a contextual space for what has traditionally been perceived as aberrant sexuality. Her mother's tenuous responses to the lesbian daughter's desire reflect both a tradition of *omertà* about personal matters and a misunderstanding on the daughter's part in interpreting the revelatory nature of the mother's quotidian exchanges. For each writer, such interventions unhinge normative relationships between mothers and daughters within traditional American family dynamics, intensifying the daughter's desire for the mother she cannot have.

If the literature of Italian America has also been chiefly a literature of generations (explicitly due to the migration experience), then it can be argued that Carole Maso, Mary Cappello and Alison Bechdel engage and rewrite generational histories, but from a distinctly queer perspective. As Ann Cvetkovich explains of Bechdel's first memoir, *Fun Home*, the author joins other lesbian artists who "rewrite queer generational histories," claiming her father's queerness "for herself and hence for history, insisting that his story be incorporated into a more fully historicized present but also that its unassimilability be acknowledged in order to problematize the present."[10] Writers of Italian America have also invoked images of unassimilability with regard to the immigrant generation, cognizant of the host culture's nativism and its explicit pathologization of immigrants "along the axis of gender."[11] *Ghost Dance, Night Bloom* and *Are You My Mother?* explore the intersection between sexual identity and its relation to the generations before, suggesting a consanguinity between family and sexual cultures, exacerbated by the struggle to assimilate American ways.

In an effort to claim the queer generation from whence she comes—the generation of the lesbian feminist, Alison Bechdel extends these concerns about unassimilability in *Are You My Mother?* Perhaps outmoded to queer millennials, lesbian feminism continues to shape the works of Maso, Cappello and Bechdel, whose narrative constructions serve to create intimacy with their mothers by dismantling traditional barriers erected by heteronormative expectations. Each writer ultimately bears witness to her mother's gender and sexual identities, "seeking to be the sympathetic witness" to the mother's "rich and contradictory" stories.[12] As third-generation lesbian daughters who witness imperilled family dynamics, these writers portray extraordinary devotion to mother figures. Such devotion simultaneously reflects the fruitful outcome of scholarly interest in the mother–daughter bond. As Patrizia Sambuco explains, "the coincidence of the publication of a corpus of women's writing on the mother–daughter relationship and the development of a feminist theorization of the maternal does not necessarily imply a relation of cause and effect between feminist theories and women's writing but bears witness to a more general cultural sensibility in favour of the revaluation of this formerly neglected relationship."[13] Maso, Cappello and Bechdel are self-reflexively engaged by feminist and psychoanalytical theories, helping to demystify and reimagine structures of language and kinship, institutions that oppress their mothers. A substantial area of scholarly inquiry and creative experimentation, mother–daughter studies has enlarged an understanding of a union that has often been misunderstood and undervalued. It is no exaggeration, as Adrienne Rich famously wrote, that "this cathexis between mother and daughter—essential, distorted, misused—is the great unwritten story."[14]

By establishing primary relationships with women, Carole Maso, Mary Cappello and Alison Bechdel intensify the magical bond they share not only with their biological mothers but also their literary female forebears. From a traditionally psychoanalytic perspective, these writers over-identify with their birth mothers, gesturing toward a continued desire for women and suggesting "other possible subjective economies based in women's relationships," as Hirsch explains in her examination of literary mother–daughter plots.[15] Adrienne Rich observed that "the relationship between mother and daughter has been profoundly threatening to men,"[16] and the writers under consideration depict outright conflict and/or unsettled relations within patriarchal family structures. The writers' level of commitment to understanding their mothers' family situation never diminishes in adulthood as their dis-identification with heterosexualism paradoxically increases their focus on the mother.

Committed to writing experimental narratives that are self-reflexively discursive, these writers produce meta-texts that disrupt linear narrative and offer both an implicit and explicit critique of the institution of the family and the larger American culture under late capitalism. My own

190   M. J. BONA

choice to discuss different genres—novel, memoir and graphic memoir—emerges from a recognition that these writers implement a style of confessional discourse that unifies them in revelatory ways. As Nancy K. Miller says of autobiographical memoirs, "the female autobiographical self comes into writing, goes public with private feelings, through a significant relation to an other. Feminist critics have been making the case for a model of a relational self at the heart of the autobiographical project for over two decades."[17] This is but one of the projects Maso, Cappello and Bechdel pursue through the mother–daughter plot in their confessional narratives. Each writer also deploys and reimagines the figure of the female artist through references to Virginia Woolf's classic, *To the Lighthouse*. In reconstructing a maternal genealogy, the writers revise the Mrs Ramsay–Lily Briscoe relationship in Woolf's text by exploring desire in complex ways. As Woolf memorably wrote in *A Room of One's Own*, "A woman writing thinks back through her mothers."[18] As the lesbian daughters of second-wave and second-generational mothers, these writers think back through their mothers as daughter-lovers who remain committed in adulthood to their artistic mothers.

CAROLE MASO'S EROTIC LOVE SONG: *GHOST DANCE*

Vanessa Turin, the first-person narrator of *Ghost Dance*, describes her mother always in exceptional terms: outlandish, exotic, mysterious and distant. Vanessa's girlhood desire to be embraced by her mother is always belied by her mother's *sui generis* brilliance as the already famous poet, Christine Wing. Working with a ferocity bordering on the unbearable, Christine believes that "there is no rest from perception."[19] Christine's struggle with the dual demands of motherhood and creativity is captured in the objective correlative Maso implements of the Topaz Bird. Invented by Christine for bedtime stories to help Vanessa and her younger brother, Fletcher, not *sleep* but rather *cope* with her "inexplicable sadness or rage or joy," the mother understands that the Topaz Bird is the "wild, brilliant Bird of Imagination." Speaking through metaphor to children who cannot fathom the depths of her mental anguish, Christine repeats this refrain as a revelatory confession that both apologizes for her maternal behaviour and absolves her from the traditional demands of motherhood: "You must never forget ... that the Topaz Bird means us no harm."[20] Significant for Vanessa will be the bird's relation to the healing capacity of storytelling, which will ensure a future without her distant but beloved mother. After all, the Topaz Bird is the invention of Christine *Wing*, who is always already taking flight away from her family.

When the narrative begins, Vanessa is returning to college at Vassar—her mother's alma mater—and sees her mother for what will be the final time before they part ways at Grand Central Station, she to Poughkeepsie and Christine to coastal Maine. Though Vanessa makes oblique references to the mother's death throughout her long-year's journey into night, Maso's portrayal of bereavement ranges from forms of madness (and addiction) to ritualized practices that will finally contain Vanessa's grief. Only by heeding the "call of stories"[21] will Vanessa be able to proclaim a voice of mortality for her mother, allowing her to resist self-immolation, and instead achieve appropriative uses of voice, which have in common emancipatory aims for the bereaved daughter of the Turin family. That Vanessa's surname signifies the cultural centre of the Piedmont region is no coincidence in Maso's *Ghost Dance*. Maso's paternal grandfather came from northern Italy and she considers Italy her "cultural home."[22] Despite an outward appearance of high culture and elegance the place name suggests, the Turin family in America is subject to critique by Maso as she "explores the cracks and disturbances behind the perfect proportion [father, mother, and one child of each sex] and beauty that the Turin family enacts."[23]

Vanessa Turin's journey in Maso's novel will require her to piece together, through fragments of memory and invention, the story of her family's life, with special emphasis on her mother's suffering. Divided into five parts, *Ghost Dance* begins in Vanessa's recent past, but then in Parts Two and Three, returns to both maternal and paternal grandparental generations, to explore the reasons underlying her mother's sorrowful girlhood and her father's suppressed *italianità*. Vanessa suspects both parental stories hinge on immigrant responses to America, which required a destructive abrogation of cultural identity. A child of German and Armenian ancestry on her mother's side and Italian ancestry on her father's side, Vanessa and her brother, Fletcher, probe the silences informing both parents' reticence regarding their pasts. Vanessa's Italian grandmother functions throughout *Ghost Dance* as a stabilizing presence for her grandchildren; Maria Turin combines reverence for traditional forms of mothering alongside an acceptance of difference, qualities Vanessa treasures in her. Vanessa's father's remoteness causes his children to invent homework assignments just to hear him speak. In Michael Turin's refusal to provide information about one of their prefabricated assignments—their "family tree"—Vanessa and Fletcher construct a past that clarifies their father's silence. As Maso herself says of *Ghost Dance* "[T]he way to resist [silence], is very much what [the] book is about. To live next to silence, but to speak."[24]

Parts Four and Five of *Ghost Dance* delve further into Christine Wing's childhood, her mental illness, her lover Sabine and, finally, Vanessa's overt disclosure of her mother's tragic death by fire. We learn in Part 5 that the family's 1973 Pinto is rear-ended at a toll-booth; the gas tank erupts into flames and Christine is said to have died instantaneously in the back seat. Vanessa must ultimately learn to love her mother from afar; as a third-generation witness, she must accept the fact that she can neither save her mother nor know with certitude the intricate reasons informing her behaviour. As Pipino explains, Vanessa nonetheless takes on the role of "third-generation 'rescuer,' unearthing the treasures that cannot be thrown out, tracing her family's history and identities ... [in order to] unravel and unearth ... family legends ... to answer the question: 'How do you get a point of view? ... How do you know something for sure?'"[25]

Carole Maso's *Ghost Dance* captures the fragmentation that occurs as a result of mother-loss. Unable to function as a caregiver in any practical way, Christine nonetheless remains the lodestar of the Turin family, all of whom end up lost and broken after her untimely death. For the purposes of this chapter, I will focus my comments specifically on Vanessa's reconstruction of her mother's life in order to learn to love Christine in life rather than wanting to die. As Sandra M. Gilbert explains, it is not unusual in yearning to "enter an open doorway into death and *be* dead with someone much loved."[26]

Part Two of *Ghost Dance* begins with Vanessa's confessional voice: "it will be one year since I last saw her."[27] Sounding eerily close to the formulaic practice of the Catholic confessional, Vanessa proceeds to make only tacit references to her mother's childhood, choosing instead to delve into the arguably less painful generational story of her father's Italian immigrant parents. Vanessa's grandfather, Angelo, provides his grandchildren with a migration story that suppresses Italian heritage to the detriment of his wife and the generations that follow. Despite the fact that she is compelled to deny her *italianità*, Maria Turin remains the exemplar of traditional motherhood: "Consistent and brave, she was the watchdog of a rationality in a largely irrational family."[28] Without the practical examples of useful knowledge passed down by Vanessa's paternal grandmother, the narrator might not have had the emotional fortitude to sustain the double loss of her beloved mother, who suffered from bouts of madness and who died tragically.[29] As Louise DeSalvo explains, "if Vanessa is to grow beyond the world of her mother and beyond her tortured life of drugs and abusive sex to a creative life ... she will have to manage the very difficult task of separating what can be useful to her in the example of her mother's life and what is potentially ... lethal."[30] Responding to her mother's otherworldly voice, which she hears urging her, the narrator, to "Go now .... There is no other way," Vanessa in Part Three delves deeper to reimagine a past she did not live in order to live in a present she cannot bear.[31]

Parts Three and Four of *Ghost Dance* reveal a childhood damaged by the untimely death of Christine's mother, who suffered rheumatic fever as a child, weakening her heart. A childhood overshadowed by a mother's illness, Christine attempts to save her mother in her own way: through words that will "save her life; she would make her well—with words."[32] The illness of Christine's mother unleashes grandiose assimilation dreams in her father, as he exploits his young daughter's beauty, taking her to New York commercial studios for modelling gigs. Ostensibly to pay the hospital bills but equally to fulfil his rags-to-riches dreams, Sarkis vainly hopes to turn his daughter into a child star, bigger than "Shirley Temple, bigger than Judy Garland."[33] Defying her father's American dreams, Christine "cultivates an oppositional, intellectual persona, wearing cheap eyeglasses purchased from Woolworth, reading poetry."[34] Christine will continue her struggle with the larger culture's construction of feminine ideals, affecting her subjectivity as both a mother and a poet. Taking a cue from her own mother, whose bearing of children likely exacerbated her heart condition, Christine refuses the psychiatrist's advice that she have an abortion because of precarious mental health. She insists: "I will have children. I will write poetry."[35] In Vanessa's imagined conversation between Christine and Sarkis, Christine's father does not value the birth of her daughter, saying, "'What good are girls?' ... Let me know if you have a son.' 'No, Father,' she said, and she did not call him when Fletcher was born the next year."[36] Despite Christine's limitations as a mother, she never favours one child above the other due to gender or personality, a stark contrast to Helen Bechdel's preferential treatment of her sons over her daughter, Alison. Differently from her mother-in-law, Maria, Christine offers Vanessa an alternative trajectory in matters of both love and art.

A paradigmatic example of this occurs in the Turin household at a highpoint of the Catholic calendar: Christmas. During this liturgical season, Christine performs all the festive duties expected of traditional mothers:

shopping, baking, wrapping and sending cards: "For one month each year my mother and grandmother would become friends. They sat side by side, putting cloves in oranges, hanging boughs of pine, discussing the Christmas Eve dinner."[37] Equally illuminating is the narrator's witnessing of her grandmother's scepticism toward institutional Catholicism when she attends Latin Mass with her. Vanessa realizes that the hierarchy of the Catholic Church would not accept the relationship of Florence and Bethany, two of Christine's closest friends (professors from Vassar), a lesbian couple who attend Christmas Eve dinner annually with the Turin family, "those gentle, large-hearted women, those solid citizens, satisfied, intelligent, calm, like no one else I have ever known. I cannot remember a Christmas without them."[38]

To reinforce a maternal literary legacy in *Ghost Dance*, Maso revises the dinner party scene in Woolf's *To the Lighthouse* by merging the figures of the mother and artist at the Christmas Eve dinner within the figure of Christine Wing: "She put her spoon down and moved her plate slightly, asked for the cream and sugar, and arranged those two pieces at an angle not far from her plate. She was setting up the rocks. She was seeing it now, the wintry coastline of Maine," reuniting with her long-time lover, Sabine.[39] Vanessa perceives her mother here as a lover, but inchoately she also receives the gift of imagination, allowing her to envisage a future collaboration with her mother as a sister artist. Rachel Blau DuPlessis' definition of reparenting is useful here as it relates to such a collaboration: "[T] he female artist is given a way of looping back and reenacting childhood ties, to achieve not the culturally approved ending in heterosexual romance, but rather the reparenting necessary to her second birth as an artist."[40] Perhaps the only way Vanessa can have a lesbian daughter's relationship to her mother is for that mother to be a lesbian lover herself, but the struggle to be both mother and poet within heterosexual marriage nearly kills Christine, despite Michael's support. A year after her mother's death, Vanessa visits Sabine, who represents both a mother and a lover to the bereft daughter, Vanessa (whose first name recalls Virginia Woolf's sister, Vanessa Bell, a painter). After they make love, Sabine enables Vanessa's experience of reparenting that will be necessary to her birth as an artist. Vanessa's desire for motherlove transcends boundaries, but Sabine re-establishes them by reminding her lover's daughter that "we must learn to love her from here."[41] By narrative's end, Vanessa achieves this transformation with the help of her brother and the guidance of Italian grandparents devoted to ritual, to which I return in the conclusion.

MARY CAPPELLO'S FAMILY ROMANCE: *NIGHT BLOOM*

In an autobiographical essay later expanded in *Night Bloom*, Mary Cappello writes "my mother writes the letter that I dream. Like a walk in the garden, it is not a grand gesture, but it is profound. The letter means that someone else is walking with her, that she will be there in the morning, that I can sleep."[42] Despite enduring agoraphobia and depression, Cappello's mother protected her daughter from the most dangerous outcome of her struggle: suicide. Not until Cappello is in college does her mother announce her decision to live, monumental news for both women, making Cappello aware of her mother's "one-time desire to die."[43] Unlike Vanessa's childhood experience of her mother's recurrent bouts of madness in *Ghost Dance*, Mary's is balanced early in life by her mother's outward ability to survive the most baneful aspects of an unhappy marriage and motherhood under patriarchy. Cappello suggests that her mother manages to achieve this stability through what Irene Gedalof describes in the context of women's migration processes, "everyday acts of embodied repetition."[44] Cappello argues that her mother's forms of suffering were not "failings but responses, conditions, ways of saying," somatic responses to childhood poverty. The daughter learns to read the language of creativity within her mother's embodied repetitions, whether through domestic chores or letter-writing: "When my mother painted the walls of our cramped home orange and blue, she was trying to let enter the sun, the moon." Despite incessant worries about her mother, the girl-child Mary lets "the blue surround me like a tidal comfort as I tried to fall asleep.... It's past midnight, and I still can't sleep ... until I hear the tiny tic of gas stove, and smell of coffee percolating. Now I know my mother's pen is moving across the page: my mother writes the letter that I dream."[45] Similar to Maso's and Bechdel's intensely focused relationships with their mothers, Cappello's childhood is equally marked by the daughter's desire to read the language of her mother's pain; as such, she wants to be the one who saves her mother.

Calling for a more theorized analysis about the role of reproduction in migration, Gedalof refers to feminist philosopher Adriana Cavarero's reevaluation of the mythic figure of Penelope, engaged in the "unending work of weaving and reweaving," to think differently about matters of time and place of reproduction in order to "complicate our understanding of the meaning of repetitive, reproductive practices undertaken within the domestic sphere ... for ... there is always the possibility of a repetition that

196 M. J. BONA

undoes, a repetition that communicates agency and produces something new and challenging."[46] Cappello implements something new through the trope of the garden, which links generations and rituals of preservation in *Night Bloom*, thereby revaluing Italian American family customs and a maternal space that unites thought and matter. In doing so, the author simultaneously pays homage to two literary foremothers, Virginia Woolf, who cherished and wrote in her garden at Monk's House, and Alice Walker, whose mother's garden uncovers unheralded creative acts: "our mothers and grandmothers have ... handed on the creative spark, the seed of the flower they themselves never hoped to see: or like a sealed letter they could not plainly read."[47]

Daughters have both resisted and discovered their mothers' gifts, opening the sealed letter to reveal creative acts unsung. Such is the focus of Mary Cappello's *Night Bloom*, which contextualizes her family's migration experience within a discourse of ethnic identity, focusing on the long-term effects of working-class identity on generations that follow, experiences which resonate also with the Black American woman's experience of motherhood and oppressions both racial and gendered. In homage to her migrating forebears and a mother who saved material remnants of immigrant writing, Mary Cappello's *Night Bloom*, like *Ghost Dance*, also engages in the work of recovery with the memoirist acting as third-generation rescuer. *Night Bloom* carefully explores several intersecting relationships: between family and neighbourhood; between working and middle classes; and between a "lesbian great granddaughter" and the family to whom she bears witness.[48]

Mary Cappello tells the story of extended family without excluding excruciating facts on the aftershocks of migration: poverty, fear and psychic pain. For all the eloquence and creativity Cappello attributes to her mother—"laughing, talking, performing, reciting poetry, singing"—Rosemary "rarely talked about growing up in poverty," refusing to burden her children with stories of "how living with the threat of losing one's heat, water, electricity, and not having enough food to eat can easily engender states of terror."[49] In this way, Rosemary Cappello parallels Helen Bechdel's reticence, both mothers harbouring fears and anguish they deliberately choose not to share with their children. The memoirist Cappello must then literally translate her family's story, her grandfather's Italian writing, in order to interpret the language of her mother's "body in terror."[50] Rather than consulting psychology texts, as Bechdel does, Cappello turns to the shared family language (consulting gardening manuals!) to examine maternal Neapolitan and paternal Sicilian forebears—all committed to gardening.

Cappello's memoir constructs sexuality along the lines of family genealogy, identifying her queerness *within* family personalities, modelling her development on their non-conventional habits of mind and heart. Cappello de-centres authorial control in *Night Bloom* by placing her maternal grandfather's and mother's stories next to hers, destabilizing hierarchical notions of selfhood over family. In an attempt to link her story to his, Cappello incorporates into her memoir her cobbler grandfather's journal entries, his daily acts of survival written on the materials of his trade—the tabs used to mark down the repair job to be done—alongside his hopeless feelings of vulnerability when struggling to feed an impoverished, immigrant family. Absorbing her grandfather's working-class ethos and activity of journal writing, Cappello creates a literary collage by uniting the voices of three generations of writers: grandfather, mother and daughter. By doing so, Cappello unearths the linked connection between ethnicity and sexuality through three generations of shared letters, content that contains "unspeakable truths and inappropriate yearnings":

> My immigrant heritage is marked by inappropriateness, delegitimized sound, call it the noise of my grandfather's desire to make a living crafting shoes, my mother's desire to be accounted for as a woman, of my desire to love other women, of our collective desire to be writers in an American culture that stifles the imagination of difference.[51]

By relocating queerness within her Italian American family, Mary Cappello achieves important aims in *Night Bloom*, enhancing not only the mother-daughter bond but also queer sexuality for unconventional family members: "In 'becoming queer,' I was becoming what my Italian American forbears denied about themselves even as they provided the example. In becoming queer, I see myself as having made something wonderful out of an Italian American fabric, the Italian American weavers of which were too ready and willing to discard."[52] As Anne-Marie Fortier explains, by "exploring the intersections of immigration, ethnicity, and sexuality, Cappello interrogates the very construction of Italian patriarchal culture.... She thus reveals the intricate web of connections between ethnicity and homophobia, and suggests that queer is an American construct that serves to keep the Italian immigrant at a distance, 'out of place,' by exhorting prescriptions of gendered and sexual norms."[53]

Cappello's narrative structure in *Night Bloom* emulates the shape that many traditional immigrant novels take; however, as third-generation queer daughter, Mary redeems not only immigrant ancestors, but also

198 M. J. BONA

those represented by her mother's second generation, who inherited "the pain or deformation caused by the material or laboring conditions" of her peasant forebears.[54] Cappello reverses the traditional sloughing off of the parental generation, attributing part of her mother's artistry to an indigent childhood and a strategy she adopted to cope with an untenable marriage: "More hippy than happy homemaker ... my mother nevertheless struggled daily as so many women still do, with the oppressive nature of domestic Law.... [S]he sent out lifelines in the form of letters, so many match stems, sometimes blazing, sometimes quickly spent, in the dark."[55] Cappello interprets traditionally unheralded women's art—gardening, quilting and cooking—as part and parcel of her mother's creative arsenal and of equal measure with her letter and poetry writing.

The artistry of Rosemary Cappello's gardening ritualized through the night-blooming cereus plant becomes an act of communion with her daughter, replacing old-world fatalistic fears with energetic observation. In the conclusion, I reprise Cappello's garden trope and the flower rituals it generates, uniting mother and daughter across several boundaries. Suffice to say here that in *Night Bloom*, Mary Cappello presents an example of a new-world Italian American mother, who instils artistic vitality in her daughter. Rather than tell her child to "*Mangia! Mangia!* (Eat! Eat!), my mother told me in English to 'look.' She was always commanding me thus, with exuberance, and especially before flowers and paintings.... One must always retain the capacity to be astonished."[56] In search of her mother's garden, Mary Cappello finds her own. *Night Bloom* embraces the trope of desire, for the memoir simultaneously functions, Nancy Gerber explains, as a "mother-artist" text, rupturing "notions of hegemonic heteronormativity. Desire is figured in the mother-artists' relationship to language," and, I might add, in their relationships to daughters. For the queer artist-daughter, the mother becomes the subject of "her own story, an artist in her own right."[57]

LOVING HELEN: ALISON BECHDEL'S *ARE YOU MY MOTHER?*

Chronically frustrated by Helen's maternal care, Alison Bechdel is the lesbian daughter who remains the lover manqué. In vain desiring Helen's approval of her sexual and artistic choices, Alison remains in middle age at times paralysed by her mother's uniform responses to her daughter's choices, though Alison cannot stop herself from seeking her mother's approval. In this way, Bechdel reiterates the psychic framework of her first graphic memoir, *Fun Home*, a story about her father's bisexuality and death when she was in college.[58] *Fun Home*'s engagement with trauma "puts pressure on dominant conceptions of trauma's unrepresentability" as Hillary Chute argues.[59] In "thinking about why there are so many graphic narratives about trauma," Cathy Caruth writes, "'to be traumatized is precisely to be possessed by an image or an event.'"[60] If Alison is haunted by imagined scenes of her father's closeted queer identity and death in *Fun Home*, she extends her preoccupation in *Are You My Mother?* to a prior trauma, the primal separation from her mother's womb/body. As Lisa Diedrich argues, the passage from the first memoir to the second "echoes the shifting preoccupations in the history of psychoanalysis: from oedipal father to pre-oedipal mother."[61] Typical of second-wave feminism's mantra of making the personal political is Bechdel's decision "to push beyond the limits of the personal and [think] about women's art as linked to the mother-daughter psychodrama."[62]

While she admits to having "elaborately avoid[ed] the story of me and my mother," Bechdel shifts in her recent memoir to her "complex and inscrutable" mother in order to scrutinize their relationship, implementing Donald Winnicott's psychoanalytical theories to serve "as a structure for [her] book."[63] As critics observe, Bechdel's book is conceptually recursive, "a meta-book about the writing of both memoirs," as JoAnne Ruvoli comments.[64] Generously inserting excerpts by canonic writers and psychoanalysts, Bechdel overlays her text with myriad references to Virginia Woolf, Adrienne Rich, Freud, Alice Miller, Dr. Seuss, A.A. Milne and Anne Bradstreet to name just a few. Helen Bechdel employs the term "metabook" to describe her daughter's memoir, which illuminates not only her perspicacity, but also Alison's recognition of the high-level reading habits of her English teacher mother, aligning her with recognized scholarly figures and the distinguished Helen Vendler, whom her mother desired to become.

While not an acclaimed critic, the person Alison's mother did become is complex and creative, admired by her daughter in several ways throughout *Are You My Mother?* As a muse figure, Helen launches Alison's thousand ships, the author's non-linear and layered experimental style an homage to her equally multifaceted mother. As Ruvoli explains, "the one reader of *Fun Home* that matters most to Bechdel—[is] her mother, Helen Fontana Bechdel," who remains "a powerful, but elusive presence."

200 M. J. BONA

Shifting the narrative focus to the maternal in her second memoir, Bechdel portrays a mother who continues to retain her illusiveness, perhaps representing "a woman of her generation" (born in the 1930s).[65] A combination of the mother's era, a small-town milieu (that exacerbated the pressure to repress unconventional sexuality), a move from a working-class to a middle-class identity, and an Italian ethnicity under erasure all account for Helen's difficulties in coping with her daughter's desire.

In her epigraph to *Are You My Mother?* Alison Bechdel signifies the primacy of Virginia Woolf as her literary maternal forebear, quoting from *To the Lighthouse*: "For nothing was simply one thing." This announcement serves as Bechdel's philosophical mantra. Late in Woolf's novel, this quotation appears after Mrs Ramsay has died (and the First World War and ten years have intervened), and the grown children finally take the long-anticipated boat trip to the lighthouse with their autocratic father. After experiencing childhood disillusionment of imagining but not experiencing the trip to the lighthouse, upon approach, James thinks to himself: "So that was the Lighthouse, was it? No, the other was also the Lighthouse. For nothing was simply one thing. The other Lighthouse was true too."[66] As the lighthouse symbolizes at least two different perceptions of time, Woolf manages to conceptualize its movement as forms of consciousness, as Michel Serres explains, between the discontinuous, but intermittent, a process that never ceases, and continuous, stretching out over long periods of time. Like the lamp of the lighthouse that marks its "rhythmic measure ... a process that never ceases be its *tempo* fast or slow," the idea of time itself continues to present itself in intersecting thoughts of past and present in *To the Lighthouse* (p. 277).[67] Likewise, Bechdel's memoir juxtaposes childhood memories (including thoughts and feelings she attributes to her mother) alongside present maternal conversations and past and present analysis in therapy sessions.

Trying to cope with her mother's disapproval of her lesbianism and her art, Alison Bechdel recalls the crucial metaphor of the lighthouse by Virginia Woolf, who achieved the following in her art and life: (1) she revolutionized the novel form; (2) she wrote an autobiographical novel about both parents, liberating herself from them; (3) she loved other women sexually; (4) and she created an artist figure in Lily Briscoe who expresses both an exploration of autonomy and a recursion to the figure of the mother, also conceptualized as an artist in *To the Lighthouse*. Juxtaposed to the children's boat trip to the lighthouse are Lily's shore reflections, the painter crying out for "Mrs. Ramsay! ... Mrs. Ramsay!" as she moves closer to achieving her artistic vision.[68]

Are You My Mother? registers a conception of time that is concurrently continuous and discontinuous, Bechdel measuring out the rhythmic pulsations of her work vis-à-vis past memories and present conversations with her mother. In a confessional mode cum-therapy, Bechdel unflinchingly portrays a middle-aged woman still calling out for her mother, and feeling like her precursor, Lily Briscoe, annihilated as much by her mother's absence as by her presence. Bechdel's second memoir comprises seven chapters, each framed by a dream Bechdel narrates and visually renders on a black background, and each ending with a two-page spread of images that, as Ruvoli explains, "echo and refract the patches, webs, silence, words, and artifice that permeate the rest of the narrative and bind the mother and daughter. As [Lynda] Barry might say, each image also has significant trouble behind it."[69]

An exceptional example of Bechdel's turmoil graphically rendered occurs in the final frame of Chap. 4. Unable to forgive herself for not being present to console her mother on the night she asks Bruce for a divorce, Bechdel torments herself textually and graphically in this frame. A single image on a two-page spread illustrates Bechdel's ongoing guilt over not answering a phone call from her mother in college, decades after the event occurs. Further irony: her mother had been calling an old dorm phone number, yet this knowledge does not assuage Alison, who laments, "I wasn't there when she had needed me," punishing herself in three repeated caption rectangles: "One ring reverberating into another. And another. And another." Coloured in black, grey and red, Bechdel's frame suggests both photographic precision and the persistent reminder of her mother's unmet desire scrolled horizontally in capital red letters across the frame and the phone on its hook:

IINNNGGGDRRIIINNGGDRRIII

That the letters are capitalized in a gradient colour of red, cordovan or maroon, epitomizes Bechdel's self-torment as this is also the colour her mother uses to respond to Bechdel's drafts—it is both the colour of correction and of menstrual blood. Such consanguinity is not lost on the author, for her mother's need is perceived by Bechdel as simultaneously both disciplining and excessive.[70]

This is but one example of the lesbian daughter's tendency toward intensive empathy for her mother's plight and it parallels in its obsessional fervour the responses of daughters Vanessa Turin in *Ghost Dance* and Mary Cappello in *Night Bloom* to what they imagine is their mother's anguish.

Genie Giaimo attributes Bechdel's self-driven torment about her mother to an "overdeveloped theory of mind [that] allows her to create worlds containing minute details of her characters' psychology ... but it also drives her obsession with finding referential certainty through autobiographical artifacts."[71] Bechdel frames a memory of hearing her mother's sobs when she, Alison, is 5 years old with an excerpt from Woolf and a case study from Winnicott: both literary and psychological archives invite Bechdel to probe intensively the persistent if not obsessional thoughts about her mother's sorrows and, correspondingly, the author's own unmet desires. Woolf's literary exorcism of her parents in writing *To the Lighthouse* and Winnicott's breakthrough therapy with a toddler's suffering after her mother's recent childbirth, serve to frame Alison's relationship to her mother, intensifying her preoccupation with her mother's feelings. Despite Alison's overdeveloped awareness of her mother's psychological states and cognitive processes, she manages simultaneously to assert and to reveal the benefit that being a lesbian has had on her psyche, helping her to transcend sheer intellectualization: "But now I speculate that being a lesbian actually saved me.... If it weren't for the unconventionality of my desires, my mind might never have been forced to reckon with my body."[72] As Heike Bauer asserts, "where 'queer' is a term associated with movement and crossing of boundaries, Bechdel nevertheless emphasizes that her lesbianism—which she calls 'the central organizing principle of [her] existence'—guides the direction of her travels."[73]

Bechdel's unconventional desires direct her compulsion to document dreamscapes and a vast arsenal of materials to produce what Diedrich calls "a veritable archive of thinking and feeling."[74] Inscribing repetition as "a kind of obsessive embodiment," as Chute describes Bechdel's drawing of archival materials, the memoirist re-inhabits spaces as a form of reproduction, therefore moving her closer to her mother.[75] Within that treasure trove is stored Helen Bechdel's unconventional desire. A post-Second World War generation mother, Helen's maternal work in fact abets her artistic talents, and I would submit that her artistry is informed by an Italian American heritage under partial erasure. Committed from the outset to rupture notions of heteronormativity, Bechdel refigures desire in her mother's relationship to art forms that include writing, performing and cloth-working. The queer artist-daughter documents Helen Fontana Bechdel as an artist in her own right, one whose sewing activities connect her to Italian migratory experience in which handwork constituted one form of cultural production that undergoes transformation in a small-town setting.

The extended family culture of Mary Cappello's second-generation mother, Rosemary, the latter's marriage to a Sicilian man, and the ethnically diverse neighbourhood [where she lived and brought up her children?] invited Mary to maintain an identity inflected by *italianità*.[76] In contrast, Alison Bechdel's mother, Helen, is represented in relation to several artistic forms—sewing, costume designing, acting, piano playing and writing—ostensibly disconnected from a heritage that likely made such work possible. Why is this so? Perhaps her marriage to Bruce and small-town America de-emphasized an Italian connection, but Helen Bechdel ultimately claimed it herself on behalf of none other than her friend, actor-comedian, Dom DeLuise, to whom she paid tribute in the *Centre Daily Times*, the newspaper of State College, PA, and for whom she wrote regular articles and reviews. Recalling when they met (at the Cleveland Playhouse), Helen writes, "We had a lot in common. We were the youngest members of the group. We were second-generation Italian Americans. And we both liked to eat and showed it."[77]

Alison Bechdel makes sundry references to her mother's Catholic upbringing, juxtaposing re-drawn First Communion photos of both daughter and mother over a two-page spread, describing her mother's physiognomy in terms similar to her own: "She's dark, pale, shy. All the things I disliked about my own appearance."[78] Inheriting a passion for opera from her father, Andrew Fontana (who was featured as a solo baritone in concerts and radio broadcasts), Helen's multiple creative interests are frequently reproduced throughout *Are You My Mother?* Bechdel refers to her mother's artistry using cloth-working metaphors culled from actual experience and dreams: patching, mending, costume-making and spider web dreaming. In one of their daily conversations, Alison recalls her mother's costume designing for a fashion show, using "mother/daughter models," with "costumes from her personal collection." Pulling out a childhood dress made by her mother, Alison describes its "au courant" style and "mod stripes." What breaks Bechdel's heart is her mother's demonstration of maternal care: "On the inside, there's an iron-on patch as familiar as my own hand. This evidence of my mother's care is wrenching."[79] Suffering depression after her parents died, and a difficult marriage, Helen Bechdel, by sheer force of will, demonstrated this important fact to her daughter: "*the life we save is our own.*"[80]

Implementing reading as a form of maternal mending, Helen, in her usual fashion, offers her daughter revelatory information from a writer she admires, Dorothy Gallagher, whose well-respected biographies reveal a writer known for restraint and whose subjects of biography are worthy of

204 M. J. BONA

an "admirable libretto."[81] In the concluding pages of *Are You My Mother?* Alison interprets her mother's reading as a form of healing: "'The writer's business is to find the shape in unruly life and to serve her story. Not you may note, to serve her family, or to serve the truth, but to serve the story.' Family be damned.... The story must be served."[82] In a final allusion, Bechdel references her mother's singing the inspired aria, "Là ci darem la mano" ("There we will give each other our hands"). An *opera buffa*, *Don Giovanni* (*Il dissoluto punito*), with a libretto by Lorenzo da Ponte, is "raised to sublimity by Mozart's music."[83] This reference allows Alison Bechdel paradoxically to end on a comic note, sharing her mother's delight regarding the staging of the opera as bedroom farce, sitting comfortably alongside the *donné* of her memoir, "Don Giovanni is in perpetual pursuit of his mother, too."[84]

WRITING THEIR WAY HOME: CLOSURES AND THE MOTHER'S RETURN

In her examination of "narratives of queer migrations," Anne-Marie Fortier examines the idea of homecoming and asks, "Is it possible to relocate queerness in the home without rendering 'home' as a site of justification, but rather as a site of possibilities and constraints?"[85] These writers offer sites of possibility in their narrative endings, reprising the mother–daughter plot, as Rachel Blau DuPlessis has shown, to "sever the narrative from formerly conventional structures ... and consciousness about women."[86] In each ending, the authors re-witness their mothers in action, revealing subversive strength through acts of mothering toward daughters desperately in love with them.

Through the creation of Christine Wing in *Ghost Dance*, Carole Maso both "reinvents and challenges the traditional Italian mother/Madonna icon," despite the fact that Christine is neither Italian American nor particularly maternal.[87] Christine's beatific return at novel's end is Maso's homage to a tradition she embraces through critique. *Ghost Dance*'s ending is as operatic as Puccini, Maso inventing a queer rendition of a bohemian's garret for her protagonist, Vanessa Turin, so that she will survive mother-loss and pull herself up "out of [her] mother's body, which lay motionless in the snow."[88] Meeting her brother at his third-floor walk-up during a New York snowstorm, Vanessa reunites with Fletcher to perform the ghost dance ritual, learned from Grandpa Angelo, after he renounced his Italian heritage for what he considered a more genuine, Native

American one. Of importance here is Vanessa's witnessing her mother's return in the form of the Topaz Bird, Maso reconstructing the story of the Annunciation by combining both the angel Gabriel and the Blessed Virgin Mary within the figure of one mother, Christine Wing. As though to reinforce the impossibility of maintaining the ideal Madonna/mother figure here on earth, Maso portrays an artist-mother, whose tragically foreshortened life underscores the danger of traditional expectations placed upon women. In making the choice to live, Vanessa says to her spirit mother, "'We can't come yet, Mommy.... We must live.' And she knows it is true."[89] By saying good-bye, Vanessa sustains her relationship with her beloved mother; at the same time, she manages to collaborate alongside her brother to bring that relationship to an end.[90]

Though less operatic, Mary Cappello's conclusion of *Night Bloom* equally inspires as the author relocates queerness in the garden and through her mother's cultivation of the night-blooming cereus plant, "the flower [that is] queer. In Freudian terms, it's polymorphously perverse. Undomesticated it fails to grow in a containable direction, and one wrong pruning can prevent it from yielding a flower."[91] An "unflinching totem" in her family, the night-blooming cereus is like a "magic wand with no right way to use it," evincing different meanings in each gardener's hand.[92] The lessons of carefully plying one's trade are those Cappello learned exceptionally well from her maternal grandfather and mother, Rosemary. As a result, the memoirist is able to conceive and construct a home space that is a site of possibility and memory, teaching her to carry the lessons of the garden over the thresholds of "the hallowed halls of academia," night-blooming cereus plants in tow: "The gardens I grew up in stood for willfulness, patience, and an abiding love of changing forms."[93]

In the final pages of *Night Bloom*, Cappello explains how she extends in adulthood the flower rituals performed by her mother when Mary was a child. With her lover, Jean, and with friends who attend her night-blooming cereus parties, Cappello pays a final tribute in *Night Bloom* to her mother who roused her girl-child from sleep to partake in a ritual as unconventional as the undomesticated plant and in a "hopeless neighborhood where nothing was meant to bloom."[94] Providing her daughter with an example of unusual beauty, Rosemary Cappello embraces the "witchy, bewitching ... hideous monstrosity of a plant," fully understanding the magnificence of its secret: its nocturnal flowering.[95] Anticipating a time when she will have the strength to watch the white, fragrant, flower nod its head and die, Mary Cappello holds off narrating this event, but knows that, like her mother, she will also learn how to say good-bye.

Alison Bechdel reprises a scene of the crippled child game she played with her mother in the concluding pages of *Are You My Mother?* Referencing Winnicott's use of play as a therapeutic technique practised with children patients, Bechdel stages this final scene, "for both theatrical and therapeutic effect," employing "graphic play as healing play."[96] Utilizing a bird's-eye view in the final double-page spread of mother and daughter, Bechdel bifurcates the aerial view with a high-angle shot that reveals a young mother, Helen Bechdel, arms akimbo, guiding her charge. The pages are slightly off-centre and weighted toward the mother, and this final image in black, as Ruvoli explains, "controls the reader's focus. The diagonals of the cabinets, oven and table create an internal arrow that baby Alison is crawling toward.... [T]he directional page design of the arrow suggests she is moving away from the mother."[97] Attributing her mother's willingness to play the "crippled child game" as simultaneously the "moment my mother taught me to write," Bechdel recognizes that her mother's generosity enables the creative trajectory that becomes her daughter's life.[98] In being able to "get up now," Alison Bechdel will be able to say good-bye to her mother, always knowing that it was Helen Fontana, who "has given me the way out."[99]

NOTES

1. I use the word "lesbian" to refer to the primary way these writers identify their orientation in their narratives. I use the term "queer" more largely to refer to the ways in which heteronormative discourse has been challenged in debates about sexualities across historical, cultural and textual landscapes.
2. Giorgio, "Mothers and Daughters in Western Europe," p. 29.
3. Marianne Hirsch's *The Mother/Daughter Plot* continues to be essential reading for interpreting the ideology of motherhood as it intersects with a range of women's English and American novels and for feminist revisions of psychoanalytic thought within that literature.
4. The term *italianità* has been adopted by scholars developing the field of Italian American literary studies to describe the meanings related to an imagined or recovered cultural identity.
5. Giunta and Sciorra, *Embroidered Stories*, p. 3. Alison Bechdel confirmed her mother's Italian American roots in an email to the scholar, JoAnne Ruvoli. Email correspondence with Ruvoli, 6 February 2015.
6. I reference the subtitle of Richard Alba's work, *Italian Americans: Into the Twilight of Ethnicity*. Alba argues for a diminished relation to ethnicity in later generations of Italian-descended Americans.

7. For my attempt to undo the essentialism that attends requests to write about the defining features of an ethnic group, see my "On Being an Italian American Woman." For an examination of complementary forms of mothering in literary Italian America, see my "Mothers and Daughters."

8. For edited collections on media representations of Italians and Italian Americans see *Anti-Italianism: Essays on a Prejudice*, ed. Connell and Gardaphé; and *Making Italian America: Consumer Culture and the Production of Ethnic Identities*, ed. Simone Cinotto.

9. See Quinn's "'We Were Working on an Erotic Song Cycle'," p. 94. While Maso makes no overt connection to Italian American heritage in *Ava*, Quinn reads it as part of a third-generational response, revealing an "Italian American female aesthetic." Quinn places the novel within the parameters of "the cultural marker of *italianità* in order to reveal the ways in which Maso's work is ethnically and formally expansive" (pp. 94, 93). I take several cues from Quinn and my essay is indebted to her work.

10. Cvetkovich. "Drawing the Archive," p. 124. Cvetkovich explains that the focus on "secrecy and shame attached to Bechdel's father's sexual life make[s] it function like occluded trauma and suggest[s] the relevance of witness to a range of seemingly ordinary contexts," p. 113.

11. According to Katrina Irving in *Immigrant Mothers*, feminization of immigrants from southern and eastern Europe "ultimately set the discursive stage for a full-blown nativist argument," advocating "curtailing immigration in order to protect the native vigor of Anglo-Saxons from contamination by weak, effeminate aliens," p. 19. Irving's thesis delineates how "immigrant maternity, became an entrenched site of representational struggle within the public discourse of immigration," p. 3.

12. Cvetkovich, "Drawing the Archive," p. 113.

13. Sambuco. *Corporeal Bonds*, p. 6.

14. Rich, *Of Woman Born*, p. 225. According to Brenda Silver, Rich's statement on the relationship between mothers and daughters is "one of the most widely cited statements to come out of the [North American] women's movement" (Silver, "Mothers, Daughters, Mrs. Ramsay," p. 265).

15. Hirsch, *The Mother/Daughter Plot*, p. 10.

16. Rich, *Of Woman Born*, p. 226.

17. Miller, "The Entangled Self: Genre Bondage in the Age of Memoir," p. 544.

18. Woolf, *A Room of One's Own*, p. 96.

19. Maso, *Ghost Dance*, p. 49. Maso has authored ten books, seven of which are novels. She is known for her experimental prose, a willingness to break with conventional narrative, and a mixed-genre style that is equal parts poetic and allusive.

20. Maso, *Ghost Dance*, pp. 8, 16, 10.

208   M. J. BONA

21. I borrow this description from the title of Robert Coles' book, *The Call of Stories: Teaching and the Moral Imagination.*
22. Pipino, "*I Have Found my Voice*", p. 149. I am indebted to Pipino's analysis of *Ghost Dance*; the quotation from Maso is from a telephone interview Pipino conducted with the author on 8 April 1999.
23. Pipino, "*I Have Found my Voice*", p. 156.
24. Maso, "Interview by Nicole Cooley," p. 34.
25. Pipino, "*I Have Found my Voice*", pp. 149, 150.
26. Gilbert, *Death's Door: Modern Dying and the Ways We Grieve*, p. 3.
27. Maso, *Ghost Dance*, p. 65.
28. Maso, *Ghost Dance*, p. 79.
29. Maso claims that her mother, a nurse, was her first and only mentor: "She took me very seriously ... demanded that I come home with all A's. I worked hard and took myself very seriously—it became very bound up in my love for her" (Maso, "Interview by Joyce Hackett," p. 68).
30. Louise DeSalvo, "'We Will Speak and Bear Witness': Storytelling as Testimony and Healing in *Ghost Dance.*" In contrast to DeSalvo, who argues that Vanessa must separate herself from her mother to begin her healing process, I argue that Vanessa's understanding of separation is influenced by her lesbian love, complicating the separation process and enhancing her desire to reclaim her mother through creativity.
31. Maso, *Ghost Dance*, p. 103.
32. Maso, *Ghost Dance*, p. 111.
33. Maso, *Ghost Dance*, p. 182.
34. Pipino, "*I Have Found My Voice*", p. 155.
35. Maso, *Ghost Dance*, p. 256.
36. Maso, *Ghost Dance*, p. 212. Disappointed in America, Sarkis Wing changes his surname back to the Armenian Wingarian, returning to his home country never to see his daughters again.
37. Maso, *Ghost Dance*, p. 232.
38. Maso, *Ghost Dance*, p. 234.
39. Maso, *Ghost Dance*, p. 237. In the celebrated dinner party scene of *To the Lighthouse*, compare Lily's thoughts: "In a flash she saw her picture, and thought, Yes, I shall put the tree further in the middle; then I shall avoid that awkward space.... She took up the salt cellar and put it down again on a flower in pattern in the table-cloth, as to remind herself to move the tree" (p. 128).
40. DuPlessis, *Writing Beyond the Ending*, p. 94.
41. Maso, *Ghost Dance*, p. 258.
42. Cappello, "My Mother Writes the Letter That I Dream," p. 133. Mary Cappello has published five works of non-fiction prose. Cappello's university webpage describes her work as "creating forms of disruptive beauty,

QUEER DAUGHTERS AND THEIR MOTHERS: CAROLE MASO, MARY... 209

figuring memory in the information age, bringing incompatible knowledges in the same space, and working at the borders of literary genres." (http://web.uri.edu/english/meet/mary-cappello/)

43. Cappello, *Night Bloom*, p. 122.
44. Gedalof, "Birth, Belonging and Migrant Mothers," p. 82.
45. Cappello, *Night Bloom*, pp. 74–75.
46. Gedalof, "Birth, Belonging and Migrant Mothers," p. 92.
47. For archival photographs of Virginia and Leonard Woolf's garden at Monk's House in the village of Sussex, see Caroline Zoob's *Virginia Woolf's Garden*. The quotation is from Alice Walker's *In Search of Our Mothers' Gardens*, p. 240.
48. Cappello, *Night Bloom*, p. 11.
49. Cappello, *Night Bloom*, pp. 126–27.
50. Cappello, *Night Bloom*, p. 127.
51. Cappello, *Night Bloom*, p. 73.
52. Cappello, *Night Bloom*, p. 181.
53. Fortier, "'Coming Home': Queer Migrations and Multiple Evocations of Home," p. 417. Fortier mistakenly locates Cappello's memoir in working-class South Philadelphia. Cappello grew up in Darby, a working-class suburb different than South Philly, where Mary's father's side of the family lived. Mary spent ample time with her Sicilian relatives in South Philly and with her mother's Neapolitan side of the family in Darby. I am grateful to South Philly native and poet, Maria Famà, for these details.
54. Cappello, *Night Bloom*, p. 43.
55. Cappello, *Night Bloom*, p. 70–71.
56. Cappello, *Night Bloom*, p. 252.
57. Gerber, *Portrait of the Mother-Artist*, pp. 12, 5.
58. Alison Bechdel was first known for her long-running serial comic strip, *Dykes to Watch Out For*. Her acclaimed *Fun Home* explores her relationship with her father, Bruce Bechdel, whose homosexuality undergirds the author's focus, including the uncertain nature of his death. Bechdel's follow-up to her "father-book," *Are You My Mother?*, was published when her mother was alive and this "affect[ed] the story," as Mary E. Barber clarifies in her review of the book (p. 124).
59. Chute, *Graphic Women*, p. 182.
60. As quoted in Chute, *Graphic Women*, p. 183.
61. Diedrich, "Graphic Analysis: Transitional Phenomena in Alison Bechdel's *Are You My Mother?*," p. 185.
62. Bilger, "The Other Shoe Drops," p. 14.
63. As quoted in Grace Bello's "Materfamilias," p. 35.
64. Ruvoli. "Review of Alison Bechdel's *Are You My Mother?*."
65. Ruvoli, "Review of Alison Bechdel's *Are You My Mother?*."

210   M. J. BONA

66. Woolf, *To the Lighthouse*, p. 277.
67. Serres, "*Feux et Signaux de Brume*: Virginia Woolf's Lighthouse," p. 110.
68. Woolf, *To the Lighthouse*, p. 269. I am indebted to Phyllis Rose's *Women of Letters: A Life of Virginia Woolf* for an interpretive biography of Woolf.
69. Ruvoli, "Review of Alison Bechdel's *Are You My Mother?*"
70. Bechdel, *Are You My Mother?*, pp. 158–59.
71. Giaimo, "Psychological Diffusions," p. 43.
72. Bechdel, *Are You My Mother?*, 156.
73. Bauer, "Vital Lines Drawn from Books," p. 269.
74. Adapting Ann Cvetkovitch's terminology about drawing the archive, Diedrich reveals at least "three levels of obsessive-compulsive documentation" at play in Bechdel's memoir, explaining it as "a meta-obsessive-compulsive documentation of the process of documentation itself." Diedrich. "Graphic Analysis," p. 186.
75. Chute explains, "By embodied I mean not simply *concrete*, but that everything Bechdel represents—from letters to diaries to photographs—is drawn by hand.... She inhabits the past ... by giving it visual form, but further by the embodied process of reinscribing archival documents" (Chute, *Graphic Women*, p. 183).
76. Bechdel by contrast grew up in Beech Creek, PA, a borough of Lock Haven, PA, with a racial makeup of over 90 per cent white. Bechdel's grandparents, Rachel Victoria Rohe and Andrew Fontana, whose marriage was mostly likely considered "mixed" during a period in America history when exogamy was considered unseemly, met in the town of Bellefonte and were employed by the Bush House Hotel ("Obituary for Helen Bechdel").
77. Helen Bechdel, "Remembering a Friend from the Theater."
78. Bechdel, *Are You My Mother?*, pp. 88–89.
79. Bechdel, *Are You My Mother?*, p. 109. Helen Bechdel's talents as a costumier were posthumously on display in "A Costumer's Legacy: Helen Fontana Bechdel" at the Mifflinburg Buggy Museum. The exhibit featured costumes from plays in which Helen performed. See "Buggy Museum Exhibit Remembers Helen Bechdel."
80. Walker, "Saving the Life that Is Your Own: The Importance of Models in the Artist's Life." In Walker, *In Search of Our Mothers' Gardens*, pp. 3–14.
81. Daniel Aaron says this in his review of Gallagher's biography of Carlo Tresca. A parallel to Helen Bechdel's own *sprezzatura* in the face of extremity is Aaron's description of Gallagher's style in writing about a figure like Tresca: "Dorothy Gallagher's ... almost laconic, recital of his flamboyant career ... is anything but operatic; in fact, it reads like an inspired police report," (Aaron, "Who Killed Carlo Tresca?," p. 43).
82. Bechdel, *Are You My Mother?* pp. 283–84.

83. As quoted in *The New Grove Book of Operas*, ed. Stanley Sadie, p. 165.
84. Bechdel, *Are You My Mother?* p. 286.
85. Fortier, "'Coming Home': Queer Migrations and Multiple Evocations of Home," p. 408.
86. DuPlessis, *Writing Beyond the Ending*, p. x.
87. Pipino, "*I Have Found My Voice*", p. 154.
88. Maso, *Ghost Dance*, p. 267.
89. Maso, *Ghost Dance*, p. 275.
90. Mourning rituals, Susan Letzler Cole explains, are performances of "ambivalence on behalf of an absent presence" (Cole, *The Absent One*, p. 1). This is the paradox of grieving Maso portrays in *Ghost Dance*.
91. Cappello, *Night Bloom*, p. 258.
92. Cappello, *Night Bloom*, p. 253.
93. Cappello, *Night Bloom*, p. 254.
94. Cappello, *Night Bloom*, p. 259.
95. Cappello, *Night Bloom*, p. 258.
96. Diedrich, "Graphic Analysis," p. 189. Diedrich explains, "The game becomes an orthopedic treatment that eases Alison's feelings of being hobbled," p. 202.
97. Ruvoli explains, this image contrasts "the final image in *Fun Home*, where Alison is airborne and leaping back, but into … the arms of the father. In *Are You My Mother?* the color of the mother's shirt forms a kind of triangle … and her arms are placed in a position that can be read anatomically as a female uterus. It is almost a figurative birthing scene." Email correspondence with JoAnne Ruvoli, 30 July 2015.
98. Bechdel, *Are You My Mother?*, p. 287.
99. Bechdel, *Are You My Mother?*, p. 289.

BIBLIOGRAPHY

Aaron, Daniel. "Who Killed Carlo Tresca?" Review of *All the Right Enemies: The Life and Murder of Carlo Tresca*, by Dorothy Gallagher. *New York Review of Books*, 15 June 1989: pp. 43–45.

Barber, Mary E. Review of *Are You My Mother? A Comic Drama* by Alison Bechdel. *Journal of Gay & Lesbian Mental Health* n. 17 (2013): pp. 124–26.

Bauer, Heike. "Vital Lines Drawn from Books: Difficult Feelings in Alison Bechdel's *Fun Home* and *Are You My Mother?*." *Journal of Lesbian Studies* n. 18 (2014): pp. 266–281.

Bechdel, Alison. *Are You My Mother? A Comic Drama*. Boston: Houghton Mifflin Harcourt, 2012.

———. *Fun Home: A Family Tragicomic*. Boston: Houghton Mifflin, 2006.

212   M. J. BONA

Bechdel, Helen. "Remembering a Friend from the Theater." *Centre Daily Times*, July 17 2009. Accessed July 27, 2015.

Bello, Grace. "Materfamilias." Review of *Are You My Mother? A Comic Drama* by Alison Bechdel. www.publishersweekly.com. p. 35.

Bilger, Audrey. "The Other Shoe Drops." Review of *Are You My Mother? A Comic Drama* by Alison Bechdel. *Women's Review of Books*, September/October 2012: pp. 13–14.

Bona, Mary Jo. "Mothers and Daughters." *The Routledge History of the Italian Americans*. edited by William J. Connell and Stanislao Pugliese. New York: Routledge, 2018.

———. "On Being an Italian American Woman." In *The Italian American Heritage: A Companion to Literature and Arts*, edited by Pellegrino D'Acierno. New York: Routledge (Garland Reference Library of the Humanities), 1998, pp. 61–68.

"Buggy Museum Exhibit Remembers Helen Bechdel." *The Express*, 27 June 2015. Accessed August 3, 2015.

Cappello, Mary. "My Mother Writes the Letter That I Dream." *VIA: Voices in Italian Americana*. 7, n. 2 (Fall 1996): pp. 125–134.

———. *Night Bloom*. Boston: Beacon Press, 1998.

Chute, Hilary. *Graphic Women: Life Narrative and Contemporary Comics*. New York: Columbia University Press, 2010.

Cinotto, Simone, ed. *Making Italian America: Consumer Culture and the Production of Ethnic Identities*. New York: Fordham University Press, 2014.

Cvetkovitch, Ann. "Drawing the Archive in Alison Bechdel's *Fun Home*." *Women's Studies Quarterly* 36. n. 1 & 2 (Spring/Summer, 2008): pp. 111–128.

Cole, Susan Letzler. *The Absent One: Mourning, Ritual, Tragedy, and the Performance of Ambivalence*. University Park: Pennsylvania State University Press, 1985.

Coles, Robert. *The Call of Stories: Teaching and the Moral Imagination*. Boston: Houghton Mifflin, 1989.

DeSalvo, Louise. "'We Will Speak and Bear Witness': Storytelling as Testimony and Healing in *Ghost Dance*." *Review of Contemporary Fiction* n. 17 (Fall 1997): pp. 144–156.

Diedrich, Lisa. "Graphic Analysis: Transitional Phenomena in Alison Bechdel's *Are You My Mother?*" *Configurations* 22, n. 2 (Spring 2014): pp. 183–203.

DuPlessis, Rachel Blau. *Writing beyond the Ending: Narrative Strategies of Twentieth-Century Women Writers*. Bloomington: Indiana University Press, 1985.

Fortier, Anne-Marie. "'Coming Home': Queer Migrations and Multiple Evocations of Home." *European Journal of Cultural Studies* 4, n. 4 (2001): pp. 405–24.

QUEER DAUGHTERS AND THEIR MOTHERS: CAROLE MASO, MARY... 213

Gedalof, Irene. "Birth, Belonging and Migrant Mothers: Narratives of Reproduction in Feminist Migration Studies." *Feminist Review* n. 93 (2009): pp. 81–100.

Gerber, Nancy. *Portrait of the Mother-Artist: Class and Creativity in Contemporary American Fiction*. Lanham: Lexington Books, 2003.

Giaimo, Genie. "Psychological Diffusions: The Cognitive Turn in Alison Bechdel's *Are You My Mother? A Comic Drama*." *The European Journal of Life Writing* Volume II (2013): pp. 35–58.

Gilbert, Sandra. *Death's Door: Modern Dying and the Ways We Grieve*. New York: Norton, 2006.

Giorgio, Adalgisa. "Mothers and Daughters in Western Europe: Mapping the Territory." In *Writing Mothers and Daughters: Renegotiating the Mother in Western European Narratives by Women*, edited by Adalgisa Giorgio, pp. 1–45. New York: Berghahn Books, 2002.

Giunta, Edvige and Joseph Sciorra, ed. *Embroidered Stories: Interpreting Women's Domestic Needlework from the Italian Diaspora*. Jackson: University Press of Mississippi, 2014.

Hirsch, Marianne. *The Mother/Daughter Plot: Narrative, Psychoanalysis, Feminism*. Bloomington: Indiana University Press, 1989.

Irving Katrina. *Immigrant Mothers: Narratives of Race and Maternity, 1890–1925*. Urbana: University of Illinois Press, 2000.

Maso, Carole. *Ghost Dance*. Hopewell, NJ: Ecco, 1990.

———. "Interview by Nicole Cooley." *American Poetry Review* 24, n. 2 (1995): pp. 32–35.

———. "Interview by Joyce Hackett." *Poets and Writers* 24, n. 3 (1996): pp. 64–73.

Miller, Nancy K. "The Entangled Self: Genre Bondage in the Age of Memoir." *PMLA* 122, n. 2 (March 2007): pp. 537–548.

Obituary, Helen Fontana Bechdel. "In Memory of Helen Fontana Bechdel." Wetzler Funeral Home, Inc. Accessed July 27, 2015.

Pipino, Mary Francis. *"I Have Found My Voice": The Italian-American Women Writer*. New York: Peter Lang, 2000.

Quinn, Roseanne. "'We Were Working on an Erotic Song Cycle': Carole Maso's *AVA* as a Poetics of Female Italian-American Cultural and Sexual Identity." *MELUS* 26, n. 1 (Spring 2001): pp. 91–113.

Rich, Adrienne. *Of Woman Born: Motherhood as Experience and Institution*. Tenth Anniversary Edition. New York: Norton, 1986.

Rose, Phyllis. *Women of Letters: A Life of Virginia Woolf*. New York: Oxford University Press, 1978.

Ruvoli, JoAnne. "Inter-ethnic Space in *Fun Home* and *Dykes to Watch Out For*." In *Approaches to Teaching Alison Bechdel's Fun Home*, edited by Judith Kegan Gardiner. New York: Modern Language Association, forthcoming.

———. Review of *Are You My Mother? A Comic Drama* by Alison Bechdel. *Packington Review* n. 4 (Spring 2013). Accessed July 10, 2015.

Sadie, Stanley, ed. *The New Grove Book of Operas*. New York: St. Martin's Press, 1997.

Sambuco, Patrizia. *Corporeal Bonds: The Daughter–Mother Relationship in Twentieth-Century Italian Women's Writing*. Toronto: University of Toronto Press, 2012.

Serres, Michel. "*Feux et Signaux de Brume.*" Virginia Woolf's Lighthouse." *Substance: A Review of Theory & Literary Criticism* 37, n. 2 (2008): pp. 110–131.

Silver, Brenda R. "Mothers, Daughters, Mrs. Ramsay: Reflections." *Women's Studies Quarterly*. 37, n. 3 & 4 (Fall/Winter 2009): pp. 259–274.

Walker, Alice. *In Search of Our Mother's Gardens*. San Diego: Harcourt Brace Jovanovich Publishers, 1983.

Woolf, Virginia. *A Room of One's Own*. New York: Penguin Books, 1963 (orig. ed. 1928).

———. *To the Lighthouse*. New York: Harcourt, Brace & World, Inc., 1955 (orig. ed. 1927).

CHAPTER 9

Beyond the Stereotype: The Obstacle Course of Motherhood in Italy

Chiara Saraceno

Conflicting Representations

In February 2014, in Lombardy, a young man on the run from prison was recaptured within a few hours: the newspapers reported that he had taken refuge at his mother's house. This sentimental and ill-considered "return to *mamma*"—more so than those instances of mothers who bitterly defend their violent children at any cost, still often encountered in both Italian iconography and real life, although a clear minority—seems to confirm all the stereotypes regarding "the Italian *mamma*" and "*mammismo*" as particularly characteristic, not so much of Italian mothers, but of their sons. These are often labelled "*bamboccioni*" or "*mammoni*" because they are perceived as being perpetually looked after by their *mamma*: by a mother who, in her turn, seems to have no real outside interests beyond the over-zealous care of her (male) children. In 2007 Tommaso Padoa Schioppa, the respected Treasury Minister who coined the unfortunate but popular idea of the "*bamboccioni*" ("overgrown children"), called on mothers to make their sons leave home rather than continue to look after them. He implied that the primary reason for young men's difficulties in

---

C. Saraceno (✉)
Collegio Carlo Alberto, Turin, Italy
e-mail: chiara.saraceno@unito.it

© The Author(s) 2018
P. Morris, P. Willson (eds.), *La Mamma*,
Italian and Italian American Studies,
https://doi.org/10.1057/978-1-137-54256-4_9

215

achieving independent living was their dependence on maternal care, rather than the problems of finding reasonably stable and well-paid work, minimal protection from unemployment, and an expensive and limited market in rented accommodation.[1] To add to this picture, the Ecclesiastical Court of Liguria recently confirmed that a psychological and emotional dependence on one's mother can be a reason for annulling Catholic marriage, in that a spouse who was very dependent in this way would be incapable of genuine marital union. Leaving aside a cynical interpretation of this decision, which further widens the range of reasons for annulment and thus helps it to compete with divorce (still opposed by the Catholic Church), this court's declaration sees an overly close relationship between a mother and her son as the potential source of a serious personality disorder.

While over-involved mothers have come to be blamed for their sons' lack of independence, those who do not devote themselves exclusively to looking after their children also risk accusations of causing damage. Should a child or young person run away from home, or exhibit some sort of problem, their mother's behaviour is still the first thing to come under scrutiny; when a young person's difficulties become a news item, journalists are often quick to link these to their mother being in employment.

More generally, when there are complaints that children or young people are inadequately supervised, or left entirely to themselves, although "family" or "parents" may be mentioned, it is in reality mothers who are being judged. As a result, they are caught between the risks of being either excessively present and involved or excessively absent, or over-willing to delegate their responsibilities to others. The debates and differences of opinion that can be found on Italian "mums' blogs," are a good representation of the inconsistencies of images and advice, where the only consistent feature is the view of mothers and their behaviour as the main, if not only, determinants of their children's welfare.[2]

In the context of these conflicting representations of the mother–child relationship, fathers appear either as victims (excluded from their wives' attention, as they are devoted instead to their children), or as responsible for a lack of authority over both children and mothers,[3] or sometimes, if they take care of their small children, as pitiful would-be mothers (*"mammi"*) who cannot possibly succeed, and who thus endanger their children's balanced development.[4] In what they say explicitly or simply imply, these images contribute to the symbolic and emotional repertoire that mothers in Italy are confronted with, and also to the constraints that

Italian women encounter on the road towards motherhood. In particular, the belief that the mother, not the father, is principally responsible for a child's wellbeing and psycho-social development, for better or worse, can operate as a powerful disincentive to any woman with an awareness of her own limitations, and at the same time can unsettle anyone who is considering reconciling motherhood with other activities or interests. This same belief also constitutes a powerful cultural and value-based legitimization of the view that services that look after children, for example childcare for the under-3s, full-day school arrangements, and summer camps and activities for children and adolescents, are a replacement for the absent mother. As a result, the legitimacy of these services is undermined when they have to compete for public resources.

This chapter examines the problems of becoming and being a *mamma* in Italy, caught between expectations of omnipotence and a lack of practical support. In contrast to that of most of the other contributions to this volume, the focus will be on empirical data on the behaviour of women and mothers, and on context. We will therefore be examining family arrangements and engagement in the labour market on the one hand, and, on the other, whether and how social policies support motherhood and the reconciliation between family and paid employment.

THE SMALL FAMILY OF THE "*MAMMA FORTE*"

The image of Italy as the land of the *mamma* has a paradoxical contrast in the image of its "*culle vuote*" ("empty cradles"). For years, Italy has had one of the lowest fertility rates in the world, although it no longer leads the field: it has been matched, and in some cases overtaken, by Spain, Germany, the Netherlands and several post-communist countries of Eastern Europe. It also provides a prime example of the inversion of the relationship between fertility rates and female employment, a process that occurred in developed countries during the last two decades of the twentieth century.[5] While in the 1970s Italy's fertility was still relatively high and female employment low, by the mid-1980s its female employment rate and its fertility rate, at about 1.5 children per woman, were both among the lowest. The fertility rate continued to fall until 1996, reaching 1.19 children per woman. It then slowly rose (mainly because of the higher rate for migrant women), but remained below 1.5. More recently, the trend has again been downward. In 2016, Italy's overall fertility rate stood at 1.34 children per woman; it was only 1.26 for Italian nationals,

218   C. SARACENO

but 1,97 (a substantial fall on previous years when it was constantly above 2) for non-nationals.[6] The average age of women at the birth of their first child has risen, from 28.2 in 1995 to 31 in 2015 (32.2 for mothers with Italian citizenship), and there has been a steady increase in births to those aged over 35.[7] The decrease in births in recent years has been particularly rapid in the Italian South, where over a short period the fertility rate has been falling to meet that of the Centre and North, despite (or perhaps actually because of) much lower rates of female employment.

In 1997 the demographer Massimo Livi Bacci was already wondering whether Italy was facing a sort of reproductive anorexia.[8] Another demographer, Gianpiero Dalla Zuanna, has written about the "strong family and its few children."[9] By this he meant that Italian families (or parents) were so overburdened with responsibility for their children's future, and for such a long time, that having a child, and even more so having more than one, is psychologically as well as materially demanding. The excessive expectations that people have regarding families is a strong disincentive to having children. These expectations are even enshrined in law: Article 433 of the Civil Code lays out responsibilities, defining these widely, for the maintenance of children (and grandchildren) in case of need, well beyond their legal majority. They are also implicit in the weakness, if not absence, of policies to support young people's independence from their families of origin, such as housing policies and social safety nets in case of unemployment. These expectations relate to both fathers and mothers (and to some extent also grandfathers and grandmothers), but they also have a gender-specific nature, in that the care needs of offspring—from infants to older children—are considered and dealt with all but exclusively in terms of what is expected of mothers. It is the availability of their time that is regarded as potentially problematic, even when support measures are offered. Article 37 of the Italian Constitution in fact only mentions the existence of essential family responsibilities for mothers and not for fathers.[10] This has provided a constitutional basis for measures to support motherhood, and in particular for maternity leave for women employees, with the guarantee that their jobs can be retained. However, it has also indirectly legitimized neglect for the rights and responsibilities of fathers, not only as breadwinners but also as care providers.

The belief that the psychological and physical wellbeing of children, especially when small, is predominantly, if not exclusively, the responsibility of their mother is also widely endorsed by public opinion. Italy is among those countries where a high percentage of people believe that children of

BEYOND THE STEREOTYPE: THE OBSTACLE COURSE OF MOTHERHOOD... 219

pre-school age suffer if their mother works.[11] Perhaps to mitigate this "suffering," in recent years the meticulous "educational protocol" implemented across all nurseries and the first year of infant school, both public and private, has prescribed a slow process of introduction, lasting two weeks and ideally involving just one family member; in reality this is generally the mother, as fathers generally prefer to avoid a totally female environment where they are seen as a rare breed.[12] Moreover, with reference to the need to protect children, both their independence and the ability of older children to look after them have in recent years been constrained. Until the end of the 1970s, children could still go to school on their own in their third year of primary school. At the age of 14 or 15, if not earlier, they were seen as capable of looking after their younger siblings, including taking them to school and collecting them. It is certainly true that traffic was much lighter, although there were also fewer traffic lights. Even today, around Europe, children aged between 8 and 10 can commonly be seen going to school on their own, or accompanied by older brothers or sisters rather than adults. In Italy, by contrast, teachers must not hand over a child at the school gates to a sibling who is not an adult, and children cannot go to or from primary school on their own, not even in their fourth or fifth year, whatever the distance or the features of the journey between school and home. Parents who have sent their child to school on their own, in a village, have even been contacted by Social Services and warned that they could be reported to the Juvenile Court for child neglect.

This idea of children's "neediness" and the risks of their "premature" independence of movement has not resulted in an extension of the school timetable, nor in the provision of activities that could be undertaken at school by those children without an "authorized adult" who can collect them at 12.30. Instead, the parents have to shoulder the burden of making arrangements, and may feel guilty for their failure to meet the expectations of their availability that are implicit both in school arrangements and in the shortage of care services covering early childhood. Having two children of different ages attending different schools or services can become a complex challenge, if not a nightmare, even for a housewife, let alone for a woman who has to juggle her work timetable with varying school hours, especially school finishing times. Because it is the demands on mothers' time that have changed, due to an increased participation in the labour market that has reduced their ability to meet those implicit and explicit expectations, it is mothers who are identified, and identify themselves, as being primarily responsible.

220   C. SARACENO

As Loredana Lipperini has recently observed, young Italian mothers have limited room for manoeuvre between an updated "maternalism," which brings together the enduring stereotype of the sacrificial mother and all-consuming motherhood with the equally all-consuming idea of children's needs, and the new model of the super-mum, who keeps on top of everything—children and work—thanks to her sheer energy and will-power.[13] These two models of super-motherhood, which are only superficially conflicting, can also be found in other countries; they are challenging (as well as hazardous) for any woman to pursue in any context, but especially so in a country like Italy where ideology and policies too often combine to create a very hostile environment for any type of mother.

THE ENDURING PROBLEM OF RECONCILING MOTHERHOOD AND PAID EMPLOYMENT

Levels of female employment in Italy rose steadily from the second half of the 1990s until the crisis of 2007, especially among young women with small children. This related to various factors, notably the rising level of female education from the late 1970s onwards and the ensuing closure of the gender gap in educational achievement. Within couples, there has been increasing parity in education. In particular, situations where the man has a higher educational qualification than the woman have decreased, while instances of the converse have increased. Increasing numbers of women thus possess the attribute—educational attainment—that in Italy, more than in many other countries, facilitates women's ability to enter and remain in the labour market even when they have family responsibilities.[14]

However, Italy remains one of the few European and OECD (Organisation for Economic Co-operation and Development) countries where marriage, not just having children, causes women's departure from the labour market, especially if they have low education and particularly in the South, where the figures for female employment are very low. In the years after 2000, in the 35–44 age range, employment rates at the national level were 83 per cent for unmarried women without children but only 75.4 per cent for married women without children. They were 56.9 per cent for married women with children, and 40.5 per cent for those with three or more children. Moreover, almost one woman in five left or lost her job when her child arrived.[15] According to a longitudinal study, of those women who had a child in the 2009–10 period 64.7 per cent had been employed at the start of their pregnancy, while 53.6 per cent were

BEYOND THE STEREOTYPE: THE OBSTACLE COURSE OF MOTHERHOOD... 221

employed two years later.[16] Of new mothers who were no longer working, 56.1 per cent said that they had spontaneously resigned, mostly (67.1 per cent) over difficulties in reconciling paid work with family responsibilities. Only a minority (13.5 per cent) gave lack of satisfaction with their job or their pay as the reason for leaving the labour market altogether. The risk (or choice) of leaving employment is particularly high among women with low levels of education, whose employment opportunities are limited to low-paid jobs requiring minimal qualifications. However, it also affects women with more qualifications. According to the most recent survey by the AlmaLaurea consortium on employment outcomes after university, five years after graduating 73 per cent of women who did not have children were employed, compared to 63.3 per cent of those who did (and 88.9 per cent of male graduates with at least one child).[17]

Leaving the labour market for family reasons is not a recent phenomenon, and does not relate exclusively, nor even principally, to the protracted economic crisis experienced by Italy since late 2007. Rather, it seems to have structural features and affects all age cohorts, not having significantly less incidence in the younger generations despite their higher proportion in paid employment.

Clearly, there is no simple causal relationship between the birth of a child and leaving employment. These two events may in fact be parts of a complex and diverse chain of circumstances and micro-decisions, without any direct causality. Moreover, the women who leave work may, for example, have cultural characteristics, such as models of gender identity and the family, that differ from those shared by the women who retain employment. Whatever the causes, in the second decade of the twenty-first century motherhood and employment are experienced as incompatible, on a more or less temporary basis, by a significant proportion of Italian women at the height of their reproductive capacity. For women under the age of 34, it is only among those who are neither employed nor in education or training that the majority (57.2 per cent in 2013) have a child. The decision to leave the labour market, or to not enter it before taking on maternal responsibilities, may be intended as a temporary measure within a sequential model that envisages the establishment of a family and paid employment as separate life stages. In Italy, more than in other countries, however, this decision may prove definitive, not only because of the nature of labour demand and the rigidities of work organization, but also because the system of services and compulsory education offers such minimal support for reconciling family and employment.

We are, therefore, witnessing the persistence of old models of family organization, based on a strong gender division of labour, but also changes to these models, largely prompted by changes in women's time organization. However, these are not always accompanied by adequate care services or adjustments to social timetables (school hours, for example), nor by changes in the division of family labour. This lack of adjustment in part explains the marked reduction in fertility rates discussed earlier.[18]

This is not only a product of social policies, which will be discussed in the next section. It is also due to resistance to changes in the gender division of labour within households. Various studies, including some comparative ones, have reported that within Italian families men give very limited help to women either with domestic tasks or with looking after children and other family members who require care.[19] This is reflected in the differences in workload between men and women within the family, including when the women are in employment. In particular, studies of time allocation carried out by ISTAT from the 1990s onwards, examining both paid employment and unpaid work within the family, show that employed women who also have family responsibilities on average work between 9 and 11 hours each week more than men, despite having on average fewer paid working hours and less travel time to work.

A comparison between the survey of the mid-1990s and that of 2013–2014, however, shows changes in both female and male behaviour. Women in employment reduced the time spent on domestic tasks in the narrow sense (but not on childcare), while men, and especially young men, increased the time spent with their children, although without reducing time spent in paid employment.[20] This shows that in young families with small children and two working parents, time use had to some degree changed: more went on care and relationships, and less on domestic tasks. Moreover, counter to commonly held beliefs, the hours spent with children had not decreased: children may, in fact, enjoy a greater amount of paternal time. This is particularly true for families where the parents have a medium or high level of education, or have jobs that require good qualifications but are not too exacting in career terms. Fathers in very demanding professions or careers do not in fact have much time for their children.

Employment insecurity due to short-term contracts, which is particularly high among younger adults, may be a restraining element as regards both the decision to have children and the trend towards greater equity in the division of labour and family responsibilities. Uncertainty and vulnerability in employment may in fact discourage negotiations on working hours and limit the take-up of parental leave even when people are entitled to this. In addition, as there is a greater concentration of women in temporary employment contracts, with the instability that this implies, and, as women experience more difficulties in transferring to more stable and protected employment,[21] there may be greater prioritization of paid male employment within a couple's strategy, in an era in which the labour market guarantees increasingly fewer places as "male breadwinner" to the younger generations of men.

THE LIMITED AND UNEVENLY DISTRIBUTED RESOURCES FOR RECONCILING MOTHERHOOD AND EMPLOYMENT

Social policies, especially those supporting the reconciliation of family and paid employment and the realignment of the gender division of unpaid work within the family, have been unable to keep pace with changes either in women's engagement with the labour market or in the labour market itself, in spite of some important innovations, especially as regards maternity and parental leave.

Until as late as the 1970s, Italy had relatively generous maternity leave in terms of both length and remuneration: five months could be taken, at 80 per cent of normal pay. There was also an optional longer period of six months leave, albeit with pay at only 30 per cent. In addition, nursery school places for children aged 3–5 were widely available, catering for 70 per cent at the national level and above 90 per cent in some central and northern cities and for the older children in the age range.[22] In subsequent years, the right to maternity leave and related pay has been extended to various types of women workers: not only the self-employed, but also, in an increasingly fragmented labour market, different kinds of semi-independent collaborators and temporary workers. In theory, all legally employed women workers should now have these rights. Moreover, any woman who has not paid sufficient contributions to have the full right to maternity pay can request a maternity grant of €1916.22 in total, as long as she has paid the equivalent of at least three months of contributions between 18 and 9 months prior to the birth. Finally, there is a second and smaller maternity grant (€1545.55), paid out by local councils but funded centrally. This is intended for women who have worked but not made the minimum level of contributions for the first grant, and for those outside the labour market. This second grant, unlike the first, is only paid if family income is below a specified threshold, and therefore is not an unconditional right. Both these grants were introduced in 1999 by the first Prodi government. Law n. 53/2000 and the subsequent unifying legislation on maternity and paternity (Law n. 151 of 26 March 2001), moreover, adjusted the regulations on leave, awarding rights to working fathers as well and bringing the amount of parental leave up to ten months in total (only the first six months qualifying for pay, at 30 per cent, and only if taken within the first six years of the child's life). This time can be allocated between the parents, neither of whom can take more than six months leave during the child's first twelve years. Recognition of a father's rights was an important innovation, although it came late relative to many other European countries and is limited by the low level of remuneration. In a cultural context where a male worker who gives up work to look after children is still viewed with suspicion, and especially where there is increasing insecurity in the labour market, these financial limitations have in fact been a powerful disincentive to the take-up of parental leave by fathers.

Thus in Italy, in theory, women in regular or irregular employment and unemployed women in low-income families all have access to some form of financial support in cases of pregnancy and motherhood. If in employment they also have, in theory, the right to retain their job during their leave. The reality, however, is somewhat different. Many skilled workers and self-employed women cannot allow themselves a break of five months from work, much less a longer period. The possibility of taking on a temporary replacement, allowed for in law, is generally impractical for the self-employed, and for those whose professional reputation is their biggest asset. Semi-independent collaborators, similarly, for financial or professional reasons cannot always afford to be out of the labour market for very long. The increase in temporary work contracts also puts many women at risk of losing their job after maternity. This risk is also incurred by many women on permanent contracts, in an explicitly or implicitly illegal manner. At the point of recruitment they are sometimes forced, entirely illegally, to sign an undated resignation letter which can be used later to force their departure in case of pregnancy. Alternatively, during their leave or on return to work, they may be subjected to bullying with varying degrees of subtlety. There may also be financial inducements, of varying generosity, to leave voluntarily. These phenomena are not quantifiable, although they are regularly reported. In terms of individual women's lives, a striking collection of evidence is presented by Chiara Valentini who documents the difficulties experienced, across social classes and professions, in becoming a mother in Italy.[23]

As regards quantitative data, important evidence is provided by the proportion of employment contracts that are terminated because of maternity, which has consistently been between 8 and 10 per cent over time. These endings can even occur during the so-called "protected" period (pregnancy and the first 12 months of the child's life), during which a woman cannot be dismissed. According to ISTAT's 2008–9 survey of time use, about 800,000 mothers, of all ages, said that at some point in their working lives, during or after pregnancy, they had been either dismissed or put in situations that forced their resignation. This represented 8.7 per cent of mothers who were working or had previously been in work.[24]

Tensions and conflicts over the use of time and the priorities for mothers are particularly acute in the early years of their children's lives, when Italian services offer the least assistance.[25] While the availability of infant school places for children between the age of 3 and primary school entry now covers more than 90 per cent of children nationally, services for children under 3 are still scarce, generally expensive, and markedly unequally distributed across regions. At the national level about 23 per cent of the under-3s are provided for, but the figure is around 10 per cent for the South.[26] Here, moreover, infant schools, for children aged 3–5, still often only operate on a half-time basis. Regional differences are also apparent in compulsory schooling, the availability of full-time places being much more widespread in the North and Centre than in the South. In 2012–13, 30 per cent of primary school classes, nationally, were full time. This proportion was above 40 per cent (but below 50 per cent) in some central and northern regions (Lombardy, Lazio, Emilia Romagna, Tuscany, Piedmont and Liguria) but only in one southern region (Basilicata). In Campania, Molise and Sicily it was below 8 per cent.[27]

These differences in the provision of services for children correspond to differences in the rates of female employment, which are much lower in southern regions. However, children's services should not only be ways of resolving the problems of working mothers. They should also be vehicles of equal opportunity for children, reducing the differences in opportunities for balanced growth and for skill development that result from inequalities in family circumstances, as well as helping parents with their educational responsibilities. As poverty, especially child poverty, is concentrated in the South, these services should in fact be more rather than less widespread in

226 C. SARACENO

southern regions, where parents, especially mothers, find themselves more isolated in coping with circumstances that are generally more difficult than elsewhere, over and above the issue of unemployment.

In addition, the largest concentration of very young mothers is to be found in the South. Births to women under the age of 18 have in fact markedly decreased at the national level, falling by more than two-thirds compared to only 15 years ago, but here they have remained a significant phenomenon. In 2012, for example, they represented 0.8 and 1.5 per cent of all births in Campania and Sicily respectively, compared to 0.2 per cent in central and northern regions.[28] For the most part these young mothers were married (often in fact because of the pregnancy),[29] but they were often in families where their partner did not have regular employment, and was sometimes absent due to imprisonment.[30] In Catania, Syracuse, Palermo, Foggia, Brindisi, Crotone, Naples and Enna, births to mothers under the age of 20 accounted for more than 30 per 1000, whereas in the Centre and North the only city with a rate above 20 per 1000 was Piacenza. Data gathered from birth records in 2010 showed that four in ten young mothers had a low level of educational attainment, and sometimes had not actually completed compulsory schooling (lower secondary school to the age of 15). Almost 20 per cent were still attending school. Only 5 per cent were in employment, 17 per cent were unemployed and 51 per cent were classified as "*casalinghe*" ("housewives"), but in reality swelling the ranks of the "NEET"—not in education, employment or training—although often, unlike their male peers in the same situation, already weighed down by family responsibilities.[31] The lack of services for younger children leaves these young mothers and their offspring without reference points and assistance outside family networks, which cannot always help them.

This situation presents a sort of vicious circle. The services for early childhood, but also full-time school places, are regarded first and foremost as services for mothers in employment and only secondly, and then not always, as an opportunity for the children. This weakens their legitimation, not just on the level of social policy but also on the cultural and symbolic level.[32] Even among employed mothers, the belief often prevails that "*la nonna*" (grandmother) is a better choice than a nursery, not just because of the obvious issues of cost and flexibility (grandmothers do not have to be paid and will also look after children who are ill) but also for emotional reasons. In Italy, more than elsewhere, grandparents are in effect a crucial resource for managing the everyday life of families with small children, particularly when the mothers are employed, and are not just for dealing with emergencies.[33] One has only to look at the groups waiting for children coming out of nurseries, infant schools and primary schools: there is a preponderance of grandmothers and grandfathers, rather than mothers and fathers. However, it should be noted that the behaviour of grandparents indicates a change: while over time the percentage who contribute in some degree to the care of their grandchildren has increased, the percentage of those doing this full time has fallen.[34]

Obstacles to Motherhood

In Italy, as in almost all EU countries, the number of children people would like to have is now higher than the number they actually do have.[35] For both men and women within couples the number of children wanted averages 2.1, in contrast to the markedly lower fertility rate, without any significant variation across social class. There may be various reasons for this gap: it cannot simply be attributed to practical difficulties, as the desired number of children may be at odds with other aspirations that are equally strong, if not stronger. An examination of the disparity between the intention to have a child in the near future and the actual fulfilment of this intention may prove more helpful. A longitudinal survey by ISTAT, published in 2003, reported that a quarter of women aged between 18 and 49 had intended to have a child (whether or not their first) within the next three years, with no significant difference across social classes.[36] However, more than half were unable to realize this intention. The distribution of this inability across social groups appears far from random, indicating that material constraints were in operation. Women with higher levels of educational attainment and medium or high social status were the most likely to have had children within the three-year period. Of those women who had wanted children, 68.2 per cent of university graduates and 54.4 per cent of those who had completed upper secondary school actually had a child, as against 37.8 per cent of those who had simply completed lower secondary school; 76.1 per cent of managers, entrepreneurs and independent professionals had a child, followed by 58.2 per cent of middle managers and other staff, 52.4 per cent of self-employed workers and assistants, and finally 43.2 per cent of manual workers.

228 C. SARACENO

While being in employment sometimes hinders fulfilment of the wish to have children, having low job security is even more of a deterrent than having reasonably stable employment, and may lead to postponement of the decision. In 2013, in the 25–34 age group, 34.1 per cent of women who had permanent jobs already had a child, compared to 23.8 per cent of those on fixed-term contracts.[37] This may throw some light on the sharp drop in fertility in the South within the most recent generation, as in this context paid work is in short supply and often insecure, for both men and women. For young women who want paid employment, not having a child may represent a sort of extreme preventative measure, as well as being necessary in view of the shortage of resources, to ensure that when they enter the labour market they will not have this additional constraint.

Fulfilment of the wish to have children may, however, be frustrated by factors that are more fundamental than difficulties in reconciling family and employment, or financial constraints, and which relate to reproductive capacity in physiological terms. The question of whether there is an absolute right to have children, even when there are difficulties of a physiological nature, remains an open one. All countries respond to this with, on the one hand, rules governing adoption—who can adopt and on what conditions—and, on the other, regulations governing access to the various techniques of assisted reproduction. Italy has some of the most restrictive regulations regarding both adoption, an option for married couples only, and assisted reproduction, which under Law n. 40 of 2004 was doubly restricted. Access to these techniques has only been legally possible for an established (not necessarily married) heterosexual couple, and then only if the couple were still of childbearing age and were confirmed as being unable to have children. Furthermore, assisted reproduction could only take place with the biological contribution of both partners, without recourse to donors. This assistance was thus not available to couples where one or both partners were infertile, nor to couples where both partners were fertile but where one or both were carriers of a serious genetic disorder, as they were technically able to have children. A recent judgment of the Constitutional Court (9 April 2014), on a case brought by three different couples, ruled that in cases of absolute sterility the ban on using donors of cells was unconstitutional.[38] The Court ruled out also another ban, for people who are fertile but carriers of serious genetic conditions, referred to it by a court in Rome. This followed an application by a woman, herself healthy but a carrier of Becker muscular dystrophy (passed down by her father), and her husband, who had been denied access by a hospital to both assisted reproduction and pre-implantation genetic diagnosis. Even when these prohibitions are removed, those on women without a partner and on same-sex couples will still remain. Anyone with sufficient means can get around this double ban by going to a country like Spain where these obstacles do not exist. An internet search on *"riproduzione assistita"* (assisted reproduction) will quickly reveal a flourishing market outside Italy that is particularly aimed at potential Italian clients, exploiting the restrictive legislation operating on Italian soil. However, this is not an option for everyone, from either the financial or the logistical point of view: there are the direct costs of the procedure, and then allowances have to be made for travel and stays that may often have to be repeated, entailing not only substantial additional expenditure but also potential absences from work, primarily for the would-be mother but also for her partner. In regard to same-sex couples, moreover, it should be remembered that they have no legal status in Italy. The same-sex partner of a woman who has had a child through assisted reproduction using a donor (in a country where this is legally possible) thus has no legal recognition as a parent, even though the decision to have a child was taken together and the responsibility for care and bringing up the child is shared.[39] On the level of everyday relationships with their wider families, friends, and the schools the children attend, this is often irrelevant, to the extent that the non-biological mother is frequently recognized and welcomed. Two-mother couples (more than two-father ones) have, in fact, become much more visible in recent years. However, the lack of legal recognition can have very negative consequences, for the non-biological mother and the child, if the couple subsequently separates or if the biological mother dies.

CONCLUSIONS

In the country that in the international imaginary has been "the land of the *mamma"* par excellence, with all its positive and negative values, becoming a *mamma* has in fact become increasingly difficult. This is indicated by the demographic data, which for decades have placed Italy among the countries with the lowest fertility in the world. It is indicated by data on the employment of mothers, which show how difficult it is to combine participation in the labour market and responsibility for care of the family, and how leaving the labour market due to having children is still a widespread phenomenon. It is indicated by the data on poverty, which show how this increases as the number of children rises, to the extent that Italy has one of the highest levels of child poverty among European countries, and one of the largest differences between adult and child poverty. Stereotypes both of the "good *mamma*" and of the Italian family, which take as given both a long-standing inter-generational solidarity and the gender division of labour and responsibilities, seem to legitimize the cautiousness, if not the absence, of policies that might meet the needs and expectations of women who want to reconcile motherhood with other matters, especially participation in the labour market and financial independence. Difficulties in the labour market further accentuate the tensions and the obstacles encountered both by mothers and by those aspiring to motherhood. At the same time, Italy is one of the European countries with the most legal barriers for those who want to become mothers (or in fact fathers) but have difficulties of a physical or genetic type, or are not in a heterosexual relationship. Italy's legislation both on adoption and, especially, on assisted reproduction is among the most restrictive. Rather than being "the land of the *mamma*," from this perspective Italy seems instead to present a hostile environment for the achievement of motherhood.

Translated by Stuart Oglethorpe

NOTES

1. See, for example, the recent survey carried out by the Istituto Giuseppe Toniolo, *La condizione giovanile in Italia.*
2. On the phenomenon of blogging mothers, see Stadtman Tucker, "Mothering in the Digital Age."
3. See, for example, the polemical work by Polito, *Contro i papà.*
4. A finding that the excessive presence of fathers creates insecure children emerged from research by HelpMe, an association of volunteer psychologists, coordinated by Massimo Cicogna, and attracted some press interest (see for example "Gli esperti contro i 'mammi'," *Il Corriere della Sera*, 25 April 2000). However, this finding is problematic because the study very simplistically confused indicators of care-giving with indicators of over-protectiveness.
5. See Kohler et al., "The Emergence of Lowest-Low Fertility in Europe during the 1990s."
6. It should be noted that while non-native women have more children than native Italians, their children run twice the risk of poverty in a country where the rate of child poverty is already very high. Fifty per cent of non-native

children and young people are in poverty as against about 25 per cent of native Italians (the latter being especially concentrated in large families and in the South). See Lemmi et al., "Povertà e deprivazione."

7. ISTAT, "Natalità e fecondità."
8. Livi Bacci, "Esiste davvero una seconda transizione demografica?"
9. Dalla Zuanna, "The Banquet of Aeolus." See also Dalla Zuanna and Micheli, *Strong Family and Low Fertility: A Paradox?*; Saraceno, "Il paradosso riproduttivo."
10. Having specified the principle of equal pay for female and male workers in the first paragraph, in the second the article states that "working conditions must allow fulfillment of [the woman's] essential family function and guarantee particular and appropriate protection for the mother and child."
11. This relates to an item within the European Value Survey, part of the International Social Survey Programme (ISSP). Italian interviewees, along with Germans and Austrians, were those most in agreement with this statement. On the limitations of this type of question, see Saraceno, "Childcare Needs and Childcare Policies." An interesting comparative analysis of the relationship between attitudes in regard to the family, inasmuch as conclusions can be drawn from inquiries on "values," and rates of female participation in the labour market, is provided by Algan and Cahuc, "The Roots of Low European Employment."
12. In a posting on the "la27ora" page of the *Corriere della Sera* website in January 2014 (Ricci Sargentini, "I bamboccioni nascono all'asilo"), an infuriated mother wrote that in this way children learn at the nursery how to become "*bamboccioni.*" This resulted both in supportive comments and in strong criticism from other mothers and fathers. It should be acknowledged that this practice is fairly widespread across all Western European countries.
13. Lipperini, *Di mamma ce n'é più d'una.*
14. See Lucchini et al., "Dual Earner and Dual Career Couples"; Rosina and Saraceno, "Interferenze asimmetriche."
15. ISTAT, "La conciliazione tra lavoro e famiglia. Anno 2010."
16. ISTAT, *Rapporto annuale 2012*, 120. See also ISTAT, "Le difficoltà nella transizione."
17. Consorzio Interuniversitario AlmaLaurea, *Condizione occupazionale dei laureati.*
18. See also Sabbadini, "Il lavoro femminile."
19. See Del Boca and Saraceno, "Le donne in Italia tra famiglia e lavoro"; Eurostat, *Reconciliation between Work, Private and Family Life*; Del Boca and Rosina, *Famiglie sole*; ISTAT, *Rapporto annuale 2010*; Naldini and Saraceno, *Conciliare famiglia e lavoro.*
20. Capozzi, Sabbadini, Stuzzichino, "I mutamenti nella asimmetria della divisione dei ruoli nella coppia"
21. See Sabbadini, *Il lavoro femminile.*

232 C. SARACENO

22. Saraceno, *Mutamenti della famiglia.*
23. Valentini, *O i figli o il lavoro*; see also Lipperini, *Di mamma ce n'é più d'una.*
24. ISTAT, *Rapporto annuale 2010*, p. 154.
25. Naldini and Saraceno, *Conciliare famiglia e lavoro.*
26. See Istituto degli Innocenti, *Monitoraggio del Piano di sviluppo.*
27. Ministero dell'Istruzione press release, 14 September 2012. See the table comparing total and full-time classes (2007–8 to 2012–13). See also Save the Children, *La Lampada di Aladino.*
28. ISTAT, "Natalità e fecondità."
29. Families with young children and just one parent are a comparatively small percentage of all families with young children but an increasing one, particularly because of the increase in marital instability. They were estimated to be 4 per cent of all families with young children in 2001, and 7.6 per cent in 2011. See Saraceno and Naldini, *Sociologia della famiglia*, p. 47.
30. See Morlicchio and Morniroli, *Poveri a chi?*, on the case of Naples.
31. Save the Children, *L'Italia sottosopra.*
32. Various comparative studies have shown that there is a relationship, albeit not a strictly linear one, between the degree of coverage of services for early childhood and their legitimation on the cultural level. As well as Saraceno, "Childcare Needs and Childcare Policies," see Kangas and Rostgaard, "Preferences or Institutions?"; Morgan, "The Political Path."
33. Keck and Saraceno, "Grandchildhood in Germany and Italy." See also Blome et al., *Family and the Welfare State in Europe.*
34. See the data from ISTAT reported in Saraceno and Naldini, *Sociologia della famiglia*, pp. 77–78.
35. See, for example, Fahey, "Fertility Patterns and Aspirations in Europe."
36. ISTAT, "Le difficoltà nella transizione."
37. I owe these figures to the ISTAT staff who kindly did the necessary further work on the data to update and integrate the figures presented by Sabbadini, "Figli o lavoro."
38. For online press coverage of the decision, see "Fecondazione, cade divieto eterologa," *La Repubblica*, 9 April 2014.
39. The same is true for the same-sex partner of a man who has had a biological child using both a female donor and a surrogate mother.

Bibliography

Algan, Yann, and Pierre Cahuc. "The Roots of Low European Employment: Family Culture?" In *NBER International Seminar on Macroeconomics 2005*, edited by Jeffrey A. Frankel and Christopher A. Pissarides, pp. 65–109.

BEYOND THE STEREOTYPE: THE OBSTACLE COURSE OF MOTHERHOOD... 233

Cambridge (MA): MIT Press, 2007. Available online at http://www.nber.org/chapters/c0342

Blome, Agnes, Wolfgang Keck, and Jens Alber. *Family and the Welfare State in Europe: Intergenerational Relations in Ageing Societies.* Cheltenham: Edward Elgar, 2009.

Bruzzese, Dario, and Maria Clelia Romano. "La partecipazione dei padri al lavoro familiare nel contesto della quotidianità." In *Diventare padri in Italia. Fecondità e figli secondo un approccio di genere,* edited by Alessandro Rosina and Linda Laura Sabbadini, pp. 213–247. Rome: ISTAT, 2005. Available online at http://www3.istat.it/dati/catalogo/20051020_00/Arg_ediz_provv_diventare_padri.pdf

Consorzio Interuniversitario AlmaLaurea. *Condizione occupazionale dei Laureati. XVI Indagine 2013.* Bologna: AlmaLaurea, 2014. Available online at http://www.almalaurea.it/sites/almalaurea.it/files/docs/universita/occupazione/occupazione12/almalaurea_indagine2013.pdf

Dalla Zuanna, Gianpiero. "The Banquet of Aeolus: A Familistic Interpretation of Italy's Lowest Low Fertility." *Demographic Research* 4 (2001): pp. 133–162. https://doi.org/10.4054/DemRes.2001.4.5

Dalla Zuanna, Gianpiero, and Giuseppe A. Micheli, eds. *Strong Family and Low Fertility: A Paradox? New Perspectives in Interpreting Contemporary Family and Reproductive Behaviour.* Dordrecht: Kluwer Academic Publishers, 2004.

Del Boca, Daniela, and Chiara Saraceno. "Le donne in Italia tra famiglia e lavoro." *Economia & lavoro* 39, n. 1 (2005): pp. 125–140. https://doi.org/10.7384/72370

Del Boca, Daniela, and Alessandro Rosina. *Famiglie sole. Sopravvivere con un welfare inefficiente.* Bologna: Il Mulino, 2009.

Eurostat. *Reconciliation between Work, Private and Family Life in the European Union.* Luxembourg: European Commission, 2009.

Fahey, Tony. "Fertility patterns and aspirations in Europe," in *Handbook of Quality of Life in the Enlarged European Union,* edited by Jens Alber, Tony Fahey, and Chiara Saraceno, pp. 27–46. Abingdon: Routledge, 2008.

ISTAT. "Le difficoltà nella transizione dei giovani allo stato adulto e le criticità nei percorsi di vita femminili." Press release. Rome: Istat, 28 December 2009.

ISTAT. *Rapporto annuale. La situazione del Paese nel 2010.* Rome: ISTAT, 2011a.

ISTAT. "La conciliazione tra lavoro e famiglia. Anno 2010." *Statistiche Report,* 28 December 2011b.

ISTAT. *Rapporto annuale 2012. La situazione del Paese.* Rome: ISTAT, 2012.

Istituto degli Innocenti. *Monitoraggio del Piano di sviluppo dei servizi socio-educativi per la prima infanzia. Rapporto al 31 dicembre 2011.* Rome: Presidenza del Consiglio dei Ministri, 2012.

Istituto Giuseppe Toniolo. *La condizione giovanile in Italia. Rapporto Giovani 2014.* Bologna: Il Mulino, 2014.

234   C. SARACENO

Kangas, Olli, and Tine Rostgaard. "Preferences or institutions? Work–family life opportunities in seven European countries." *Journal of European Social Policy* 17, n. 3 (2007): pp. 240–256. https://doi.org/10.1177/0958928707078367

Keck, Wolfgang, and Chiara Saraceno. "Grandchildhood in Germany and Italy: An Exploration." In *Childhood: Changing Contexts*, edited by Arnlaug Leira and Chiara Saraceno, pp. 133–163. Bingley: Emerald, 2008.

Kohler, Hans-Peter, Francesco C. Billari, and José Antonio Ortega. "The Emergence of Lowest-Low Fertility in Europe during the 1990s." *Population and Development Review* 28, n. 4 (2002): pp. 641–680. https://doi.org/10.1111/j.1728-4457.2002.00641.x

Lemmi, Achille, Fabio Berti, Gianni Betti, Antonella D'Agostino, Francesca Gagliardi, Romina Gambacorta, Alessandra Masi, Laura Neri, Nicoletta Pannuzi, Andrea Regoli, and Silvano Vitaletti. "Povertà e deprivazione." In *Stranieri e Disuguali. Le disuguaglianze nei diritti e nelle condizioni di vita degli immigrati*, edited by Chiara Saraceno, Nicola Sartor, and Giuseppe Sciortino, pp. 149–174. Bologna: Il Mulino, 2013.

Lipperini, Loredana. *Di mamma ce n'é più d'una.* Milan: Feltrinelli, 2013.

Livi Bacci, Massimo. "Esiste davvero una seconda transizione demografica?" In *La società del figlio assente. Voci a confronto sulla seconda transizione demografica in Italia*, edited by Giuseppe A. Micheli, pp. 90–104. Milan: Franco Angeli, 1997.

Lucchini, Mario, Chiara Saraceno, and Antonio Schizzerotto. "Dual earner and dual career couples in contemporary Italy." *Zeitschrift für Familienforschung* 19, n. 3 (2007): pp. 289–309.

Ministero dell'Istruzione, dell'Università e della Ricerca, press release, 14 September 2012, available at: http://hubmiur.pubblica.istruzione.it/web/ministero/focus140912, date accessed 28 January 2014.

Morgan, Kimberly J. "The Political Path to a Dual Earner/Dual Carer Society: Pitfalls and Possibilities." *Politics & Society* 36, n. 3 (2008): pp. 403–420. https://doi.org/10.1177/0032329208320569

Morlicchio, Enrica, and Andrea Morniroli. *Poveri a chi? Napoli (Italia).* Turin: Abele, 2013.

Naldini, Manuela, and Chiara Saraceno. *Conciliare famiglia e lavoro. Vecchi e nuovi patti tra sessi e generazioni.* Bologna: Il Mulino, 2011.

Polito, Antonio. *Contro i papà.* Milan: Rizzoli, 2012.

Ricci Sargentini, Monica. "I bamboccioni nascono all'asilo. Le follie dell'inserimento all'italiana." *Corriere della Sera*, website (2014): http://27esimaora.corriere.it/articolo/i-bamboccioni-nascono-allasilole-follie-dellinserimento-allitaliana/

Rosina, Alessandro, and Chiara Saraceno. "Interferenze asimmetriche. Uno studio sulla discontinuità lavorativa femminile." *Economia & Lavoro* 42, n. 2 (2008): pp. 149–167. https://doi.org/10.7384/70795

Sabbadini, Linda Laura. "Il lavoro femminile in tempo di crisi." Report presented for the CNEL II Commissione: Stati generali sul lavoro delle donne in Italia,

Rome, 2 February 2012a. Available online at: http://www.slideshare.net/slideistat/ll-sabbadini-il-lavoro-femminile-in-tempo-di-crisi

Sabbadini, Linda Laura. "Figli o lavoro. La maternità negata." Paper presented at a conference with the same title organized by Gruppo Controparola, Rome, 30 November 2012.

Saraceno, Chiara. *Mutamenti della famiglia e politiche sociali in Italia*. Bologna: Il Mulino, 2003.

Saraceno, Chiara. "Il paradosso riproduttivo di una società a famiglia forte. Il caso della bassa fecondità in Italia." *La Questione Agraria* n. 1 (2005): pp. 7–28.

Saraceno, Chiara. "Childcare Needs and Childcare Policies: A Multidimensional Issue." *Current Sociology* 59, n. 1 (2011): pp. 78–96. https://doi.org/10.1177/0011392110385971

Saraceno, Chiara, and Manuela Naldini. *Sociologia della famiglia*. 3rd ed. Bologna: Il Mulino, 2013.

Save the Children. *L'Italia sottosopra. I bambini e la crisi*. Rome: Save the Children, 2013.

Save the Children. *La Lampada di Aladino*. Rome: Save the Children, 2014.

Stadtman Tucker, Judith. "Mothering in the Digital Age: Navigating the Personal and Political in the Virtual Sphere." In *Mothering in the Third Wave*, edited by Amber E. Kinser, pp. 199–212. Toronto: Demeter, 2008.

Valentini, Chiara. *O i figli o il lavoro*. Milan: Feltrinelli, 2012.

NEWSPAPER REPORTS

"Gli esperti contro i 'mammi'." *Il Corriere della Sera*, 25 April 2000.

"Fecondazione, cade divieto eterologa. La Consulta: 'È incostituzionale'", *La Repubblica*, 9 April 2014 (online), available at: http://www.repubblica.it/salute/benessere-donna/2014/04/09/news/fecondazione_cade_divieto_eterologa-83136799/?ref=HREA-1

INDEX[1]

A
Aaron, Daniel, 170
Abortion, 57, 88, 116–118, 121, 193
Abruzzi, agrarian survey findings, 165
Accati, Luisa, 43–44
Action Party, 35
Adoption, 228, 230
Advice columns, 77–100, 100n6
   See also Magazines
Aleramo, Sibilla, 16, 92, 106,
   108–114, 116–119, 121
   as cautionary tale, 110
   Una donna, 16, 92, 106, 109–111,
   113, 114, 117
Alla mia cara mamma nel giorno del
   suo compleanno, 41
Allen, Woody, 177
   New York Stories, 177
Alvaro, Corrado, 7–8, 10–11, 13, 19,
   22n32, 32–35, 44n1, 68, 77, 84,
   105, 114

Annulment, 92, 216
   See also Divorce
Antler, Joyce, 31
Archetypes
   "Great Mediterranean Mother," 30
   Jungian "great mother," 35–36
   la Mamma, 2, 162
   new bourgeois mother, 161
   peasant Italian mother, 169
   See also Stereotypes
Atanasio, Padre, 84–86
Avola, 164

B
Bagnasco, Angelo, Cardinal, 3
Bamboccione, 3, 15, 19, 40, 42,
   215–216
Banfield, Edward C., 39
Banti, Anna, 112–115, 117
   Artemisia, 114

[1] Note: Page numbers followed by 'n' refer to notes.

© The Author(s) 2018
P. Morris, P. Willson (eds.), *La Mamma*,
Italian and Italian American Studies,
https://doi.org/10.1057/978-1-137-54256-4

238 INDEX

Banti, Anna (*cont.*)
  "Vocazioni indistinte," 113–114
Barolini, Helen, 171–174
  Umbertina, 171–174
Barry, Lynda, 201
Basilicata
  agrarian survey findings, 165
  primary school provision, 225
Bauer, Heike, 202
Bechdel, Alison, 16, 185–190, 193,
  195, 196, 198–204, 206, 206n5
  Are You My Mother?, 186, 188,
    198–204, 206
  Fun Home, 188, 199–200
Bellassai, Sandro, 61
Benedetti, Laura, 118, 123
Berlusconi, Silvio, 44, 51
Bernhard, Ernst, 36–38
Birth rate, Italian, 3, 18, 39, 65, 91,
  107, 151, 217–218, 227, 229
  relationship with employment rate,
    217–218
Bona, Mary Jo, 169
Bradstreet, Anne, 199
Brava gente, 36
Bravo, Anna, 2, 8, 11, 58
Briscoe, Lily, in *To the Lighthouse*, 190,
  200–201
Brogi, Alessandro, 60
Butler, Judith, 112
Buttafuoco, Annarita, 107

C
Calabria, 150, 157n18, 157n23, 170,
  172, 173
  agrarian survey findings, 165
Calabro, John, 171
  "A Glass of Wine," 171
Calvino, Italo, 31
  The Path to the Spiders' Nests, 31
Campania

agrarian survey findings, 163
  primary school provision, 225
  young mothers, 226
Cappello, Mary, 16, 185–190,
  195–198, 201, 203, 205
  Night Bloom, 186, 188, 195–198,
    201, 205
Caruth, Cathy, 199
Catanzaro, 165
Catholicism, 56–59, 89, 174, 186,
  192–194, 203
  anti-Communism, women's role
    and, 61
  Catholic Church, 1, 32, 36–38,
    43–44, 61–62, 86, 98, 194, 216
  vision of motherhood, 1, 12, 20n1,
    63, 77–78, 81–82, 84–85,
    100n2, 151, 161, 167
Cavarero, Adriana, 80, 123, 195–196
Cavigioli, Rita, 9–10
Centro Italiano Femminile (CIF), 56,
  61, 63, 65
Chicago, 170
Childbirth, 7, 108–110, 117, 120,
  122, 164
  and leaving employment, 221
  See also Pregnancy
Childcare
  gender division of labour, 218–219,
    222–23
  provision, 17, 18, 58, 66–67, 88,
    89, 217–219, 222, 225–226
Children
  differences between number desired
    and actually had, 227
  illegitimate, 57
  See also Mother–daughter
    relationship; Motherhood;
    Mother–son relationship
Christian Democracy (DC), 12, 32,
  33, 42, 52, 56, 59, 61, 86, 100n2
Chute, Hilary, 199, 202

INDEX 239

Cinema, *see* Motherhood, representation in films
Citizenship, women's, 53–58, 60, 65, 67, 107
Civiltà materna (maternal civilization), 30, 35–40, 42–43
Cloth-working, connection to migratory experience, 202, 203
Cold War, 32, 54–56, 60–62, 77
  and gender, 62
Communist Party, Italian (PCI), 52, 56, 59–60, 62–63, 65, 78, 86, 100n2
Conrad, Joseph, 121–122
  The Secret Sharer, 121–122
Constituent Assembly, 56, 60
Constitution, Italian, 54–57, 63, 65–67
  mother's responsibilities in, 218
Contini, Mary, 15, 23n47
Culicchia, Giuseppe, *Ameni inganni*, 4, 21n13
Cusin, Fabio, 8
  L'italiano. Realtà e illusioni, 35
Cvetkovich, Ann, 188

D
Dalla Zuanna, Gianpiero, 218
Dal Pozzo, Giuliana, 86–91
Daly, Brenda, 120
D'Amelia, Marina, 7, 14, 17, 30, 53, 77, 105, 106, 114, 161
  La mamma, 7, 30
Daughters, *see* Mother–daughter relationship; Discourses, daughterly
Daughters-in-law, 82–84, 88, 93, 95, 98–99, 133, 141–143, 168–169
  See also Mammismo
de Beauvoir, Simone, 35

de Céspedes, Alba 12, 78, 89–100, 100n7
  Quaderno proibito, 12, 96–97, 99–100
De Filippo, Eduardo, 10, 133–134, 139, 140
  Filumena Marturano, 37–38, 133, 155n4
  Mia famiglia, 135
  Napoli milionaria, 134–135
  Natale in casa Cupiello, 135
  Neapolitan plays, 17
  Non ti pago, 135
De Filippo, Peppino, 41
Deledda, Grazia, 112–113
  Cenere, 113
  Cosima, 112–113
  La madre, 113
DeLuise, Dom, 203
De Maria, Beniamino, 66
De Rosa, Tina, 169
DeSalvo, Louise, 193
de Siervo, Fedele, 163
Diaspora communities, 6, 13–15
  Anglophone countries, 161–178
  Antipodes, 15, 176–177
  Canada, 171, 176
  Scotland, 15–16
  United States, 6, 16–17, 162, 165–170, 171–178, 186–187, 191–193, 196, 203
di Donato, Pietro, 167
  Christ in Concrete, 167
Diedrich, Lisa, 199, 202
Di Giacomo, Salvatore, 133
  Assunta Spina, 133
  'O voto (The Vow), 133
Di Gregorio, Gianni, *Gianni e le donne*, 4
Di mamma non ce n'è una sola, 41
Di Pietro, Alessandra, 18

240 INDEX

Discourses
  daughterly, 106, 109, 117, 119,
    123, 124n4, 125–126n49
  maternal, 13, 77–78, 106, 108,
    110, 111, 124n3
  maternalist, 53–54
  See also Catholicism, Catholic
    Church; Fascism; Feminism;
    Patriarchy
Divorce, 11, 12, 57, 87, 91, 92, 95,
    216
  See also Legislation
Domestic manuals, 79–80, 107
"Donna Letizia" (Colette Rosselli),
    80–81, 83
DuPlessis, Rachel Blau, 194, 204

E
"Economic miracle," 5, 11, 64
Education, women's, 151, 220
  right to, 63, 107
Egelman, William, 175
Elections
  election posters, 59
  1948, 32, 33, 57
  1946, 55–56
Emilia Romagna, primary school
    provision, 225
Employment, women's, 11, 18, 54,
    58, 62, 64–65, 67, 88, 91, 92,
    95, 98, 138–139, 141, 150–154,
    163, 217–227
  black market, 135
  conflict with motherhood, 219–227,
    229–230
  employment rate, women's,
    220–221
  explanation for child neglect, 216
  fragmentation of labour market, 223
  insecurity, impact on fertility and
    gender division of labour,
    222–223

maternity, risk to contracts, 224
money-lending, 136–137
pregnancy, 18
right to work, women's, 62–63
  See also Maternity leave; Noce Law
    (Law for the protection of
    working mothers, 1950)
European Union, 51

F
Faina, Eugenio, survey, 163
Falconi, Dino, see "Signora Quickly"
Fallaci, Oriana, 116–121, 123
  Lettera a un bambino mai nato,
    116–118, 121, 122
Families
  extended, 83, 88, 93, 137, 146,
    157n22, 168, 196
  family models, 147
  "intimate conjugal," 147, 156n15
  Italian, 2–3, 6, 14, 19, 119, 153,
    165, 174, 176, 218, 222,
    230
  Italian-American, 162, 174, 175
  nuclear, 39
  patriarchal, 67, 162
  patrilocal, 9–10, 23
  peasant, 9–10, 163–165
  shrinkage, 151
  See also Daughters-in-law; Diaspora
    communities; Husbands; Life
    stories; Mammismo;
    Motherhood; Patriarchy
Familism
  amoral, 39–40, 105
  Neapolitan, 134
  United States, 166, 176
Fanfani, Amintore, 52
Fascism, 9, 31, 32, 35, 36, 53, 55, 62,
    64, 105, 107, 108, 110,
    114–115, 119
  demographic campaigns, 65, 105

INDEX   241

veneration of motherhood, 9, 150
Federici, Maria, 52–53, 56, 66, 67
Fellini, Federico, 36
  I vitelloni, 40–41
Femininity, 52, 54, 60, 134, 193
  performative, 112, 125n32
Feminism, 107–108, 110, 116, 119,
    147, 185, 187, 199
  lesbian, 188–189
  1970s, 108, 118, 154, 171,
    173–174
  nineteenth-century, 107
  sexual difference, on, 107
Feminization, *see* Masculinity, Italian
Fernandez, Dominique, 38
  Mère méditerrannée, 38
Ferraro, Thomas, 169
Fertility rate, *see* Birth rate, Italian
Flaiano, Ennio, 40
Food, social consumption, 15–16
Forgacs, David, 89
Fortier, Anne-Marie, 197, 204
Forza Italia, 51
Friedman, Susan Stanford, 122
Freud, Sigmund, 36, 185, 199, 205

G
Gallagher, Dorothy, 203–204
Gallo, Vincent, 175–176
  Buffalo '66, 175–176
Gambino, Antonio, 37–39, 43,
    155n1, 155n5
Gardaphé, Fred, 166–168, 170
Garner, Shirley N., 106
Gassani, Gian Ettore, 3–4
Gatt-Rutter, John, 117
Gaudreault, Emile, 176
  Mambo Italiano, 176
Gedalof, Irene, 195–196
Gender, 8, 17, 40, 171, 188, 189,
    196, 221

discrimination, 56, 87, 92, 99,
    147–148
history of, 7, 146
inequalities, 12, 13, 220
roles, change in, 54, 143, 144, 146,
    150, 154, 222
roles, Italian, 6, 14, 32, 55, 62, 79,
    140, 178, 197
  See also Households, Italian;
    Mammismo; Patriarchy
Generations
  differences across, 13, 15, 17, 83,
    84, 90, 143–154, 171–174,
    176–177
  ties between, 10, 13, 88, 166
  See also Mother–daughter
    relationships
Giagnoni, Silvia, 177
Giaimo, Genie, 202
Gilbert, Sandra M., 192
  Gilmore Girls, The, 177
Ginatempo, Nella, 153
Ginzburg, Natalia, 36, 115–116,
    121
  "Dell'aborto," 116
  "Il mio mestiere," 115, 116
  "La madre," 115
  Lessico familiare, 115
  "Un'assenza," 115
Giorgio, Adalgisa, 107, 185
Giunta, Edvige, 176, 186
  Godfather, The, 174
Golden, Daniel, 177
Grandparents, 137, 194, 218,
    226–227
  grandmothers, 97, 147, 151, 153,
    157n18, 226–227
  identification with, 137–138
Guidi Cingolani, Angela Maria,
    61–62
Gulf War, 42
Gundle, Stephen, 89

242 INDEX

H

Heyer-Caput, Margherita, 113
Hollywood, 4, 14, 168, 175, 176
See also Motherhood, representation
  in films
Homans, Margaret, 122
Hine, Lewis, photographic images,
  166
Hirsch, Marianne, 189, 206n3
See also Mother–daughter
  relationships
Households, Italian, gender division of
  labour, 3, 18, 222, 223
Housewives, women as, 11, 19, 63,
  64, 90, 150, 153, 154, 219, 226
Husbands, 82, 92, 95, 107, 151
  absent, 145–146
  authority, 19, 87, 151, 164–165
  infidelity, 82, 84, 92
  weak, 17, 44, 138–139, 141
See also Families; Households;
  Masculinity, Italian; Mother–
  son relationships

I

Immigrant domestic workers, 18
Istituto Nazionale di Statistica
  (ISTAT), 227
Italian-Americans, 61
See also Diaspora communities;
  Families
Italian Association of Psychology, 36
Italianità, 186, 191, 192, 203

J

Jacini, Stefano, survey, 163, 165
Jewison, Norman, 176
  Moonstruck, 176
Johnson, Colleen, 175
Jung, Carl, 35–37
  archetype of "great mother," 35–36,
  38

K

Kahane, Claire, 106
Kaplan, E. Ann, 108
Kennan, George, 60
Kristeva, Julia, 121

L

Labour market, see Employment,
  women's
La Guardia, Fiorello, 61
Lawler, Steph, 106
Lazio, primary school provision, 225
Le Bon, Gustave, 35
Legislation, 13, 18, 51–69, 72n44, 89,
  151, 224
  assisted reproduction, 228
  Civil Code, responsibilities for
  children, 218
  divorce, 87
  Family Code, 57
See also Constitution; Noce Law
  (Law for the protection of
  working mothers, 1950)
Leone, Davide, Confessioni di un
  mammone, 4
Lesbians
  dual motherhood, constraints,
  185–214, 229
See also Mother–daughter
  relationships
Life cycle, women's, 140–143
Life stories, women's, 132–133,
  137–154
Liguria, primary school provision, 225
Lipmann, Walter, 5
Lipperini, Loredana, 220
Livi Bacci, Massimo, 218
Lombardy, primary school provision,
  225
Longo, Luigi, 67
L'Orfano, Francesca, 162
Loy, Nanni, 41
  Made in Italy, 41

INDEX 243

M
Machiavellianism, 38
Madonna, *see* Virgin Mary
Mafias
    American, 170, 174
    Camorra, 137
Magazines
    advice columns; *Epoca*, 12, 78,
      89–96, 98–99; *Famiglia*
      cristiana, 12, 78, 84–86, 88–89,
      98–99; *Grazia*, 12, 78, 80–84,
      86, 88, 92, 98; *Noi donne*, 12,
      78, 86–89, 91, 98, 99
    L'Espresso, 37
    Life, 89
    Look, 40
    PourFemme, 3
    Tempo Presente, 37
Mammarolo, *see Mammone*
Mammina, 82
Mammismo, 2–6, 54, 68–69, 121,
    215–216
    abroad, 13–16
    birth, 7–13, 77, 105
    emergence in United States, 14
    films and novels, in, 4–5, 40–41,
      123
    foreshadowed, 52–53
    magazine advice columns, in,
      77–100
    political discourse, in, 42
    stereotype history, 29–44
    stereotype today, 18–20
    See also Daughters-in-law; Sons
Mammo, 20, 216–217
Mammone, 3, 11, 19, 29, 40, 83,
    215–216
    See also Mammismo
Mann, Delbert, 174
    Marty, 174
Maraini, Dacia, 121–123
    Un clandestino a bordo, 121–122
Marotta, Giuseppe, 34

Le madri, 34
Marriage
    departure from labour market, and,
      220
    infidelity, 139
    male-female relationships, 145–146,
      165–166
    marital breakdown, 4
    See also Divorce; Husbands;
      Separation
Masculinity, Italian, 5, 12, 19, 21n15,
    21n16, 30, 32, 35, 53, 55,
    59–61, 168, 175
    crisis of, 5, 7, 32, 84, 90–91
    feminization, 32, 41
    inetto, 5, 84
    Italian-American, 167–168, 178
    Neapolitan, 132
    portrayal, 96–97
    "unhealthy," 31
Maso, Carole, 16, 185–195, 204–205
    Ghost Dance, 186, 188, 190–196,
      201, 204–205
Mastroianni, Marcello, 5
Maternalism, 220
    maternalist discourse, 53–54
Maternal, the, *see* Motherhood
Maternismo, 30
Maternity, *see* Motherhood
Maternity leave, 13, 18, 57, 63,
    67–68, 89, 218, 223–225
    clausola di nubilato, 68
    See also Legislation; Noce Law (Law
      for the protection of working
      mothers, 1950)
Mattei, Teresa, 56
Mazzoni, Cristina, 108, 120, 123
Men, Italian, 1, 2, 178
    changing role, 150
    male perspective, 135
    Neapolitan, 135
    view of women, 1, 90
    See also Husbands; Masculinity, Italian

244 INDEX

Merlin, Angelina (Lina), 56, 68
   legislation on brothels, 61
Messina, Elisabeth, 165–166
Migration, 15, 144, 161–163, 166,
   169, 175, 178, 186–188, 192,
   195–196, 204
   See also Diaspora communities
Miller, Nancy K., 190
Milne, A. A., 199
Mistry, Kaeten, 60
Mobility, social, 147, 151, 154, 173
Modernity, 153–154
   materialist American-style, 61
   myths of, 143
   tradition and, 79, 133, 154
Moi, Toril, 35
Molise, primary school provision, 225
Momism, 11, 14, 29–44
   first appearance in United States,
      30–31
   See also Mammismo
Montanelli, Indro, 42
Morante, Elsa, 117, 123
   La storia, 123
Mother–daughter relationship, 7,
   16–17, 81–82, 85, 87, 90,
   172–173
   friendship, as, 149
   lesbian daughters, 185–206
   mother–daughter plot, 186, 189
Motherhood
   ambivalence, 17–18
   Black American woman's
      experience, 196
   conflict and, 106
   conflicting representations, 216–217
   cult of, 107–108
   cultural models and female care,
      151, 217, 218
   excessive expectations, 218–219
   feminist perceptions, 2
   "great mother," 35–36, 155n1, 217
   hostile environment, Italy as, 230

   identity and self-definition, 108,
      111, 118–120, 123, 124, 138
   interdependence with child,
      109–110, 119
   jouissance, see Motherhood,
      pleasures of
   legal provision, 18, 151
   magazine advice columns and,
      77–100
   maternal fantasies, 110, 114, 117,
      121
   maternal genealogy, 190
   maternal thinking, 120–121, 123
   maternal voice, 108, 109, 115, 117,
      121
   Mediterranean, 11, 30, 35, 131,
      133
   middle-class archetype, 161
   "natural," 2
   obstacles, 17, 227–230
   patriotic, 30
   performative, 112
   physicality of, 109, 114, 117, 120,
      122, 123
   pleasures of, 109–111, 114, 120
   political activity, influence on, 18
   practice, 2, 115
   reconceptualizations, 117, 123,
      133, 149, 187
   reconciliation with other activity,
      217
   representation in films, 14, 162,
      174–178
   representation in literature and
      theatre, 14, 16, 34, 105–124,
      131–137, 140, 162, 166–174,
      187
   representation in literature by
      women, 4, 169
   representation on television, 14,
      162, 177
   self-sacrifice, 110, 111, 113, 114,
      118, 220

silence about, 106–108, 110
southern Italian, 10, 131, 139, 163
super-mum, 220
traditional view of, 118–119, 133,
   154, 186–187, 222, 230
transformative, 117, 122
unborn child, 85
work, relationship to, 18, 216–217,
   227
See also Discourses; Employment,
   women's
Mothers
Jewish, 4, 44n2, 177
as subjects, 106
unmarried, 34, 57, 86, 91, 98,
   113
very young, regional differences,
   226
working, *see* Employment, women's
See also Motherhood
Mother–son relationship, 7, 8, 10, 11,
   35, 44, 82–83, 93–95, 105, 113,
   133, 141, 146, 167, 168,
   170–172, 174, 177, 216
See also Mammismo
Muscio, Giuliana, 175

N
Naples
Neapolitan women, 17, 131–154,
   196
Newspapers
Corriere della Sera, 38
Guardian, 3, 52
New York Times, 55
Il Popolo, 61
La Repubblica, 37
La Stampa, 40, 170
New York, 168, 172, 173
the Bronx, 174, 176
Niceforo, Alfredo, 131–132

Noce Law (Law for the protection of
   working mothers, 1950), 52, 57,
   63–64, 67–68, 72n44
parliamentary debate, 66–67
Noce, Teresa, 52–53, 56–60, 63–64,
   66–69
Noto, 164

O
Obando, Lidia, 18
O'Hare McCormick, Anne, 55
Opera nazionale maternità e infanzia
   (ONMI), 64

P
Padoa-Schioppa, Tommaso, 3, 42,
   215
Parental leave, extension to fathers,
   223–224
See also Maternity leave
Participation, public, women's, 9, 52,
   53, 56, 58, 61, 64, 80
See also Citizenship, women's;
   Employment, women's
Passerini, Luisa, 107
Patriarca, Silvana, 6, 53, 60
Patriarchy, 7, 13, 36, 37, 41, 43,
   46n42, 67, 96, 98, 107, 117,
   119, 122, 123, 131, 162, 187,
   189, 195, 197
Per amare Ofelia, 41
Piano, Maria Giovanna, 113
Pickering-Iazzi, Robin, 117
Piedmont, primary school provision,
   225
Pipino, Mary Frances, 192
Pius XII, Pope, 43, 61
Plath, Sylvia, 187–188
Policy, social/welfare, Italian, 17, 20,
   64–65, 151, 217, 218, 222–227,
   230

246 INDEX

Policy, social/welfare, Italian (*cont.*)
  See also Childcare, provision;
    Maternity leave
Politicians, Italian women, 13, 18,
  51–69
Popular Front, 59
Postmodernism, 185
Poverty, 39, 93, 140, 147, 150,
  163–166, 196, 225, 230, 230n6
Pregnancy, 7, 18, 95, 108–110, 118,
  121–122
  impact on employment, 220–221,
    224–225
  postponement, 228
  taboo around, 118–119
Proietti, Giuliana, 11
Psychoanalysis, 36, 178, 189, 199
  mother as subject in, 106
Psychology, 5, 11, 30, 35–37, 40, 60,
  165, 196, 202
  of peoples, 35
Puzo, Mario, 168–169
  The Fortunate Pilgrim, 168–169

Q
Qualunquismo, 38
Quinn, Roseanne, 187
Quinzio, Sergio, 37

R
Rando, Gaetano, 177
Ravera, Lidia, 118–121, 123
  Bambino mio, 118–120, 122
  In quale nascondiglio del cuore,
    120–121
Reddy, Maureen, 120
Reich, Jacqueline, 5
Reparenting, 194
Repossi, Carlo, 66
Reproduction, assisted, access to, 17,
  228–230

Constitutional Court decisions,
  228–229
Republic of Salò, 31
  See also Fascism
Resistance, Italian, 31, 55
  women in, 31, 53, 56, 58–60, 64
Rich, Adrienne, 189, 199
Riis, Jacob, photographic images, 166
Risorgimento, 2, 30, 105, 108, 110,
  161
Rodano, Marisa, 59–60
Rome, 7–8
Ronzulli, Licia, 51–52, 69, 69n2
Rosenthal, Phil, 177
  Everybody Loves Raymond, 177
Rosselli, Colette, *see* "Donna Letizia"
Ruddick, Sara, 120
Ruvoli, JoAnne, 199, 201

S
Salvati, Mariuccia, 69
Sambuco, Patrizia, 189
Sanremo, Festival, 34
Saraceno, Chiara, 107
Savoca, Nancy, 176
  True Love, 176
Scattigno, Anna, 119
Sciorra, Joseph, 186
Scire, Thomas, 176
  Desolato, 176
Separation, 91, 92
  See also Divorce
Serao, Matilde, 136–137, 139, 140
  Il paese di Cuccagna, 136–137
Serra, Ilaria, 174
Serres, Michael, 200
Seuss, Dr., 199
Sex
  Allied soldiers, with, 33
  premarital, 85–86
  sexual conduct, 79, 82
  sexual fulfilment, 165

See also Sexuality
Sexton, Anne, 187–188
Sexuality
  heterosexual norm, 30, 41, 162,
    187
  male homosexuality, 31, 41, 60, 176
  queer, 197–198
  same-sex couples, 229–230
  sexual morality, 37, 147
  change in, 144
  See also Lesbians; Mother–daughter
    relationships
Sicily, 196, 203
  agrarian survey findings, 163–164
  primary school provision, 225
  young mothers, 226
Siebert, Renate, 150, 157n18, 157n23
"Signora Quickly" (Falconi, Dino),
    80–85, 87, 89–90, 92, 98
Sinatra, Frank, 175
Sociology, mother's perspective in,
    106
Sons
  "chosen one," 15, 147–148
  gay, 176
  See also Mother–son relationship
Sopranos, The, 174, 175
Sordi, Alberto, 4, 40–41
South, Italian, 10, 14, 33, 131, 150,
    154, 161, 163–165, 169, 178,
    218, 220, 225–226, 228
  See also Motherhood; Stereotypes
Space, social
  rural, 147, 156n17, 157n23
  urban, 132, 144, 149
  working-class, 144
Spackman, Barbara, 110–111
Sprengnether, Madelon, 106
Stereotypes, 5–7, 114, 117, 131, 178,
    230
  brava gente, 36
  "Italian matriarchate," 10, 174
  Jewish, 177

maternal, rejection of, 110
migrant constructions, 14, 161–178
mother-in-law, 84
representations, Naples area and,
    131–132
South, of the, 154
today, 18–20
WASP, 177
See also Families; *Mammismo*;
  Motherhood
Strecker, Edward, 31
  Their Mothers' Sons, 31
Swanson, Gloria, 172
Suffrage, women's, 55, 61

T
Talese, Gay, 169, 170
  Unto the Sons, 169
Tamburri, Anthony, 170
Taricone, Fiorenza, 107
Togliatti, Palmiro, 62–63
Tognazzi, Ugo, 41
Trade unions, women in, 58, 60
Trasformismo, 38
Turco, Livia, 18
Tuscany, primary school provision,
    225
Tutte le mamme, 34

U
Unification, Italian, *see* Risorgimento
Unione Donne Italiane (UDI), 56, 59,
    65, 86

V
Valentini, Chiara, 18, 224–225
Valentino, Rudolf, 168
Vendler, Helen, 199
Veneziani, Maurizio, 42
Vezzosi, Elisabetta, 63

248 INDEX

Viganò, Renata, 86–87, 89
L'Agnese va a morire, 86, 87
Virgin Mary, 1, 32, 43–44, 52, 81, 85,
 100n2, 166–167, 205
 See also Catholicism, Catholic
 Church
Vivanti, Annie, 111–112, 115, 116
 The Devourers/ I divoratori,
 111–113, 115

W
Walker, Alice, 196
West, Rebecca, 79–80
Widows, 94–95, 146–147, 165, 167,
 170
Willson, Perry, 58–59
Winnicott, Donald, 199, 202, 206
Women
 female ideal, 154
 mothers, as, 107
 neighbourhood networks and, 141
 peasant, 165

victims, as, 140–143
working-class, 98, 133, 136, 161
 See also Motherhood; Mothers
Woods, Kate, 176–177
 Looking for Alibrandi, 176–177
Woolf, Virginia, 190, 194, 196, 199,
 200, 202
 To the Lighthouse, 190, 194, 200,
 202
 A Room of One's Own, 190
Wylie, Philip, 31, 34, 36
 Generation of Vipers, 31

Y
Young Women's Christian Association,
 US, 55

Z
Zampa, Luigi, 40–41
 Un eroe dei nostri tempi, 40–41